THE FIRST BRIDGE TOO FAR

THE FIRST BRIDGE TOO FAR

The Battle of Primosole Bridge 1943

MARK SALIGER

CASEMATE

Oxford & Philadelphia

Published in Great Britain and the United States of America in 2018 by
CASEMATE PUBLISHERS
The Old Music Hall, 106–108 Cowley Road, Oxford OX4 1JE, UK
and
1950 Lawrence Road, Havertown, PA 19083, US

Hardback Edition: ISBN 978-1-61200-689-5
Digital Edition: ISBN 978-1-61200-6901 (epub)

A CIP record for this book is available from the British Library

Printed and bound in the United Kingdom by TJ International

Typeset in India by Versatile PreMedia Services. www.versatilepremedia.com

For a complete list of Casemate titles, please contact:

CASEMATE PUBLISHERS (US)
Telephone (610) 853-9131
Fax (610) 853-9146
Email: casemate@casematepublishers.com
www.casematepublishers.com

CASEMATE PUBLISHERS (UK)
Telephone (01865) 241249
Email: casemate-uk@casematepublishers.co.uk
www.casematepublishers.co.uk

Front cover image: A Bren gun carrier crossing the bridge soon after its capture. (Kent and Sharpshooters Image)

Contents

Introduction

As the orange sun glistens on the turquoise blue waters of the nearby Ionian Sea on a hot summer's day, it is difficult to picture that this quiet rural Sicilian landscape witnessed one of the most brutal encounters of World War II. It pitted the elite British Parachute Regiment against the equally elite German paratroopers, the Fallschirmjaeger. Both units had reputations for toughness and skill in battle gained when they had faced off in North Africa at such battles as Oudna and Tamera. The Fallschirmjaeger had nicknamed the Paras the 'Rote Teufel' (Red Devils) and in return the Paras had given the Fallschirmjaeger the equally fearsome nickname of the 'Green Devils'. These 'Devils' were set to fight each other in hellish conditions at Primosole Bridge.

The end of the beginning of World War II began with the Allied Forces chasing the German *Afrika Korps* and Italian armies out of North Africa. After the Axis powers were defeated in North Africa, the Allied armies' next logical objective was to cross the Mediterranean and attack the 'soft underbelly' of Hitler's Fortress Europe. The hard-won deserts of North Africa were now to serve as a springboard for the Allies' next move. Such was the length of the North African coastline now in Allied hands, they could choose the time and place of their battleground. The Allied planners had a choice of the south of France, the Balkans, Sicily or Italy and could begin to pinpoint the exact location that they wanted to strike next. The Axis powers, in contrast, had to spread their forces thinly all along the Mediterranean coastline, to cover all possible invasion sites.

The Primosole Bridge sits astride the gently meandering waters of the Simeto River as it flows into the Ionian Sea only two miles away. An agricultural patchwork of straw-coloured rectangular fields enclosed by grey stone walls blankets the area around the bridge, peppered by dark-green olive trees and the occasional fruit orchard. The scene is typical of this tranquil corner of Sicily. The local population continued to work their fields and graze their cattle fairly untouched by the war that was raging all around them, on the island of Malta, the sands of North Africa and the waters of the Mediterranean Sea. In the early days of the war, the locals still headed to the nearby coast to swim in the sea after work or travelled the short distance to Catania to visit the shops or trade their goods. As the war intensified, signs of the conflict did begin to appear on Sicily. The local beaches were cordoned off with barbed wire and had minefields sown on their once leisurely golden sands. As the Germans and Italians began to evacuate Tunisia the shadow of war loomed larger as local areas of military value were identified. One such valuable asset was the Primosole Bridge, which commanded access for the main highway over the River Simeto and onto the Catania Plain, linking the main points of the eastern side of the island together. In the event of an invasion the bridge was highlighted as a piece of vital ground by the Germans and Italian defenders, resulting in the construction of defences and a garrison of Italian troops being stationed permanently at the bridge, adding to the sense that the war was creeping closer to home for the local Sicilians.

Despite the business as usual atmosphere on Sicily, the Allied planners had been poring over maps and photographs of the island as part of their invasion planning. As a result, the Allied planners' magnifying glass had fallen on a very important-looking bridge – the Primosole Bridge. With Sicily's hilly interior and the active volcano of Mount Etna further north of Catania, the coastal road over the Primosole Bridge would form an important main supply route and therefore a vital strategic objective in the Allied military campaign to take and hold Sicily as a launch-pad to the invasion of Italy, in turn opening a second front in southern Europe to assist both the Russian offensive in East Europe and divert Axis forces away from the Atlantic Wall prior to an Allied invasion of France in 1944.

But how to seize and hold a well-defended bridge behind enemy lines? After witnessing the tactical surprise gained by Germany's elite Fallschirmjaeger in the early campaigns of the war, Churchill sent a message to General 'Pug' Ismay, Head of the Military Wing of the War Cabinet Secretariat on 22 June 1940, stating that 'a corps of at least 5,000 parachute troops' was required in order to hit back at Nazi Germany. As a result, the Parachute Regiment was formed. Parachute landings had previously been attempted in North Africa but the elite paras ended up fighting as infantry in some of the bloodiest encounters of the campaign. However, in Sicily, they would reprise their intended role of parachuting behind enemy lines to secure key objectives in the vanguard of a large-scale Allied invasion. In the case of the 1st Parachute Brigade of the 1st Airborne Division their daunting task would be to capture and hold the Primosole Bridge as part of the invasion of Sicily in order to facilitate the advance of Montgomery's Eighth Army, the 'Desert Rats', to advance and clear the island. Opposing them at the Primosole Bridge would be the very Fallschirmjaeger who had given rise to the elite legend of paratroopers, providing an even tougher assignment for the Parachute Regiment soldiers. The campaign in Sicily would prove to be larger in size than the Normandy landings the following year, involving 500,000 Allied soldiers battling for 38 days to seize and hold the first piece of mainland Axis territory of World War II.

The battle of Primosole Bridge is a classic story of an airborne objective providing a key linchpin in the overall plan of a large-scale invasion. The plan set out a clear objective of taking and holding the Primosole Bridge to allow for ground forces to utilise the crossing point to chase the Axis forces up the coast to Messina and eventually back to the Italian mainland. What actually transpired was a savage airborne battle of paratroopers and Fallschirmjaeger fighting hand to hand whilst both sides waited for the ground reinforcements to arrive. The similarities with later airborne operations such as Arnhem and Normandy are all too apparent with the minutely detailed plan for the British Airborne assault being in complete disarray by the time the first round was even fired as the airborne armada flew over their drop zones. A delay in ground forces reaching the lightly armed paratroopers meant that they were cut off and fighting for their lives whilst stubbornly defending their prized objective against the full force of the German and Italian forces. Lessons that were learned from Sicily seemed to have been implemented by High Command and airborne forces were supported better in later campaigns, including at Pegasus Bridge in Normandy, but these lessons were quickly forgotten — at Arnhem the battle of Primosole Bridge was played out again but on a grander scale, indeed, by the very same men who had fought at Primosole Bridge.

Primosole Bridge is a hard-won battle honour taught to the Parachute Regiment recruits in Training Depot during regimental history lessons and still discussed in the pubs of Aldershot, Dover, Colchester and St Athan. It was the first strategic use of British paratroops to take an objective by surprise and then hold the objective for land forces as part of an inter-Allied sea, air and land assault onto Axis ground, all in the face of fierce resistance by their German airborne counterparts.

As Stephen E. Ambrose states, 'bridges are always central features in war. Battles and campaigns are often decided by who holds the bridge, or seizes the bridge, or destroys the bridge'.[1] He goes on to state that the three most prominent bridge battles in World War II were Remagen, Arnhem and Pegasus Bridge in Normandy. Two of these three battles are Parachute Regiment battle honours. This is significant, as it was at the battle of Primosole Bridge that the hard-won experience of parachuting behind enemy lines to capture a bridge was developed. The next time the men of the 1st Parachute Brigade would go into action after the battle of Primosole Bridge would be Arnhem. Forever known as the 'bridge too far', Arnhem was merely the second bridge too far for the 1st Parachute Brigade. They had won and lost a bridge only a year before, that was the Primosole Bridge, the first bridge too far.

The battle of Primosole Bridge therefore deserves a detailed account of the legendary exploits of the British paras to be recorded as it was this battle that played such a significant role in shaping future airborne operations and also reinforced the reputation of the Parachute Regiment as one of the finest fighting units of World War II, in turn living up to their regimental motto of *Utrinque paratus* (Ready for Anything), a legacy that lasts to this day.

CHAPTER ONE

'Maroon Machine'

As the convoy rumbled across the last stretch of the desert the weary men in the back of the trucks could see emerging through the dust cloud ahead of them the faint outline of the tents that were to be their home for the foreseeable future. They weren't particularly excited to be arriving at their new home. They assumed it would be just another basic military camp that could wait until tomorrow to be explored. Instead the men simply welcomed the chance to rest after their recent exertions on the battlefields of North Africa. These men were the battle-hardened remnants of the 1st Parachute Brigade, an elite fighting formation that already had the distinction of earning the first three battle honours awarded to the Parachute Regiment – Bruneval, Oudna and Tamera; all within a year of the Paras coming into existence. Their reputation now went before them. Whilst they settled down for some well-earned rest and relaxation, plans were afoot for these elite men of the Parachute Regiment and Airborne Forces to once more enter into battle and play a pivotal role in the next Allied move in the liberation of Europe, the invasion of Sicily.

The 1st Parachute Brigade had been formed in late 1941, twelve months after Churchill's requirement for 'a corps of at least 5,000 parachute troops' was issued on 22 June 1940 in response to the recent German Fallschirmjaeger operations in Scandinavia and the Low Countries. Britain's initial attempts to establish a parachute-trained unit centred on commando-trained No. 2 Commando who had already been earmarked to become parachute-trained and were renamed as 11th Special Air Service Battalion. The first ever British airborne operation was carried out by 11th Special Air Service Battalion, which attempted to destroy the Tragino Aqueduct in Italy. Months later, the German capture of Crete by paratroopers in May 1941 led Churchill to add impetus to the training and expanding of Britain's parachute troops. The 11th Special Air Service Battalion was immediately expanded to form a parachute-trained brigade, to be designated 1st Parachute Brigade from September 1941. Authority was therefore given to create four parachute infantry battalions (to be designated 1, 2, 3 and 4 Para) along with parachute-trained engineers and signal troops. The call was sent out across the armed forces for volunteers to join this new pioneering airborne unit. Men with good military records and a good level of fitness were encouraged to apply. General Sir Alan Brooke, Chief of the Imperial General Staff (CIGS), appointed Brigadier Richard 'Windy' Gale as the first brigade commander of the 1st Parachute Brigade. He in turn appointed his first three commanding officers for each of the battalions (the fourth battalion had not been created at this stage). Lieutenant-Colonel Eric Down would command 1 Para, 2 Para was to be led by Lt Col Edward Flavell and 3 Para by Lt Col Gerald Lathbury (later to command the brigade in Sicily). The Regimental Sergeant Major of the brigade was appointed in the shape of ex-Grenadier Guardsman RSM Lord. It was customary for him to greet newcomers to the 1st Parachute Brigade with his standard introduction. 'My name is Lord – Regimental Sergeant Major – my initials are J. C. But don't let that fool you, for I'll have no mercy on you'.[1] The ethos of the Parachute Regiment and Airborne Forces was now beginning to form through strong and professional officers and NCOs being recruited to build the skeleton of the regiment. The toughness of its training clearly marked them out as a unit that would be at the front of any response to beating Hitler. As such, this meant not just anyone would be accepted into the regiment's ranks. Men were required to pass its tough selection process to prove that they had what it took to serve in the Airborne.

A medical was the first step on the ladder to becoming a paratrooper. It was designed to measure the men's health and fitness levels met the standards required. Men had to be between 22 and 32 years of age, though senior NCOs could be slightly older. The men also had to weigh no more than 196lb so that they could parachute with enough kit to sustain themselves in the field. An interview process was created for the volunteers for Airborne Forces, where each commanding officer would interview potential recruits for each of their respective battalions. If deemed successful at the interview, the chosen men were told to report to Hardwick Hall near Chesterfield and from there, on to Ringway airport to begin their parachute training. Nearby Tatton Park was used as the drop zone for all training jumps. Whilst at Ringway candidates were assessed on their physical fitness as well as their ability to perform the qualifying number of jumps from both balloons and Whitley aircraft. The men were all volunteers from other infantry regiments. Most men were eager to become part of a newly elite organisation, have the chance to fight back at the Nazis and also benefit from the welcome addition of extra 'parachute pay'. Initially this was four shillings per day for officers and two shillings per day for other ranks once they had completed their three qualifying jumps. However, this was soon balanced out as two shillings per day for all ranks but only after the number of qualifying jumps was increased to seven. This led to more candidates passing the course than failing, owing to the motivation of men as they fought to join an elite fighting formation and secure the extra 'para pay'. Airborne troops who travelled to the battlefield in gliders did not qualify for the extra pay though, which caused consternation between the different units within Airborne Forces.

Early paratrooper adopts correct jumping position on exiting the aircraft over Tatton Park. (Courtesy of Air Assault Museum)

Competition was tough between the newly appointed officers and NCOs of the parachute battalions to secure the best recruits for their own battalion as Major John Frost recalls from his time as 2 Para adjutant in charge of selecting men to the ranks of 2 Para:

> To me it seemed that I would never be able to get the battalion up to strength, which did not seem to be happening with the 3rd Battalion, who were also at Hardwick. Then I found out my counterpart in the 3rd Battalion had stationed a man at the entrance and told all new arrivals to report to the 3rd Battalion Guardroom. Here their RSM inspected them all and kept the best ones for himself and sent the chaff down to me! I decided to send a few men with a truck to just outside the camp and for them to pick up all the new arrivals. This worked well for a while, till the 3rd's Adjutant sent a truck even further down the road, we then called a truce and both units started to build up fairly equally.[2]

Whichever battalion the men finished up in after training, there was a single quality that all ranks of the Parachute Regiment shared, and they still do share, to this day. Lieutenant Martin Willcock remembers 'the one thing that we all had in common from the Col to the Private – was that we had JUMPED – a unique experience which we would never forget and one which made us feel the battalion was something rather special'.[3] Rivalry existed at every level and was a mark of the elite status and constant pursuit of excellence required of paratroopers. Each man was proud of his unit, whether it be his battalion, company, platoon or section, and was fiercely loyal to upholding its standards and reputation.

As Major Victor Dover also recalled when he had finished his training, 'I did not appreciate at the time (how could I?) the magnificence of the men with whom I had the privilege to serve and to call my friends. Many were to die, many were to suffer serious wounds and a number were to become legends'.[4] The volunteers who had met the call to arms for the new airborne elite were trained and at last ready to get back into the fight against Hitler.

As 1 Para had been centred around the previous 11th SAS Battalion, the new recruits, sometimes whole battalions transferred from the line infantry, were mainly placed in 2 and 3 Para. Towards the end of 1941 the battalions were rotating through parachute training a battalion at a time, increasing the numbers of trained parachutists that were now ready for action. The first unit into action would be 2 Para's C Company, now led by Major John Frost. They were parachuted into France by the RAF and captured vital enemy radar equipment from a house being used as a radar station on the cliffs above the fishing village of Bruneval. They were met on the shore by the Royal Navy and extracted with the captured radar equipment and a sole German prisoner to explain how the kit worked. This was a highly successful raid and proved the potential of inter-service co-operation for parachute- and commando-style raids on Hitler's Fortress Europe.

After proving the possibilities of parachuting into battle to maximise the element of surprise upon the enemy, the brigade was shipped to North Africa – the main land campaign of the Allied effort after being pushed out of mainland Europe via Dunkirk. The remainder of the brigade were eager to get into action, preferably by parachute, in order to put all their hard work into practice. The chance was soon to come as the Axis Forces were now on the retreat from El Alamein and heading back towards Tunisia chased by Montgomery's Desert Rats.

In support of Montgomery's easterly offensive from Egypt and with the American entry into the war after Pearl Harbor, a second front was opened to perform a pincer movement on the Axis from the west of Tunisia. Operation *Torch* was devised to invade Vichy French North Africa with troops landed directly from the United States. The 1st Parachute Brigade was deployed in support of *Torch* and conducted a series of battalion-sized parachute operations to underpin the Allied advance by capturing vitally strategic objectives. Both the Allies and Germans quickly identified

Tunis as a key to holding Tunisia. Bone airfield was situated halfway between Tunis and Algiers and became the subject of a race between competing airborne forces to parachute and capture it first. On 12 November 3 Para flew towards Bone airfield and only beat the Fallschirmjaeger of 5th Parachute Regiment there by a matter of minutes. As the men of 3 Para began exiting their Dakotas, a fleet of Ju52s with its own cargo of paratroopers was in the distance watching the drop. The Germans promptly about-turned and headed back to base knowing they had lost the race for the airfield. The first clash of British and German paratroopers on the battlefield had been narrowly avoided. However, the success illustrated by the 'vertical-envelopment' of a strategic target by only a few paratroopers had been clearly demonstrated and led to further jumps for the brigade.

Four days later, on 16 November, 1 Para was tasked to capture an important crossroads on the road to Tunis at Beja. 1 Para's Commanding officer, James Hill, flew in the lead Dakota and looked out of the plane's door for a suitable drop zone near the target as maps of the area had proved insufficient in their detail. Accordingly, when Hill decided to jump, the remainder of the following Dakotas would also despatch their parachutists. In this ad hoc manner the battalion jumped into battle in a relatively small dropping area and secured their objective. During the ensuing actions over the following days, Hill was shot three times in the chest whilst capturing enemy tanks by banging on the turret and demanding their surrender armed with just his pistol and a stick. Whilst Hill convalesced after the battle, Alistair Pearson took command of the battalion. The men of 1st Parachute Brigade were now living the dream as they began to conduct operations behind enemy lines. These airborne operations were what the men had joined the Parachute Regiment for.

A third airborne assault for the brigade was now planned for 29 November and to be led by John Frost's 2 Para. They were to secure the Oudna airfield in support of a ground offensive towards Tunis. As the planes began to taxi down the runways for take-off, men could be seen running towards the Dakotas carrying a parachute in one hand and their weapon in the other hand. 'It is not every man who will disobey orders to parachute into battle'.[5] This clearly highlights the *esprit de corps* that had formed amongst the Parachute Regiment soldiers and no man wanted to miss out on operations. 2 Para parachuted close to Oudna but were then given the news that the planned link-up with the advance by ground forces had been cancelled. The entire battalion now found itself cut off miles behind enemy lines. A legendary fighting retreat now ensued as the battalion was surrounded and had to battle against overwhelming odds to regain the Allied font line, albeit at the cost of half the battalion killed, wounded or taken prisoner. The men of 2 Para had taken to keeping a book on the odds of the officers' fortunes on the battlefield as a bit of entertainment. 'The Book', however, proved to be so accurate in North Africa that John Frost banned it. The Parachute Regiment was awarded the battle honour of 'Oudna' for this epic fighting retreat. Coupled with the Bruneval battle honour, John Frost had now been at the

Alastair Pearson, Commanding Officer 1 Para. (Courtesy of Air Assault Museum)

scene of the Parachute Regiment's first two battle honours. He, along with the majority of the 1st Parachute Brigade, would soon be at the scene of yet another, Tamera.

With the Allied push on Tunis requiring ever greater numbers of troops to fight the shrinking perimeter and therefore growing concentration of the Axis forces, the 1st Parachute Brigade now reverted to their standard infantry role and were moved into the line to fight off increasingly desperate German counter-attacks. Fighting from defensive positions astride the main roadway, the paras fought off wave after

John Frost, Commanding Officer 2 Para, seen here after the Bruneval raid. (Courtesy of Air Assault Museum)

wave of enemy counter-attacks, often with hand-to-hand fighting to repel World War I-style infantry charges aimed at over-running their trenches. Unknown at the time, the brigade was fighting off a division-sized enemy force, including their Fallschirmjaeger opponents for the first time, at odds of nearly ten to one against. It was here in the Tamera Valley that the paras acquired their nickname. Allied intelligence had picked up radio traffic from the Germans which had referred to the Parachute Regiment defenders of the Tamera Valley as the 'Red Devils'. The name was taken as a mark of respect and still stands as the regimental nickname till this day. The intercepted message was passed on to the men who had won this hard-fought recognition from their adversaries:

> From Major-General Browning to All Para Units: General Alexander directs that 1 Para Brigade be informed that have been given name of 'Red Devils'. General Alexander congratulates the brigade on achieving this high distinction.[6]

The news was met with pride, in that the Germans had paid them the respect of granting them a nickname, but also tinged with sadness at the memory of the men who had been lost in earning that hard-won respect.

The brigade also developed its war-cry in the Tamera Valley, adopted from the local Arabs who encouraged their mules into action with the call of 'Waho Mohammed'. Future enemies' first encounters with the 1st Parachute Brigade were invariably led by this North African war cry followed by a Red Devil on the charge with his weapon levelled, ready for anything. For holding their ground against these overwhelming odds, the battle honour 'Tamera' was bestowed upon the Parachute Regiment.

The two North African battle honours had come at a high price. The three infantry battalions of the brigade alone had suffered casualties as high as 1,700 killed, wounded and missing of which 49 officers and 469 other ranks were officially listed as being killed during the North African campaign – effectively a full battalion. In return, the brigade had dished out casualties on the Axis forces as high as 5,000 killed and wounded and a further 3,600 captured. The brigade was one of the most decorated in the British Army earning 8 Distinguished Service Orders, 15 Military Crosses, 9 Distinguished Conduct Medals, 22 Military Medals, three Croix de Guerre and one Légion d'Honneur.

The paratroopers and Fallschirmjaeger had by now already developed a healthy respect for each other's abilities on the battlefield. Frost recalled that 'on two occasions I felt bound to leave part of my fighting strength to protect our wounded, but in the event our German opponents turned out to be of the parachute fraternity and they took considerable trouble to look after our men whenever they could'.[7] This clearly highlights the comradeship and understanding between these two elite units, while there would be tough fights in the future they would always maintain the high standards of chivalrous combat. An even starker example of this airborne brotherhood, even between enemy combatants, was displayed after the battle of Oudna in North Africa. Men from 2 Para who had been captured were lined up against a wall. They were about to be shot when Oberstleutnant Walter Koch, commander of 5th Fallschirmjaeger Regiment and a veteran of the famous Eben Emael glider assault in Belgium, arrived. He immediately kicked over the German machine gun and, after an argument with the German commander who had ordered the deaths, turned to the 2 Para men. Koch stated that 'you are paratroopers and you put up a brave fight. You are prisoners of war and will be treated as such'.[8] The airborne brotherhood and mutual respect between the elite paratroopers had now been established and would continue throughout the war.

After the endeavours of the North African campaign, the 1st Parachute Brigade was joined by its parent division, the 1st Airborne Division, commanded by Major-General 'Hoppy' Hopkinson. The 1st Parachute Brigade was reorganising itself around its rear party headquarters at Boufarik, near Algeria. The veteran paratroopers were enjoying some 'R and R' in Algiers and other nearby towns while new recruits were brought in to replace the casualties of the previous campaign. Colonel John Frost remembers visiting the wounded in the base hospitals around Algiers: '"You'll have no trouble finding your men, they all wear their berets all the time," said one of the nurses. So indeed they did. Even in bed with their pyjamas on. In fact I heard that one tried to keep his on en route to the operating theatre'.[9] This clearly highlights the *esprit de corps* and sense of well-earned elitism that was blossoming in the ranks of the Parachute Regiment after their success and hard-won battles in North Africa. Their pride in wearing their distinctive maroon berets, the 'Maroon Machine', was a sign of the value of belonging to such an elite and respected unit. Some of the wounded would return in time for the Brigade's next action, some, due to the severity of their wounds, would not. Replacements, both experienced and inexperienced men, began arriving

Bill Yeldham, Commanding Officer 3 Para with The Officers' Mess, 3rd Parachute Battalion, Spalding, Lincolnshire, 1944. Standing: L-R: Lts A R 'Tony' Baxter (2 Pln, A Coy, wounded in the legs), Collett (A Coy), Archibald (HQ Coy), S W Burnard (QM, 1st Sea tail.), 'Alex' Vedeniapine MM, G M 'Gerry' Infield (8 Pln, C Coy), S WA Bennett (MTO, 1st Sea tail.), 'Dixie' Dean (DCM. HQ-Coy), Stanley Gillespie (Mortar Pln, PoW), 'Johnny' Pryce (RSO, PoW), J A S 'Jimmy' Cleminson MC (5 Pln, B Coy, awarded the MC), E 'Jimmy' James MC (MiD. 4 Pln, B Coy, PoW), L W 'Len' Wright (9 Pln, C Coy, wounded and taken PoW at Arnhem Bridge 20 September 1944), Derrick J Bentham (A/ADJT UK based), M J 'Dickers' Dickson (MMG Pln, PoW), Gordon Hill (6 Pln, B Coy, KIA) and B P 'Bertie' Ash (3 Pln, A Coy, PoW & cited for a Military Cross.)
Sitting: L-R: Capts J 'Sandy' Rutherford (RMO taken PoW with the wounded), W H ' Chippy' Robinson (2iC C Coy), G L W 'Pat' Street MC (2iC HQ Coy, OC 1st Sea tail), Maj Peter H Waddy (B Coy, KIA 18 September 1944), Maj M Dennison (A Coy), Maj R 'Dicky' Lonsdale DSO, MC, Lt Col E C 'Bill' Yeldham, Capt Charles Seccombe (ADJT, wounded, lost both his legs), Maj J I 'Happy' Houston (OC, HQ Coy, KIA 20 September 1944), Maj Alan Bush (OC C Coy, took over as Bn 2iC, wounded in both legs and awarded the MC), Capts R P C 'Pongy' Lewis (2iC C Coy, took over as OC, wounded in the legs and back at the Van Limburg Stirum School), R 'Roddy' Thessiger (2iC A Coy, WIA, PoW) and Edward 'Bill' Phillips (Padre, taken prisoner with the wounded at St Elizabeth's Hospital). (Courtesy of Air Assault Museum)

to make up the losses from recent fighting. Even parachute training courses were being cut short in order that men arrive in-theatre in time for upcoming operations. 'Exceptional measures were taken including getting down the time of Hardwick Hall and Ringway courses and the presentation of Parachute Wings after only 5 qualifying jumps'.[10] They would now continue their training for real on the battlefield.

Among the new batch of officers was a new second-in-command of 2 Para, Major John Lane, and two other experienced officers; Major Dickie Lonsdale was to be officer commanding 'A' Company and Major Tony Fitch was to be officer commanding B Company (Fitch was later killed at Arnhem whilst commanding 3 Para). Captain Victor Dover, who had been wounded in action along with Captain Doug Crawley, was appointed as the 2 Para adjutant with Doug Crawley appointed

Gerald Lathbury, Commanding Officer of 1st Parachute Brigade. (Courtesy of Air Assault Museum)

as Fitch's second-in-command for B Company. Both the new recruits and the old hands were keen to get back up to fighting strength as quickly as possible in expectation of their next deployment.

Whilst fighting at Oudna and Tamera, the 1st Parachute Brigade was replaced in the division's orbat by the newly formed 3rd Parachute Brigade, led by the former 3 Para CO, Brigadier Gerald Lathbury. However, the division's order of battle was reconfigured for their anticipated next operation with the men of the division being briefed on 11 February that they weren't about to be shipped back home but instead were briefed about an anticipated operation somewhere overseas in June or July time. The 1st British Airborne Division now comprised the 1st and 2nd Parachute Brigades and also the glider-borne troops of 1st Airlanding Brigade. Lathbury officially now took over command of the 1st Parachute Brigade in North Africa on 28 April 1943 from Flavell.

On 9 March 1943, 1st Airborne Division, with the exception of 3rd Parachute Brigade (already in theatre), two battalions of 1st Airlanding Brigade and the Airborne Light Tank Squadron, was ordered to mobilise by 1 May for operations in North Africa. The majority of the division sailed from England in two convoys, 2nd Parachute Brigade arriving at Oran on 26 April and 1st Airlanding Brigade a month later on 26 May. Others flew out from Salisbury Plain to the new division staging area including Major-General Browning who would help to start plan the airborne element of the invasion. The 1st Parachute Brigade travelled by train from Boufarik, changing trains at Perreguax onto a smaller-gauge railway line, and eventually arriving at Mascara on 10 May to rejoin the rest of the 1st Airborne Division in Western Algeria, where it was undergoing training.

The 1st Parachute Brigade had now settled into their tented camp, which was centred around the small hamlet of Matemore as, in timeless army tradition, they eased into a routine of training and listening to rumours of their next deployment. The men weren't to know it yet but they would have only two months in which to prepare for their next and biggest operation. The village had been controlled by the French prior to the start of the war and a small airfield already existed at Mascara. The French air force had previously discounted other areas around Mascara as suitable for airfields due to their prevalence of malaria-carrying mosquitoes, but US engineers had started to carve airfields out of the desert which began to resemble rudimentary working airstrips with basic tented accommodation. The surrounding area was flat wine-growing country with few obstacles such as stone walls dividing the fields, trees or telegraph poles and so proved to be ideal ground for the parachute and glider troops. During their down-time the men were driven to the waters of the Mediterranean Sea, only thirty minutes away by truck, or they could visit the American cinema at the Thiersville airstrip. The chance to recuperate after the

The red and green devils first clashed in North Africa. Here a member of 2 Para is being interrogated by a group of Fallschirmjaeger. (Courtesy of Air Assault Museum)

North African campaign was welcomed but the men would have felt these good times were the calm before the storm and it wouldn't be long before the top brass sent them into action again. Rumours were rife amongst the men as to their next destination. Their recent exploits could have earnt them a period of home leave and let some other units take their turn in the fighting but most felt they were being kept in Africa for the next strike at the Axis, somewhere in the Mediterranean. The airborne units had been well utilised in capturing key objectives during the Oudna battle and then proved their worth as elite infantry around Tamera. These two skills combined would surely serve to make them a key unit in any upcoming invasion force. The men's guesses ranged from southern France, to Sardinia, Sicily, the Italian mainland, the Balkans or Greece. The Allied deception plan had worked extremely well. Not only did the Axis forces not know where the next move would be, neither did the men of the Allied armies.

CHAPTER TWO

'Stepping Stone to Italy'

During the final months of the North African campaign, with Rommel's Afrika Korps on the retreat back to Tunisia, the Allied strategic planners were already turning their thoughts to where to strike next in the Mediterranean Sea. Churchill pressed for invasions of the Dodecanese Islands, the Balkans and the Greek mainland, as well as the large islands of Corsica, Sardinia and Sicily. After much discussion with President Roosevelt in Washington between December and January 1941 it was decided that the Allies would focus on defeating Germany before Japan. The Americans, led by the Joint Chiefs of Staff (JCS), were given strategic responsibility for the Pacific area of operations whilst the British, led by the Chiefs of Staff (COS) were given strategic responsibility for Europe and the Middle East. The forthcoming next step against Germany in the Mediterranean would therefore fall under British command. As a recognition of Britain's experience in the war so far it maintained the command for the Mediterranean theatre but as mutual recognition of the men and materiel entering the theatre from the United States it was decided to create the Combined Chiefs of Staff (CCS) with representatives from both the JCS and COS. Lieutenant General Dwight D. Eisenhower would be the overall commander of the European Theatre of Operations. The policy stated that the leader and their deputy should be of different nationalities. General Sir Harold Alexander was therefore appointed as his deputy.

As the sun set on the North African campaign, culminating in the capture of 100,000 Axis soldiers, Churchill and Roosevelt, with the CCS in tow, met at the Casablanca Conference, 14–24 January 1943. Over the course of the next ten days the plans swung constantly between next objectives. With both the British and Americans decided that Germany must again be the focus of the next operation, the Mediterranean was decided as the next area of operations. The deciding argument was again to relieve the pressure on the Eastern Front and also to allow more time for a build-up of Allied forces prior to the invasion of Northern France. The final decision weighed the advantages of securing Sicily or Sardinia or both simultaneously. The joint invasion (Operation *Influx*) of both islands was deemed to be too resource-intensive to be feasible. Therefore, the decision was whether to focus on either Sardinia or Sicily. Sardinia (Operation *Brimstone*) provided a base closer to attack Rome next; it also offered a springboard with which to invade Corsica and then southern France. However, the invasion of Sardinia as well as Sicily would require extra men and machines, which the three arms of the services could ill-afford at this stage. Sicily (Operation *Whipcord*) could be captured and provide a base of operations from which to strike at the Italian mainland using far fewer resources. The capture of Sicily would also open up sea lanes between Gibraltar and the Suez Canal and there was potential to precipitate the overthrow of Mussolini if the war was brought to Italian soil. The CCS decision was close but Sicily was their eventual preferred option. This was presented to Churchill and Roosevelt for final approval on 22 January. The prime minister and president were in unison and made a joint decision: *Whipcord*, now renamed *Husky*, would be taken forward. The final target of the next Allied blow was to be Sicily, with the island now given the code-name 'HORRIFIED'. A top-secret message was duly sent to Eisenhower in North Africa stating that 'the Combined Chiefs of Staff have resolved that an attack against Sicily will be launched in 1943 with the target date as the period of the favourable July moon'.[1]

Deception plans to mask the Allies' intention to invade Sicily and Italy formed part of a concerted intelligence and disinformation operation named Operation *Barclay*. The intention was to promote to the Germans that the next major Allied attack would be in Sardinia, Greece or the Balkans. The deception plan was led by British MI5's Twenty Committee (so-called as it represented the Roman numerals for twenty, XX, and also stood for 'Double Cross' due to its use of double agents). The idea was to plant a dead body with false secret documents purportedly from Allied Combined Operations Headquarters along the Spanish coast where, the Allies believed, it would be handed over by Spanish authorities to German military intelligence, the *Abwehr*. The plan, code-named Operation *Mincemeat*, was the brainchild of two British intelligence officers, Flight Lieutenant Charles Cholmondeley of the RAF attached to Section B1 (a) of MI5 and Lieutenant Commander Ewen Montagu, a Royal Navy intelligence officer. They eventually found a suitable corpse at a London mortuary, later named as Glyndwr Michael – the 'man who never was', a homeless man reportedly found suffering the effects of consuming rat poison in a King's Cross warehouse. He was subsequently given a new identity of Acting Major William 'Bill' Martin of the Royal Marines, attached to the Combined Operations Headquarters. On 19 April HMS *Seraph*, a British submarine, left its Scottish base and headed for the Spanish coast near Huelva with its unusual cargo. The crew were only told that the capsule they were carrying contained Top Secret meteorological equipment. The crew approached their final destination, one mile offshore the Spanish coastline near Punto Umbria. At 04:30 they released the body into the sea and also a dinghy half a mile further south. By 09:30 the tide had washed both man and dinghy ashore where they were discovered by local fishermen. In the coming days Top Secret ULTRA intercepts from Allied intelligence picked up signals from the *Abwehr* in Spain reporting the discovery back to Berlin. The ruse had been believed. Sicily was discounted as the next possible Allied objective, with German troops consequently sent to reinforce the Balkans and Sardinia and even a flotilla of R boats being deployed away from Sicily to instead plant new minefields around the Greek mainland.

Meanwhile on the other side of the Atlantic, American officials approached the notorious Mafia boss 'Lucky' Luciano who was at the time incarcerated for running a prostitution racket. Officials requested his help in preventing pro-Nazi sympathisers working in the Mafia-controlled unions on the eastern seaboard of America from passing information that could be used by U-boats waiting off the shore to target Allied convoys. Luciano was also believed to have strong connections to the Sicilian Mafia and in turn they were reportedly tasked by Luciano to provide intelligence on the defences of Sicily and attempt to subvert the Italian troops based there, later supported by rumours that Allied planes during the invasion were dropping gold flags with a black 'L' for Luciano on villages prior to the American troops approaching. This was the signal for the local Mafia to arrange for the Italian defenders to disappear or surrender. The Americans were also approached by the British Special Operations Executive (SOE) who questioned whether the Mafia could be useful in the upcoming Sicilian invasion. 'We have some evidence as to (a) separatist tendency in Sicily started by former members of disbanded mafia. Military events might quickly emphasise such tendencies'.[2] The Sicilian Mafia, it was hoped, would be transformed into a short-term guerrilla force, similar to the French Resistance, able to pass on intelligence, cut enemy communications and even attack enemy forces.

The planning for the invasion of Sicily now moved onto the details of the invasion itself. The basic plan of the outline of the Sicily invasion had been agreed at the top level. With the main commanders still engaged in action in North Africa, the detailed planning of the Operation *Husky* was passed to British Major-General Charles Gairdner. He set up his planning headquarters at the *Ecole Normale* in the town of Bouzera just outside Algiers. The first factor to consider was geography. Sicily's geography dominated the strategy adopted by both the attacking and defending forces. The island is a rough triangle shape with its eastern coast nearest Italy measuring 125 miles whilst the other two coasts are around 175 miles in length. The 2-mile-wide Straits of Messina separate the islands from the Italian mainland. The British-held island fortress of Malta was only 55 miles to the south. The island has a narrow coastal plain which then rises quickly into the rugged hilly interior of the island, criss-crossed with valleys and ravines. Villages and towns were dotted across these hills with winding roads connected the conurbations. The east side of the island is dominated by Mount Etna, an active volcano of 10,922 feet (3,329 metres) height. The slopes of Mount Etna run down towards the sea, with the city

General Montgomery (right) seen inspecting Parachute Regiment soldiers later in the war. He was the British Forces commander for *Husky* and concieved the plan for Operation *Fustian*. (Battlefield Historian Ltd @ battlefieldhistorian.com BHC 002035)

of Catania, including a population of 100,000 people, at its feet. To the north of Catania is the port and capital city of Messina, to the south the port of Syracuse. In the far north-west of the island lies the port and city of Palermo. These three main cities and other major ports and towns, all situated on the flatter coastal plain, were connected by the island's only main road network. Due to the hilly terrain of the island these roads crossed rivers and valleys, necessitating the construction of key bridges. Three of these key bridges were on the road between Catania and Syracuse. One of these bridges was the Primosole Bridge.

The overall plan for the units to be involved in the invasion of Sicily, the 'stepping-stone' between Africa and Europe, had now been completed at the top level of the Allied Supreme Headquarters with General Eisenhower in overall command. His Deputy Commander-in-Chief was General Sir Harold Alexander who commanded the ground forces, collectively named the Allied 15th Army Group.

The campaign called for an army boundary to be established between the two armies, running north to south through the middle of the island, with Montgomery's ultimate objective to land in the south-east between Pachino and Syracuse and then capture Messina in the east with the ultimate goal of closing off any escape route to the Italian mainland for the remaining Italian and German forces. General George Patton's objective was to land in the west between Licata and Scoglitti and mop up further resistance on his way to Palermo. Montgomery's army was initially

Gen Harold Alexander (left), the ground force commander for 'Husky', in conversation with Gen Dwight D. Eisenhower, the Allied Supreme Commander in the Mediterranean. (Battlefield Historian Ltd @ battlefieldhistorian.com BHC 003023)

code-named as part of Task Force 545, with the American force code-named Task Force 343. At Montgomery's insistence, this was changed to an over-arching Task Force East with Montgomery's army now renamed to its preferred 'Eighth Army'. Patton, not to be outdone, renamed his force as the US Seventh Army and was part of Task Force West.

The Eighth Army consisted of two corps. Firstly XIII Corps, under Lieutenant-General Miles Dempsey, comprised the 5th and 50th Divisions along with the 4th Armoured Brigade. Secondly was XXX Corps led by Major-General Oliver Leese and consisted of the 51st Highland Division, 1st Canadian Division (included at the insistence of the Canadian Prime Minister, William Lyon Mackenzie King), 231st (Malta) Brigade and the 23rd Armoured Brigade. The 1st Airborne Division and 78th Armoured Division were to be held in reserve in North Africa until the landings in Sicily were underway and objectives then identified for these reserve divisions.

Patton's US Seventh Army was split into three groups. The first two groups were commanded by General Omar Bradley and consisted of 'Cent Force' which was centred around the 45th Division and 'Dime Force' which was based on the 1st

Infantry Division ('The Big Red One') supported by two Ranger battalions. The third group was named 'Joss Force' and comprised of the 3rd Infantry Division again supported by a Ranger battalion. Held back in reserve in North Africa were the 82nd Airborne Division and the 9th Infantry Division.

In addition to the seaborne landings, there were also to be airborne landings during the invasion. The US 82nd Airborne Division would initially be held in reserve but then land in support of the US Seventh Army, whilst the British 1st Airborne Division were to conduct brigade-sized landings along the eastern coast to support the Eighth Army by capturing a series of three bridges. The scarcity of bridging equipment available to the Allies meant that replacement bridges could not be built to create further crossing points on the island, therefore taking control of the existing bridges became a top priority to maintain the momentum of the invasion. The 1st Airborne Division was, therefore, given three objectives: firstly, Operation *Ladbroke* involved the seizing of the Ponte Grande, a road bridge south of Syracuse, which was to be taken by the 1st Airlanding Brigade commanded by Brigadier Philip Hicks in a glider assault; secondly, Operation *Glutton* was to target the port of Augusta, code-named SNOWBOOTS, and was given to the 2nd Parachute Brigade; thirdly, Operation *Fustian* covered the Primosole Bridge (the bridge itself was code-named 'MARSTON') and was to be the objective of the 1st Parachute Brigade. The 4th Parachute Brigade was to be held as divisional reserve. In addition, No. 3 Commando was to take the Ponte Dei Malati bridge over the River Leonardo near Lentini, the other major bridge on the Syracuse–Catania road. For this operation 1st Airborne Division was placed under the command of Montgomery's Eighth Army.

Operation *Fustian* was to be the biggest Allied airborne operation to date. Its intention was to deliver into battle by air nearly two thousand paratroopers at night to their objectives over 400 miles away and behind enemy lines. This would be the first time that an operation this size had been attempted by moonlight and as part of a major Allied invasion.

The 1st Parachute Brigade's task of capturing the Primosole Bridge was a vital objective, as it was the only crossing point over the Simeto and led directly into the open countryside south of Mount Etna on the Catania Plain. Three rivers, the Simeto, Dittaino and Gornalunga, straddled the south of the plain but flowed together into the Simeto only two kilometres from the coast. This therefore presented the opportunity for the Allies to cross onto the plain by capturing just Primosole Bridge. Its capture would give the Eighth Army access to the flat terrain of the plain and enable them to continue their advance northwards by spreading out their armoured units, far preferable to the alternative of becoming bottle-necked on the narrow coastal road. The plain, measuring 20 miles wide east to west and 8 miles long from north to south, was the only real area of terrain on the island where the Allies could use the space to out-flank the enemy and hasten their advance towards Messina, other than by using amphibious landings to get behind the enemy lines. The tables could be turned on the German and Italian defenders who were expected to use the bottleneck at Simeto to control the troops moving inland from the southern beaches. With the capture of the plain the Allies would instead be able to bottle the Axis forces up in Catania on a narrow front whilst using the plain to outflank the enemy and move its forces up to create a strong staging area with shorter lines of supply. The thin coastal strip surrounding Sicily only allowed troops to move laterally up and down main highways but access to the plain would allow Montgomery to also move his forces laterally across the chess board of Sicily. Alternatively, the bridge's destruction would seriously hamper the advance of the British on Sicily and keep them bottled up below Catania. On a personal level, it would also slow Montgomery's advance and potentially lead to Patton outpacing the British advance towards the ultimate prize of the island's main port, Messina. Once the 1st Parachute Brigade had captured the bridge, they would then have to defend it until relieved by units of the Eighth Army advancing from the landing beaches.

The naval task force was assigned to the command of Admiral of the Fleet Sir Andrew Cunningham, known to the men as 'ABC'. His job was to command the invasion fleet at sea, land the troops and then provide fire support from the big guns of the Allied ships offshore. The Mediterranean Air Command was under the RAF's Air Chief Marshal Tedder and was to provide fighter cover to supporting bombing raids and also to bring in paratroopers and gliders for the airborne operations.

Initially disagreement about how best to gain a foothold and proceed across Sicily was centred around the scope of the operation. The *Husky* plan called for widespread landings along the entire south-east coast and then a general advance in a northerly direction, with the Americans steering for Palermo and the British for Messina. Montgomery began sowing the seeds of his personal and professional clash with Patton. Montgomery was fresh from the North African campaign where he had earned worldwide fame as the 'Victor of Alamein'. Patton was coming late to the party and would have to play a subordinate role to Montgomery until later in the war. Montgomery devised an adaptation to the overall plan. He called for a scrapping of the westerly landings. Instead the US Seventh Army should be landed closer to his landing area and be deployed to protect his left flank whilst he made a dash for Messina. He eventually cornered Eisenhower's Chief of Staff, General Walter Bedell Smith, in the toilets of the *Ecole Normale* just prior to a meeting Eisenhower had organised to settle the plans at his Headquarters. Montgomery proceeded to explain his plan to Bedell Smith in the lavatory mirror by blowing on it to create condensation and then sketching out his plan. Alexander and Eisenhower met the next day after hearing all sides of the argument the previous day. They decided to adopt Montgomery's revised plan to concentrate forces and push towards Messina.

Sicily's defence was led by General Alfredo Guzzoni with two corps of the Italian 6th Army numbering 200,000 Italian troops Despite the large numbers of men, only half were front-line infantry soldiers organised into four divisions. The remainder were local militias of conscripts who mainly guarded ports and static infrastructure sites. This force was further reinforced with German troops. The main German formations were the Hermann Goering Panzer Division and the 15th Panzergrenadier Division with a combined strength of 160 tanks and 32,000 men and further supported by 30,000 Luftwaffe ground personnel. Guzzoni would use the inferior Italian troops to guard the coastline and inflict initial losses on any Allied landings. The German

The architects of Operation '*Husky*' (seated from left to right) Anthony Eden, Britain's Foreign Secretary: Field Marshal Alan Brooke, Chief of the Imperial General Staff: Prime Minister Winston Churchill; Gen Dwight Eisenhower, Supreme Commander Morth africa: (standing left to right) Air Marshal Arthur Tedder; Admiral Andrew Cunningham; General alexander; and Gen Bernard Montgomery. (Battlefield Historian Ltd @ battlefieldhistorian.com)

and Italian troops would be based further inland and then rushed to meet the Allies once they moved off the beaches.

To keep the Axis forces guessing where the next blow would fall, the Allied planners employed the RAF and USAAF in bombing targets across Italy and also in Greece. The air forces were able to attack on two fronts as planes flew from England against targets in northern Italy and from the North African desert against southern Italy and Greece. Airfields on Sicily were the primary target whilst the beaches themselves were left relatively unscathed so as to preserve an element of surprise as to the landing sites.

By 10 July, only two airfields in Sicily remained fully operational and over half the Axis aircraft based on Sicily had been forced to leave the island. Between mid-May and the invasion, Allied airmen flew 42,227 sorties in support of Operation *Husky* and destroyed 323 German and 105 Italian aircraft, for the loss of 250 aircraft, mostly to anti-aircraft fire over Sicily.[3]

Staging operations began in May against the small island of Pantelleria, some 70 miles (110km) south-west of Sicily and 150 miles (240km) north-west of Malta, to prevent the airfield there being used in support of Axis troops attempting to withdraw from North Africa. It also subdued any potential anti-aircraft defences that could potentially interfere with the airborne armada being prepared for the Sicilian invasion. On 13 and 31 May the cruiser HMS *Orion* bombarded the island and from 6 June, Allied attacks increased. On 11 June, after a naval bombardment and seaborne landing by the British 1st Infantry Division (Operation *Corkscrew*) the island garrison of 11,399 men surrendered, with the only British casualty being a single soldier who was bitten by a mule.[4] The Pelagie islands of Lampedusa and Linosa, some 90 miles (140km) west of Malta, followed in short order on 12 June. As the staging operations were underway to prepare for the invasion, the men of the invasion force were also being prepared for battle.

CHAPTER THREE

'Battle Prep'

From 19 June to 5 July the 1st Airborne Division undertook the 1,200-km journey from Mascara in Algeria by road, rail and air to a new assembly area at M'saken, a small hamlet between Kairouan and the coastal town of Sousse in Tunisia. It was from here that the 1st Airborne Division would train for and then launch their forthcoming operation. The Kairouan area consisted of 18 airstrips, measuring 6,000 feet (1,800m) long by 300 feet (90m) wide, constructed by army engineers over the previous weeks. These sparse and dusty desert airfields were manned by the 38th RAF Wing along with the US 51st Wing. Six of the 18 airstrips were 20 miles (32km) to the south and assigned to the 1st British Airborne Division, lettered from A to F, with the remaining 12 assigned to the American 82nd Airborne Division. Airfields A–D were further assigned to the parachute troops whilst E and F were assigned to glider training and operations.

The area was chosen to host the 1st Airborne Division for two main reasons. Firstly, it redeployed the airborne troops into an area where they could train and rebuild their strength away from the congestion of air and ground space in Tunisia by other Allied units. Secondly, it provided a visible reminder to German intelligence that an Allied airborne formation was training within striking distance of several likely next targets.

Prior to the move to M'saken, on 17 May, whilst the men were still guessing where they were headed next, the forthcoming operation and intended targets were revealed to the brigade commanders. Each in turn could now start the men training for their upcoming missions by using scenarios closely resembling the real thing but without giving too much information away. Lathbury devised a series of exercises for 1st Parachute Brigade, code-named *Cactus*, to slowly merge the aircrews and his paratroopers into a single well-oiled machine whilst at the same time bring both the veterans and replacements up to operational tempo. The veterans could pass on hard-won knowledge of the battlefield ranging from first-hand experience of how the Germans fought to handling captured enemy weapons.

As the brigade was brought up to full strength its 'orbat' began to settle. The 1st Parachute Brigade was commanded by Brigadier Lathbury and comprised the 1st

2nd BATTALION PARACHUTE REGIMENT, 1944

Back Row.—Lieut. J. H. A. Mousell. Lieut. J. A. Russell. Lieut. A. Roberts. Lieut. A. L. Tannenbaum. Lieut. D. M. Douglass. Lieut. J. G. Blunt. Lieut. J. T. Ainslie. Lieut. J. G. Purdy. Lieut. A. J. McDermont. Lieut. R. A. Vlasto. Lieut. C. M. Stanford. Lieut. D. E. C. Russell. Lieut. G. P. W. Ellum.

Middle Row.—Lieut. P. H. Cane. Capt. J. W. Logan, D.S.O., R.A.M.C. Capt. A. M. Frank, M.C. Lieut. J. H. Grayburn. Lieut. W. N. Dormer. Lieut. P. H. Barry. Lieut. R. B. Woods. Capt. R. E. Morton. Lieut. R. H. Levien. Capt. J. Timothy, M.C. Capt. A. J. Rutherford. Lieut. P. R. Jessop. Lieut. C. D. Briteux-Buchanan, M.C.

Front Row.—Rev. B. M. Egan, M.C., C.F. (R.C.) Capt. D. McLean. Major V. Dover, M.C. Major P. J. Albury. Major D. W. Wallis. Lieut.-Colonel J. D. Frost, D.S.O., M.C. Major A. D. Tatham-Warten. Major D. E. Cranley, M.C. Capt. F. K. Hoyer-Miller. Capt. S. C. Panter, M.C. Lieut. (Qmr). J. T. Parker.

Officers from 2 Para pictured in 1944, many were Primosole Bridge veterans. Back row: L-R - Lt Mousell, Lt J Russell, Lt Roberts, Lt Tannenbaum, Lt Douglass, Lt Blunt, Lt Ainslie, Lt Purdy, Lt McDermont, Lt Vlasto, Lt Stanford, Lt D Russell, Lt Ellum. Middle Row: L-R - Lt Cane, Capt Logan DSO, Capt Frank MC, Lt Grayburn (later VC at Arnhem), Lt Dormer, Lt Barry, Lt Woods, Capt Morton, Lt Levien, Capt Timothy MC, Capt Rutherford, Lt Jessop, Lt Briteux-Buchanan MC. Front Ror: L-R - Rev Egan MC, Capt McLean, Maj Dover MC, Maj Albury, Maj Wallis, Lt Col Frost DSO MC, Maj Tatham-Warten, Maj Cranley MC, Capt Hoyer-Millar, Capt Panter MC, Lt Parker. (Courtesy of Air Assault Museum)

Parachute Battalion (commanded by Lt Col Alastair Pearson), the 2nd Parachute Battalion (Lt Col John Frost), the 3rd Parachute Battalion (Lt Col 'Bill' Yeldham), the 16th (Parachute) Field Ambulance commanded by Lieutenant Colonel Gerard 'Ross' Wheatley, the 1st (Parachute) Squadron Royal Engineers commanded by Major William Murray and the 1st (Airlanding) Anti-Tank Battery, Royal Artillery commanded by Major Bill Arnold. Also attached for Operation *Fustian* would be No.4 Army Film and Photo Section (See Appendix A for full ORBAT).[1]

A World War II British parachute battalion had an establishment of around 550 men divided into four companies. There were three rifle companies. 1 Para's rifle companies were lettered R, S and T Companies while 2 and 3 Para lettered their rifle companies as A, B and C Companies. Each of the rifle companies was divided into a small headquarters and three rifle platoons. The rifle platoons were numbered in order across the battalion. The first company contained 1, 2 and 3 Platoons, the second company contained 4, 5 and 6 Platoons whilst the third company contained 7, 8 and 9 Platoons. The platoons had three sections; each section had a Bren

A paratrooper using a Sten gun. (Courtesy of Air Assault Museum)

machine gun and there was a platoon 2-inch mortar as well as the men's own personal weapons, mainly Lee Enfield .303 rifles and Sten guns. The fourth company was HQ Company. This company contained the battalion's support weapons overseen by a company HQ, then comprising the mortar platoon with their 4 x 3in mortars, the machine gun platoon with their Vickers machine guns, the signals platoon, administrative platoon and the intelligence section.

The individual para was armed with the Lee Enfield .303 Rifle No.4 as standard. This weapon had a 10-round magazine with an effective range of 500 yards. It was an extremely reliable bolt-action rifle with a 'pig-sticker' bayonet that could be fitted for close-quarter combat. However, in North Africa sand did cause stoppages to the bolt-action mechanism. Each rifleman carried 105 rounds of ammunition for his rifle, 55 rounds in each of the webbing pouches on his chest, plus an additional bandolier of 50 rounds if required. Each man also carried a clip of three tracer rounds to aid target recognition if needed to help other soldiers identify enemy positions.

Each man's kit was contained in his 'webbing' which was the standard-issue 1937 pattern webbing. Men also carried an entrenching tool, water bottle and haversack comprising weapon cleaning kit, rations and cooking equipment. Each man also carried a fighting knife; during the campaign in North Africa it was carried in the trouser pocket, but was found to catch against the knee. It was continued to be carried but its location was decided by the individual paratrooper.

Parachute battalions were more freely issued with the lightweight Sten sub-machine gun than regular infantry units. Each battalion was armed with an additional 429 Sten guns as a reserve. This could be interchanged with rifles as the commanding officer saw fit – on the Bruneval raid, with Major John Frost leading C Company 2 Para, every man was armed with a Sten gun. The early variants suffered from stoppages due to the rushed nature of their mass production but it was an effective weapon as its 9mm round had better stopping power than the .303 round. Fitted with a 32-round magazine, it could be fired in semi-automatic or fully automatic mode. Most Sten-carrying men carried four full magazines for this weapon plus further four magazines worth of loose ammunition.

Each section within a platoon would also have a Bren light machine gun to serve as fire support. This was again fed with .303 ammunition, the same calibre ammunition that was used by the Spitfire, with one in every five rounds a tracer round to help spot the fall of shot. The weapon was crewed by two men, one to fire and one to support the re-loading as the weapon was not belt-fed but magazine-fed. With a magazine of 28 rounds, constant changing of the magazines was required but this also meant the firers had to be more accurate and less wasteful when suppressing the enemy. The Bren was accurate out to a range of 600 yards but had a slower firing rate when compared to its belt-fed German adversary, the MG42. The loaded magazines for the Bren were shared out amongst the men to spread the weight, rather than just the Bren team carry all of the ammunition, with normally 21 magazines being carried amongst the remainder of the platoon. The Bren gun three-man team would carry four magazines each and then each rifleman would carry two magazines each for the Bren.

The paras would also carry a sidearm, most commonly the standard British-issue pistols of either a .38 Enfield or Webley revolver. After 1942 most men were issued with the American Colt .45cal automatic pistol with a 7-round magazine. The pistol would be loaded with a magazine and each man would carry a further three to five magazines in their kit. The Colt was preferred by the troops as the trigger was lighter than the Webley, meaning greater accuracy and speed of firing. A signal pistol would also be carried by a member of each platoon along with six green and six red flares for signalling purposes.

A selection of grenades would be carried throughout each unit. The No.36 Mills grenade was the most common grenade used as a high explosive. Each rifleman carried four No.36 grenades with machine gunners and specialists only carrying two. Bakelite No.69 concussion grenades were used in Africa but were not so commonly used after Sicily in favour of the No.36 Mills grenade. Smokescreens were provided by the No.77 phosphorous grenade but could also be deployed against personnel and bunkers. Thirty-six phosphorous grenades were carried by each company. Each platoon would have a 2-inch mortar for additional fire support away from the HQ Company's heavy weapons, normally a member of the platoon HQ,. The 2-inch mortar was commonly carried with six to eight white phosphorous rounds to provide hasty smokescreens, whilst the heavier barrages were provided by the 3-inch mortars. The 2-inch mortar was later adapted for parachute formations by producing a cut-down Mark VIII version reducing the barrel length from 27cm to 19cm but still giving a range of up to 500 yards (457m).

Assault platoons for Operation *Fustian* also carried two Bangalore torpedoes per each of the two assault platoons in order to blow a path through any barbed-wire entanglements.

Support weapons would be parachuted inside a container slung underneath the aircraft and released via a static line assembly by the pilot. The heavy weapons were too heavy for the individual paratroopers to jump with as the supporting jump ropes couldn't carry the weight of the kit once the rope was lowered and the additional weight would also speed up the paratrooper's rate of descent, increasing the chance of injury on landing.

The 3-inch mortar was used to fire high-explosive (HE) rounds and would break down into three parts – the barrel, base-plate and the bipod. Each man of the three-man crew would jump with their respective piece of kit. Support weapons, such as the 3-inch mortar, would be marked using white mine tape to denote a 'must-go load'. If a man couldn't jump for whatever reason, the next available man would be expected to drop his kit and jump with the 'must-go load' instead. Due to the weight of the kit, men parachuting with support weapons normally stood at the front of the stick and jumped first to avoid them struggling to make their way to the door with their heavy kit and overshoot the drop zone. The 3-inch mortar itself had a range of 1.6 miles (2.5km) and would normally be used in a mortar line comprising three mortars in total in a triangular formation around 40 metres apart, as this was the lethal radius of the high explosive rounds. This would allow for the 'beaten zone' of the rounds landing at the other end to fully encompass an enemy position and provide an overlapping killing zone. Each battalion had four 3-inch mortars.

The Vickers machine gun was crewed by four men who would break the gun down, including ammunition, into four loads for jumping. The four Vickers per battalion were water-cooled, the Vickers had been in service since World War I but was still a reliable weapon.

Anti-tank weapons were normally carried in the form of one PIAT per platoon. This fired a hollow-shaped charge up to 100 yards (91m) and was effective against most German and Italian armour. The two-man crew would share the 18 PIAT bombs per weapon around the rest of the platoon as each bomb weighed 2.2lb (1kg). Further defensive weapons were carried including the No.75 Hawkins mine and the No.82 Gammon grenade, named after Captain Arthur Gammon of 1 Para who invented the cloth-stockinette-covered bomb containing C-2 explosive. One Hawkins mine was carried per each man with a further three Gammon bombs being carried per section. The Parachute Battalion's firepower was complimented by the airlanding anti-tank battery attached to the brigade. It was equipped with the brigade's only anti-tank guns, the British 6-pounder. The Ordnance Quick-Firing 6-pounder 7 cwt, often simply known as the 6-pounder, came into service to replace the smaller 2-pounder which was proving ineffective against improving panzer armour and also allowed the 25-pounder to revert to its intended role of heavy artillery support. The 6-pounder first saw action at the first battle of El Alamein in May 1942 where it destroyed 15 enemy tanks at Gazala. It could fire both high explosive and armour-piercing rounds and could destroy any German tank of the time. However, as Panthers and then Tigers began to appear on the battlefield, it was found to be ineffective against their frontal armour, though still able to penetrate the side and rear armour plating. With a range of 8km and able to penetrate armour up to 90mm thick, the weapon provided a massive boost in firepower for the lightly armoured paratroopers. Despite

Men from 1 Para emplaning a Dakota for a training jump in North Africa. (Courtesy of Air Assault Museum)

the formation being a parachute brigade, the only way to transport the anti-tank guns and the jeeps to tow them, was by glider. Transporting artillery by air was something new to the British or any other army, and this would be the first time that any artillery guns had ever been flown into combat.

Communications were provided by a range of wireless sets from man-portable to vehicle-mounted radios. The earlier No.18 radio was replaced in North Africa by the stronger, but heavier, No.22 set. This had a range of around 1 mile but was VHF and only worked on a line-of-sight basis. This meant that its range and effectiveness were seriously curtailed in the hills of North Africa. The flatter terrain of Sicily meant it would potentially prove more effective, however, and allow for coordinated naval fire to be called in to support the paras' defensive positions and break up Fallschirmjaeger attacks.

In terms of uniform, the men were now more settled on their combat dress. Parachutist kit had been adapted over time not only following the lessons the British had learned themselves but also through adopting kit used by their enemies. The 1942-pattern Denison smock was now standard issue and was worn over the standard battledress of 'Angola' shirt, denim trousers and anklets. However, additional pockets were added to the arms and legs of the battle-dress for extra carrying ability. The early version of the Denison smock had a front zip only halfway down the front of the smock whereas later variants had a full-length zip. Many men had the tops of their socks sewn to the cuffs to provide extra wind- and water-proofing. Helmets evolved from the initial leather helmets to the cut-down para's helmet including padded interior. Another distinguishing feature of airborne troops was the universal use of the face veil, commonly known as the scrim-net which was worn either around the neck as a scarf, worn over the soldier as camouflage netting or simply added to the helmet. Lessons learned from North Africa meant the men now also added scrim nets to their helmets to distinguish themselves in the heat of battle from their Fallschirmjaeger counterparts who wore similar shaped para-helmets. Strips of hessian could be attached to the scrim net on the helmet to further help break up the outline of the helmet. Webbing consisted of the 1937 standard issue, as well as the A-frame Bergens. The helmet was often replaced in battle by the now-standard maroon beret, affectionately known as the 'Maroon Machine'. The airborne insignia of Pegasus, designed by Edward Seago, a camouflage expert serving in Southern Command, was now standard and worn on the upper left arm, with the blue 'Wings' parachutist badge worn on the upper right arm. When in battle-dress each battalion in 1st Parachute Brigade also wore their own coloured lanyard, made from the rigging lines of their parachutes and dyed: 1 Para wore green, 2 Para wore gold, 3 Para wore red and Brigade HQ wore blue. (This has since changed and in today's Parachute Regiment, 1 Para are represented by a maroon lanyard, 2 Para by a blue lanyard and 3 Para by a green lanyard.)

After their experiences in North Africa, directives were handed down to the men to establish uniformity in their carrying of equipment to ease the locating of essential kit between the men in the heat of battle. A set of 'fighting scales' was established to provide a required amount of kit and ammunition to be carried into battle and ease logistical resupply of the unit. Every man was directed to keep their medical kit in their left leg pocket. This allowed for all casualties to be quickly treated by a comrade using the injured man's own medical kit. A spare pair of socks was to be kept in their right leg pocket. In the smock was to be carried berets and water purifying kit in the inside left pocket and a tea ration in the inside right pocket. Upper outside chest pockets were to contain food rations whilst the lower pockets would contain grenades and gammon bomb fuses. The haversack on the men's webbing would last them for 48 hours in the field and contained two rations of biscuits, tinned drippings and tinned cheese plus washing and cooking kit. Longer-term kit, such as respirators and gas capes, would be left at company stores prior to deploying into the field.

Military parachuting was still very much in an experimental stage in the British Army but their parachute design was superior to that used by the Germans. British parachutes were suspended by harnesses on the shoulders, allowing the men to steer their canopy to a limited extent but more importantly allowed the British paras to hang vertically from the parachutes and so assess their flight downwards and better prepare for their landings. The British also had the luxury of having their parachutes packed and recovered from training jumps by a supporting RAF detachment. During the *Cactus* exercises there were 16 packers working in three shifts of six hours each. In this way they managed to pack 500 parachutes per day.[2] As a reminder to the packer, inside the top of every parachute was a note that read, 'Remember, a man's life depends on every parachute you pack.' Parachute failures were rare but there were instances of 'chutes not deploying properly, known as a 'roman candle'. In such situations a paratrooper could do nothing to help himself and simply fell to his death.

As well as parachuting, Lathbury slowly turned up the daily routine from fitness and weapons training to participating in larger exercises as a rehearsal for Sicily. The men's daily routine would begin with reveille at 05:00 before the heat of the day began to take effect and then rise from their sleeping bags into the semi-darkness of the morning. There would still be a chill in the air from the cold desert night. Around 05:30 the men would be formed up into their platoons or companies and then embark on an early morning run or forced march. Around the perimeter of the camp and in the surrounding hills, clouds of red dust would be kicked up as groups of paratroopers struggled in the dust and now rising temperatures to keep the pace with the leading runners. The officers would lead the run with the corporals keeping the middle of the pack of the runners up to speed, with the sergeants at the rear 'encouraging' the stragglers to not fall back. Any men who picked up injuries on the fitness would be sent limping back to camp to see the medics whilst any other stragglers who failed to keep up with the pace would find themselves at the mercy of the sergeants. Punishment could include being given extra jobs, known as 'fatigues', such as taking an extra shift on guard or cleaning the toilets. They may well also have been put on remedial fitness and taken through another fitness session later that same day or for a more prolonged period in order to bring them up to speed with the remainder of the platoon. After fitness, the men would wash and change into their battledress whilst talking through any events of the morning's fitness regime. Stragglers would normally expect to have to endure a fair amount of banter from the guys who had kept up on the run. Men would complete ablutions then head to the cookhouse for breakfast at 07:30. After breakfast the NCOs would put the men to work in groups from 08:30 to 10:30, either cleaning equipment, weapons training or other admin chores. This would take the men up to lunchtime when they would again head to the cookhouse before being 'stood down' for the remainder of the day. The men would then use this opportunity to take a siesta in the shade of their tents away from the heat of the midday African sun. The afternoon would be whiled away with games of cards, sport, reading or even finding local wildlife, such as scorpions and spiders, and then setting them together in empty ration boxes to watch the resulting effects. Such boredom was usually countered by driving the men to the sea at Sousse to spend the afternoon swimming.

The men were accommodated in tents and marquees scattered around the airfield and in the olive groves that surrounded the perimeter of the airfields. They used the trees to hang their tents from and slept in green camouflaged sleeping bags on

Paratroopers charging an enemy position during training in North Africa. (Courtesy of Air Assault Museum)

the ground. Conditions were harsh with strong and hot winds blowing constantly a layer of sand over everything, including the men's food, with the crunch of grit in every mouthful of food being common. Each man had his water rationed to only one pint per man per day, requiring them to queue up for their water ration each time the water bowser trucks arrived at the brigade headquarters from their latest resupply trip. Washing and shaving were therefore not as rigidly enforced, in turn attracting masses of flies.

Apart from home-made entertainment the men were spending their days by waking early and completing route marches before the heat of the day kicked in. They then completed admin tasks and other training until midday before whiling away the hours in the heat of the afternoon by sleeping or relaxing. Aside from the heat and flies, another hazard of the desert was the 'Dust Devil' normally kicked up by the engines of a departing aircraft and then spiralled into a mini-tornado, causing amusement as men chased after their kit across the base.

The men of the 1st Parachute Brigade were concentrating on training that was more specific to their upcoming task. Four major exercises were carried out during July, named *Cactus I, II, III* and *IV*, with the units now regaining their pre-North African campaign strength and cohesion. The men were briefed that the aim of the exercises was to focus on parachuting again after their recent role as static front-line infantry living in defensive positions. The men had to retune their airborne skills through this series of exercises.

However, unknown to anyone else in the brigade, Brigadier Lathbury had received Operation Order No.14 – the plans to seize and hold the Primosole Bridge in Sicily – and the exercises would be used to start to drill the men in their roles for the upcoming plan that Lathbury had already began finalising. *Cactus I* on 10 June was a battalion-size jump by 3 Para, offering the pilots their first chance to drop the men in a mass jump. Of the 35 aircraft in the exercise, seven dropped their men off target, incurring 23 light casualties.[3] *Cactus II* gave the pilots more practice to hone their skills of dropping parachutists on target. 2 Para were parachuting this time, led by pathfinders marking the drop zone, followed by a march to a pre-designated target position. It was a more accurate drop this time with one serious casualty and three light casualties incurred. Next it was the turn of 1 Para along with Brigade HQ to jump. *Cactus III* began to resemble a rehearsal for the upcoming airborne operation. Once on the ground, men from 1 Para would advance with engineers to capture and hold a target, followed by the men of 2 and 3 Para as reinforcements. The addition of the brigade HQs would mean there would be more scrutiny of the pilots and paras on this exercise. Time was getting short until they would be embarking on the real thing and the pilots in particular had to start improving their delivery of troops accurately to the drop zone. For this jump 47 aircraft were provided, 38 from 60 Group and nine from the newly arrived 296 Squadron which would be completing their first air drop in North Africa. The exercise was not hailed as a success by brigade HQ who considered the 296 Squadron drop as 'most inaccurate' leading to one serious casualty and 28 light casualties.[4] Dropping accuracy didn't improve much with *Cactus IV*, a full brigade-size jump undertaken at night by 109 aircraft. Fourteen serious casualties and 55 lighter casualties were incurred and caused many to wonder what the drop would be like under enemy fire if the troops couldn't be delivered accurately and safely during daylight hours under training conditions.

When the air drop for *Cactus IV* is broken down by battalion it is clear to see the effects of a dispersed drop.[5]

UNIT	Aircraft (A/C) dropped on correct DZ within 5 minutes of correct time	A/C dropped on wrong DZ	A/C dropped on no DZ or at wrong time	A/C not dropped for various reasons
1 Para	7	19	4	1
2 Para	19	-	5	2
3 Para	6	-	25+	1
Fd Sqn RE	1	3	-	-
Para Fd Amb	-	4	-	-
Bde HQ	3	3	3	-

These figures are spookily similar to the figures for the actual drop on Sicily and show the detrimental effects on an airborne formation if they are not accurately put down in the right place from which to begin their battle. The table clearly shows that 2 Para was dropped largely intact and on time and allowed them to form up better and move off the drop zone quicker than the other battalions. 1 Para was widely dispersed but the figures for 3 Para show just what a disaster their drop had been. They had been dropped in 500–2,000 yards south of their drop zone and at the wrong time due to the pilots confusing lights on the ground with that of the drop zone marking lights, effectively taking one third of the brigade's fighting strength off the battlefield before the fighting had even started. The small number of aircraft that did correctly drop their troops on time and on target highlights that only a small fraction of the brigade was delivered to where it needed to be on landing. This was just a training exercise, with enemy activity, the men could expect even more chaos for the real jump ahead. Therefore the men were expected to anticipate this situation and use their airborne initiative to put these obstacles behind them and start tabbing towards their objective to join the fight.

The parachute units carried out a total of 8,913 descents and exercises were carried out up to brigade level. Casualties were incurred, with two killed and 100 seriously injured, as well as a parachuting trial involving a donkey, which was ultimately unsuccessful.[6] The brigade was now training with the crews of the US 51st Wing, commanded by Colonel Ray Dunn, and their C-47 Skytrains, known to the British as 'Dakotas' and nicknamed the 'Gooney Bird' by the Americans. This was to be the same aircrew and aircraft that would deliver them to their targets in the upcoming Sicily campaign. The more widespread use of the American Dakotas for forthcoming operations allowed for an improvement in the speed of despatching troops from the aircraft as the paratroopers could now exit the aircraft from the side door of the Dakota from a standing position, which meant a more concentrated dispersal of troops over a drop zone due to a faster exit. Previously, when parachuting from Whitley and Albemarle bombers, paratroopers had to hop forward from a sitting position on the floor of the aircraft, known as bunny-hopping, and then exit the aircraft through a cut-out hole in the floor of the aeroplane. The only draw-back to the new Dakota aircraft was the addition of a long-range fuel tank fitted to the inside of the aircraft, which reduced space and providing a flammable hazard if being shot at. Although the airborne troops and aircrew trained and socialised together, the airborne troops even at this stage questioned the navigational abilities of the US aircrew. This sense of foreboding crisis, unfortunately, was later largely to be proven to be correct. The American aircraft flew in a 'V' formation comprising five aircraft, due to a shortage of navigators. The navigator would be situated in the lead plane of the 'V' with the remaining four aircraft in the formation following. If contact was lost with this lead aircraft, there was no real contingency for the other aircraft to accurately plot their way to their designated drop zones. This would prove to be a hugely significant factor in the widespread delivery of the paratroopers in the invasion.

The use of aircraft to support airborne operations was still contentious for some, notably Air Marshal 'Bomber' Harris of the RAF who insisted that every plane should be focussed on the destruction of German cities to end the war more quickly. 'Parachute or glider operations are not a practical operation of war…the weather in Europe is unsuitable for airborne operations…airborne troops could not be employed with any material contribution to victory … the only alternative (to using bombers to drop parachutists and tow gliders) was to set up a separate transport force'.[7] Competing ideas from the Allied leadership persisted on all topics throughout the war, particularly in the upcoming invasion of Sicily between Generals Montgomery and Patton. Montgomery liked to use his airborne troops to lay a carpet for his ground forces to advance. Patton instead liked to use his paratroopers as a mobile reserve to be parachuted in behind friendly lines to bolster the front line.

Brigadier Lathbury slowly increased the tempo of training whilst realising that the men still need a break after the endeavours of their recent fighting and also for the new replacements to bed in. Recreational visits were allowed with day trips organised to the local towns, such as Mostagenen and Sidi bel Abbes, to allow the men to barter with the locals for souvenirs and extra rations, or just for a spot of tourism. Training consisted of fitness training, manoeuvres from individual to battalion level and also weapons training. Lathbury insisted on each man being able to use the weapons of the enemy due to the chance that parachute-dropped weapons canisters might not be retrieved once on the drop zone. For night jumps, the weapons containers were trialled with white and black paint in a dazzle pattern to aid their location. Later, small blue lights were attached to the containers to further aid recognition of them during night jumps. This trialling of kit and technique continued by all units whilst they were in North Africa, derived from their experiences of jumping into battle so far in the war. This again highlights the infancy of parachute operations. At this stage, under Lt Col John Frost's direction, 2 Para also began trialling jumping with their kit attached to their legs via rigging lines taken from unserviceable parachutes, to be lowered on a rope attached to their parachute harness once their parachute canopy had deployed, as opposed to dropping weapons containers for each stick. Previously Sten guns and pistols could be tucked into each man's uniform to be jumped with but heavier or longer weapons would have to go into the weapons containers. At night, and under fire, these weapon containers were commonly lost or time was wasted locating them, only for men to eventually take the first weapon that they came across. That weapon would not be zeroed to the particular soldier's

Two paratroopers lying behind fold in ground whilst a third stands and throws a No.36 grenade. (Courtesy of Air Assault Museum)

requirements which led to a loss of accuracy when fired. Personal weapons would now be packed into a valise and attached to the side of the kitbag. Jumping with their kit attached would be trialled for the first time in combat in 2 Para's next operation and would prove to be so successful that it is still employed by all airborne forces across the world to this day.

The commanders of 2 Para also began to use sound in order to rally men at the rendezvous (RV) on the drop zone (DZ) after the battalion had jumped. Lt Col John Frost had been serving in Iraq with the Iraq Levies when the war broke out. He was posted back to his parent unit, The Cameronians, when his contract with the Levies expired in October 1940. As a leaving gift, he was presented with an inscribed copper hunting horn with the words 'Capt JD Frost with best wishes from the Members of the Royal Exodus Hunt'.[8] The battalion commander used his hunting horn when rallying the troops to the muster on drop zones, as John Frost recalls, 'in the still African night we found this far quicker than rallying to light or smoke'.[9] This was a lesson learnt from recent fighting that would allow quicker arming and organising by the para formations once on the ground. Later at Arnhem, 2 Para would rally to the sound of Frost's hunting horn on the drop zones.

The American 82nd Airborne Division, commanded by General Matthew Ridgway, was situated in the desert near 1st Airborne Division and training for its upcoming assault on Sicily. The 82nd Airborne was also finding Kairouan a tough place to be staying. Food supply problems meant that they were having spam for breakfast, lunch and dinner. Eventually, General Ridgway, the divisional commander, ordered $1,000 of the divisional welfare fund to be used 'to provide a beef dinner with "all the trimmings" and one bottle of warm beer per man'.[10]

The paras did have the pleasure though of watching the men of the 1st Airlanding Brigade and their associates from the RAF and USAAF assemble the newly delivered Horsa and WACO gliders. Many of the troops, and even the glider pilots, had never seen these American Waco gliders before, which were built by the Weaver Aircraft Company (WACO) in Ohio, and yet they were due to glide into Sicily in them in only a few days. Officially named the Cargo Glider 4A, shortened to just the CG-4A or usually just the WACO, the glider was built to deliver a jeep and its crew to the battlefield. Once landed, the jeep would drive forwards out of the glider towards the cockpit whilst the nose of the glider simultaneously lifted via a pulley to allow the jeep to exit. The first glider was towed from Ghana to Thiersville by Lieutenant Allan of the USAAF. The first batch had been delivered to the West African port of Accra but most of the consignment had been damaged by sea water, leaving only one serviceable glider with which to fly to Thiersville and begin training the Glider Pilot Regiment on its use. However, this token appearance of a single glider fuelled the military rumour machine – there would definitely be an airborne element of wherever the next major Allied operation was to be. The American WACO gliders were much smaller than their British Horsa counterparts and were known as Hadrians rather than Wacos when in British service. The Horsa was designed to carry both a jeep and the 6-pounder field gun that it towed or 32 fully equipped troops. It would be released as close as possible to its target to reduce its gliding time over enemy territory. Once released it would glide down to earth at a 45-degree angle, coming in to land at speeds of up to 80 knots before ideally stopping within 175 metres.

In contrast, the WACO could only carry either the jeep or the 6-pounder, not both. Alternatively, it could carry between 14 and 18 fully equipped troops. Therefore, due to the shortage of tug aircraft the Horsa was generally given priority due to its heavier payload of men and material. American pilots were attached to the British Glider Pilot Regiment to provide a minimal level of training on the Waco gliders. Lieutenant Allan at first had only his single WACO glider with which to give flights to prospective WACO pilots. However, over the coming days a second consignment of WACO gliders began to arrive at La Senza airfield. The glider pilots had to assemble their own aircraft, which arrived still in their containers. Each glider was packed into five containers, flat-packed into their 70,000 parts. Each glider took 30 men one whole day to assemble, usually beginning with the American engineers having to read the instruction manual first and then supervising its construction. Soon enough though, the gliders were being constructed on an ad hoc assembly line and then flown onwards to the airfields for further training and operations.

Some Horsa gliders were flown directly from England in two legs as part of Operation *Buzzard*. It was the longest flight made by gliders during the war. Of the 30 gliders that left England, only 19 made it to Africa.[11] The remainder were either shot down by roaming Luftwaffe fighters, or ditched on route due to technical difficulties. As the men constructed the gliders they then lived in the empty WACO containers in which they had been delivered. They would soon be flying over this same stretch of water on their way to join the fray of the battle of Sicily.

On 6 July, the paras' training camp was rocked at 14:30 by the explosion of the nearby divisional ammunition dump, some 800 tons of ordnance, which was the entire supply of ammunition for the upcoming operation. Nissen huts nearest the dump were flattened in the blast which continued to burn until 22:00. Major Smith, 3 Para's second-in-command, was also hospitalised with serious head injuries. Alastair Pearson remembers 'somebody in another battalion thought the best way to clear a cactus hedge was to set fire to it. The wind caught the flames which ignited the divisional ammunition dump and produced a major fireworks display'.[12] No one was charged with starting the blaze but 3 Para were the closest battalion to the dump at the time! The losses were replaced in time for the invasion of Sicily but it added to the men's eagerness to get out on to the battlefield as it couldn't be any worse than waiting around in the hot and dusty North African desert.

The men were now fit and ready for combat again after five weeks of training. The replacements were keen to get into the thick of battle as that was the reason they had volunteered to join the Parachute Regiment, and the old hands were now rested and were again keen to get to grips with the enemy, on Axis home ground for the first time. The division was joined by 4th Parachute Brigade, less 11th Parachute Battalion which had remained in Palestine to carry out a number of minor airborne operations, to act as a reserve for future operations if required. During the final days of training the brigade received a visit at 11:30 on 8 July by General Montgomery. He drove his jeep into the middle of the hollow-square of men on parade and implored them to break ranks and gather around his jeep as he delivered his pep talk. He had arrived wearing a maroon beret with the 'wings' parachutist's badge as a cap badge. As Victor recalls, 'I think some of the soldiers thought that this was carrying 'morale technique' a little too far, and I recall a sergeant who was standing next to me saying, 'I bet he couldn't jump off the jeep'.[13] The men were pleased that Montgomery had taken the time to pay them a visit but the rank and file were sceptical of the usual speeches made by the senior officers. They were now just keen to get on with the job, they didn't need morale-boosting talks to get them in the mood for the upcoming fight. Montgomery's visit on the 8th was the last step in boosting the men's morale before they were finally briefed on Operation *Fustian* during the evening of 9 July. Each company rotated through the operations tent to be formally briefed by company commanders and then given time to study the photographs, maps and models of the place they were being sent to, a place that they had never heard of before and from where some of the men would never return. To add to the sense that the operation was a 'go-er', two days later all men were issued with life vests for the sea crossing. The operation now had a definite sense of reality.

CHAPTER FOUR

'The Plan of Attack'

The British 1st Airborne Division's objectives had been handed down at the start of July in order that preparations could begin for their role in Operation *Husky*. The senior officers of the 1st Airborne Division warmly greeted the news that they would be used in the airborne role and employed to spearhead the ground advance by seizing key objectives behind enemy lines. This was the task that they had trained for and they knew the news would be welcomed by the men after their experiences of serving as line infantry in Africa. The planners noted that 'airborne troops are expensive formations. Their use as ordinary infantry after their special role has been completed is an unsound policy. Those taking part in the initial assaults will, after completion of their special role, be given limited tasks such as protection of a beach-head or airfield'.[1] This highlights that the Allied planners wanted to utilise and save the paras for their airborne spearhead role and, unlike the Germans, not use their specialist parachute troops as standard line infantry. This differing use of airborne troops by the Allied and German High Commands continued throughout the war, with the Fallschirmjaeger continually used as a 'firefighting' force used to plug holes in the German lines, whilst the British paras were used for large-scale airborne assaults in support of major operations.

On 1 July, Lathbury finally was allowed to start briefing his battalion commanders, only just over one week before the operation, and pass on the secret plans that he had been carrying in his head for the last few weeks. The brigade staff officers began constructing the 'Ops Room' containing detailed maps of the target area and drop zones, photographs of the bridge itself and sand-table models for the battalion commanders to start formalising their approach to their battalion objectives. The plan was then disseminated down to company commander-level by each of the battalion's commanding officers at a briefing at 20:00 on 6 July. The next evening at 19:30, each commanding officer then briefed all officers in their respective battalions so that at last they were aware of their target and what was to be expected of them. The plans and objectives were worked on by the staff officers and only passed to the men when they were finalised, so that when the time came to brief all the troops, even the lowest soldier would know their part in the overall operation and their own individual job once at their particular part of the objective.

RAF Beaufighters and Mosquitos had already taken Hopkinson, Lathbury, and Chatterton on a low-level reconnaissance of eastern Sicily on the night of 20/21st May to aid in the planning of the operation and to see the ground for themselves to ensure that it would allow for the safe insertion of both parachute and glider operations.

Hopkinson's views were that:

> in my opinion the operation can be launched with every prospect of success provided that:
> The landing area for the parachute and glider-borne troops is relatively free from enemy troops
> The opposition to be expected from enemy flak over the landing area has been largely neutralised by the measures provided for in the plan.[2]

These two fundamental points of the airborne plan would prove to be far from the ideal situation that Hopkinson had imagined for his airlanding troops. They were in fact about to be met by large numbers of elite troops firing directly at them as they attempted to land. However, with the current intelligence available to them, they believed that the objective could be taken and held until relieved by ground forces. It was now time to brief the men.

Finally, on yet another hot and dusty evening in the desert, the men were ordered to attend the planning tent to be briefed on the mission. They were about to find out just what all the hard training and preparations were leading up to. Engineer Peter Stainforth remembers the morning when the men were at last ordered to the planning tent and briefed on the mission ahead. 'The wealth of information presented, particularly by two enormous air photographs, each six by four feet (2m by 1.2m), which nearly covered one wall'.[3] Firstly, the men were briefed by company commanders on the overall strategy for the invasion so that they could see where they would fit in to the grand scheme of the battle for Sicily.

Overview

The briefing opened with the troops sworn to secrecy on what they were about to hear. It then proceeded with an outline of Operation *Husky* and their Operation *Fustian* within that theatre.

Once the general outline of the invasion was explained to the men they were immediately keen to see just what their team mission was going to be. The target was then revealed. It was to be a parachute insertion supported by gliders to take and hold a bridge to maintain the momentum of the entire British advance on Sicily. The men were excited. This was just the type of mission the veterans and replacements had hoped for. It was a big part on the big stage and was an opportunity to build on the success of their airborne and ground operations in North Africa.

Aerial photograph of Primosole Bridge. (Courtesy of Air Assault Museum)

The 1st Parachute Brigade would capture and hold the Primosole Bridge and its environs until it was relieved by XIII Corps of the Eighth Army, which would have landed three days previously as part of the seaborne landings. The aim of Operation *Fustian* was to capture the bridge in order for the ground forces to pursue their advance northwards to Messina and prevent the retreat of the Axis forces back to the Italian mainland. The 1st Parachute Brigade's plan called for simultaneous parachute drops on four drop zones both north and south of the bridge to enable the objective to be surrounded and taken from both banks of the Simeto River. This would be supported by glider-borne landings on two landing zones bringing support weapons to fend off any armoured counter-attacks. Above all else, the plan would require all the hallmarks of the airborne soldier – speed, aggression and audacity.

Therefore the 1st Airborne Division's ultimate goal was to facilitate the insertion of Eighth Army onto the Catania Plain for their drive on Messina by providing a platform over the bridges between Catania and Syracuse. However, after the invasion of Sicily began and Allied forces began to capture key objectives on the island, such as Syracuse, Montgomery was still keen for the bridge to be taken to advance his Eighth Army northwards. A subsidiary benefit of taking possession of the Primosole Bridge was to prevent the Axis forces retreating and effectively bottling them up to be captured *en masse*.

Next a ground study was provided of just what exactly a challenge the target and surrounding ground would entail.

Objective

General ground

The Primosole Bridge (code-named MARSTON) was built at a narrow point of the Simeto River (WATERLOO) between the cities of Catania and Lentini. The river here was a single body of water, the sea was to the east and several hundred metres further inland to the west where the Gornalunga canal (PADDINGTON) fed into the Simeto. There were no immediate settlements or communities around the bridge, except for a few scattered farm buildings either side of the main road close to the northern end of the bridge, comprising a couple of barns each. The bridge itself consisted of a long rectangular frame of bolted-together steel girders forming a box-like tunnel which carried a tarmac roadway of two-lane traffic with a raised path on either side. The bridge was the only carriageway onto the Catania Plain that would support the weight of the Eighth Army's 33-ton Sherman tanks. To the south of the bridge way a series of three small hills rose up over the flat terrain to give a dominating view over the area. These three hills were later to be code-named Johnny I, II and III.

The Primosole Bridge lay in the middle of a horseshoe loop in the Simeto River, the open end of which was to the north. At a distance of 700 yards (600m) to the west of the bridge the embanked Gornalunga Canal joined the Simeto from the south. To the east of the bridge the Simeto wound its way to the sea, about a mile and a half away, through marshy flats with little cover. For a distance of 1,100 yards (1km) to the east and somewhat more to the west of the bridge, a belt of vines, fruit trees and olive groves which extended 500 yards (450m) north from the north bank. At the far side of this vegetation, running parallel to the Simeto River, was a track which in places was sunken and which contained the occasional farm building.

Further north lay the Catania Plain at the southern foot of Mount Etna. The plain provided the only large expanse of flat ground on Sicily, as the remainder of Sicily's flat terrain was sandwiched between the 375 mile (600km) length of the island's coastline and its hilly interior. Capturing the Catania Plain would allow

Montgomery's tanks to spread out and flank the city of Catania, provide a left hook around Mount Etna to the north and also enable a drive onwards towards Messina. The plain was comparatively bare and was criss-crossed by a number of drainage ditches, the largest being the Fosso Bottaceto which was 10 feet (3m) deep and bordered the Luftwaffe airbases to the south of the city. Highway 114 (PICCADILLY) was the part of the island's main coastal ring-road and ran from Lentini in the south over the Primosole Bridge and northwards across the plain and up to Messina.

Defences

The Primosole Bridge had a span of 469 feet (156m and was raised 39 feet (13m above the gently flowing Simeto River. The Simeto is the second longest river on Sicily, running 70 miles (110km) in length from its source in the volcanic hills south-west of Mount Etna and emptying into the Ionian Sea just to the east of the Primosole Bridge in the Gulf of Catania. The Simeto at Primosole at this point was about 30 yards (25m) wide with a muddy bottom and banks, on which grew patches of tall reeds. At that time of the year the river, slowly moving, was around waist-deep, although in places hollows in the riverbed brought the water depth to over a man's head. Coupled with the steep, sloping banks, it was a natural obstacle to vehicles although infantry could wade through, making the bridge a key strategic asset to facilitate the moving of vehicles to and from the front line. The banks were steepest at the bridge itself but sloped more gently westwards of the bridge. The land to the north of the bridge was mainly lime and almond groves in tree-lined fields to a depth of 350 yards (400m) leading to open country beyond. The groves stretched for over half a mile (1km) in either direction on the northern bank but the ground on the southern bank consisted mainly of reeds along the riverbank before giving way to open ground southwards towards a ridgeline. The road crossing the bridge is Highway 114, running from Lentini 10 miles (16km) to the south to Catania 7 miles (11km) to the north.

To assist the Italians defending the bridge, four pillbox bunkers had been constructed, two on the north bank and two on the south bank. The concrete outside walls of the hexagonal pillboxes were painted in brown and yellow diagonal stripes and covered in camouflage netting and straw. The entrances had beaded curtains hanging down to allow some cool air to blow into the hot concrete structures during the summer months. Outside the pillboxes were staggered concrete blocks in the road to slow approaching vehicles down before they arrived at the steel barriers and barbed-wire barriers. In addition, the north side of the bridge a farmhouse acted as the garrison guard room. Surrounding both ends of the bridge were a series of deep trenches which had been well constructed by the Italians and at such a depth as to be able to withstand all but a direct airburst round exploding overhead. The whole bridgehead was ringed by a barbed-wire perimeter and patrolled 24 hours a day by the garrison sentries.

Immediately to the south of the bridge was the Gornalunga canal, and 1,300 yards (1,200m) beyond that the three prominent hills on the ridgeline, later code-named Johnny I, II and III. The hills were defended by Italian garrisons. From east to west, Johnny III was the smallest of the hills but was closest to the bridge and had a clear view straight over the bridge and northwards towards Catania in the distance. Johnny III would provide a good fire support base for the men defending against any enemy attacks at the bridge from the direction of Catania. The Italians had also noted its commanding position over the bridge and it was defended by five machine-gun posts and an artillery piece. The middle hill was Johnny I, it was also defended by Italians, supported by five machine-gun posts and a 75mm artillery piece. The elongated oval-shaped hill ran parallel to Highway 114 for 200 yards (180 metres) and could provide a commanding position to block any traffic movement on the road as well as support the bridgehead. Just below the crest of the hill were a series of shallow caves from where the defenders based themselves. These caves overlooked a raised track on an embankment (CATERPILLAR), which split off westwards from the highway and would later be used as a reference point for the paratroopers to follow from the drop zone towards the highway and bridge.

Johnny I was planned to be the main defensive position for Frost's 2 Para. The third hill was Johnny II which was similar in shape to Johnny I and lay on the western side of Highway 114 opposite Johnny I, providing additional cover onto the highway where the road split to head off south towards Lentini or westwards towards the interior of the island. Johnny III overlooked a flat plain to its north and west which would later be selected as a drop zone by both the paras and the Fallschirmjaeger. The three hills would provide interlocking arcs of fire capable of defending the area and creating a strategic defence in depth of the southern bridgehead area. The road approached from the south and then curved eastwards along the southern bank of the river, crossing the bridge and then continuing dead straight northwards along a poplar tree-lined route heading towards the Fosso Bottaceto 2.5 miles (4km) in the distance. This large ditch would later be used as a forming-up point for the Fallschirmjaeger.

The Johnny hills were defended by garrisons based on the summit and in the caves near the summit of each hill. Each summit was ring-fenced with barbed wire and had several purpose-built pillboxes on each one. Johnny I had three of these pillboxes identified from aerial photography. They were constructed 6 feet (2m) into the ground with a 5-feet-high domed roof protruding from the ground. Each pillbox contained a 47mm artillery piece or a heavy machine gun, manned by a detachment of 12 men with ammunition and food stores contained in separate rooms at the rear. Therefore 2 Para were expecting to find large platoon entrenched on the slopes of Johnny I with possible reinforcements inside the wire on the summit and with further support on the neighbouring hills. The will of the Italian defenders to fight whilst they were fairly well protected in their pillboxes could mean that they would put up a fight and not be so keen to make a dash for freedom out in the

Primosole Bridge as viewed from the southern end. (Kent and Sharpshooters Image)

open. 2 Para would have to be aggressive in routing the defenders from the hills before they could pin the advancing paras down under the weight of their dug-in heavy defensive weapons. Johnny II was assumed to have four pillboxes containing 48 defenders and Johnny III a further pillbox supported by other machine-gun positions being manned by around 50 defenders.

Just north of the bridge was a junction bearing off westwards but this was in dead ground and could not be seen from the bridge or from the south bank. The structure of the bridge was primarily designed to hold a roadway over the river and had no immediate buildings or other cover from a military perspective, other than a few whitewashed farmhouses near the north end of the bridge. As the paras and Fallschirmjaeger were later to find out to their cost when contesting the bridge, the only cover was from view but not from fire.

Insertion

The drop zones were decided by the RAF as they had ultimate control over the air insertion phase of the operation. This was a condition borne out of the initiation of the Airborne Forces that they, like their German counterparts, would fall under the instruction of the air force. The army, therefore, only had a small say in the selection of the drop zones that they would have to land on and then fight from, the over-arching decision was retained by the RAF throughout the entirety of the war. Even the RAF had doubts about delivering such a large airborne force into battle for the first time with such inexperienced air crews. As early as March 1943, four months before the operation, Air Commodore Foster of the RAF planning team believed that 'the paratroops themselves may be sufficiently well trained to carry out such an operation at night, but it is very doubtful if, the time available the transport pilots can be trained to night fly so accurately that they could time their arrival over the drop zones at minute intervals at about 300 feet (100m)'.[4] This highlights severe doubts that the 1st Parachute Brigade would be dropped accurately on their

Major-General Hopkinson briefs men from the Pathfinder Platoon prior to Operation *Fustian*. (Courtesy of Air Assault Museum)

intended drop zones. Lathbury and the remainder of the paras accepted this risk of decreased accuracy but they believed that if they could be dropped within a handful of miles of their objective, then they would still be able to navigate at speed through the night to take their given objectives.

The drop zones and landing zones would for the first time in British airborne operation's history be marked out by 'pathfinders' from the 21st Independent Parachute Company of the Army Air Corps, led by Major Lander, parachuting 30 minutes ahead of the main formation. This newly formed unit trained at Larkhill with various drop zone-marking equipment and learnt how to parachute with the kit and use it effectively, before deploying to North Africa with 1st Parachute Brigade. Along with the remainder of the brigade, the pathfinders would head out to North Africa short of men: '21 Independent Parachute Company sailed from the UK approximately 60 men short. This was fully realised but it was considered that the standard should not be lowered'.[5] This shows that the Allied planners considered quality over quantity for a unit with the important task of marking out accurately the drop zones for the remainder of a parachute brigade.

Major Lander was known to train his men hard, ensuring that the men parachuted whenever aircraft were available. It was Lander who insisted on the men jumping at night and so the final qualifying descent on the parachute training course, the night jump, was added and remains to this day. During daylight operations, they would use coloured marker panels to mark out the drop zone letter and also a 'T' shape of marker panels to indicate the wind direction to incoming pilots, allowing the planes to head into the wind thus naturally slowing them down for the jumping paratroopers.

For night operations, the pathfinders actually had to carry less burdensome kit as the large marker panels were of no use in the dark. Instead, they jumped with the newly designed 'Glim' lamps. These consisted of a heavy-duty lamp fitted with shatter-proof glass and connected to a 12-volt car battery by rubber-clad cables. The light emitted from the lamp was not visible to ground troops but was angled to meet the altitude and direction of the incoming planes. The Glim lamps were a less sophisticated fall-back system, however, as the main drop-zone-marking kit was the Eureka and Rebecca units, to be used first in Sicily. The Eureka beacons consisted of a small base unit attached to a tripod-mounted antenna. The Rebecca was a larger base unit mounted in the nose of the Dakotas but not the gliders. The Eureka units were to be parachuted in by the pathfinders and then set up on the ground. Once set up, they would send a pulsed radar signal out to a distance of 30 miles (48km). This signal would be picked up by the Rebecca beacons carried on the approaching aircraft to allow the airborne armada to home in on the drop zones. However, in addition to all the latest technology being used on the ground to direct aircraft onto their correct drop zones, the pilots were all issued with 'moonlight maps' in advance of the operation so that they could get used to looking at a black and white map of the area and pick out landmarks on the ground. The pathfinders were spread around the brigade, mainly jumping with 1 Para as it was they who would be taking the bridge and therefore needed to ensure an accurate jump. Six pathfinders would jump with 1 Para: two with the assault platoon of R Company, two with the main body of R Company and two with battalion HQ.

The plan called for an airborne insertion of paratroopers and supporting gliders carrying artillery and jeeps. The brigade had six airfields and ten squadrons of aircraft in the Mascara area dedicated for the task as follows:

Airfield A – 10 and 12 Squadrons from 60th Troop Carrier Group
Airfield B – 11 and 28 Squadrons from 60th Troop Carrier Group
Airfield C – 7 and 8 Squadrons from 62nd Troop Carrier Group
Airfield D – 4 and 51 Squadrons from 62nd Troop Carrier Group
Airfield E – One flight from 295 Squadron RAF
Airfield F – 296 Squadron, 38th Wing RAF

Plan of Attack

The brigade's plan of attack was as follows – 1 Para was to capture the bridge, with 3 Para covering the northern approaches and 2 Para covering the southern approaches. The drop would be made in three waves closely timed to follow minutes after each other. The RAF's 205th Group would provide a diversionary bombing raid on Catania airfield between 23:05 and 23:15 to try and convince the defenders that this was just a fairly normal bombing raid and not the start of a mass airborne operation. Dummy paratroopers were also to be dropped forty minutes before the real paratroopers to further confuse the enemy defenders, with 80 dummies being dropped near Ramacca airfield 28 miles (45km) to the west of the bridge and a further two loads of 80 dummies being dropped north-west of Catania.

The bridge capture called for 1 Para to be split into two halves, with T and S Companies dropping on DZ1 to the north of the bridge and R Company dropping on DZ2 on the southern side of the bridge. One platoon from T Company and one platoon from R Company of Alastair Pearson's 1 Para, together with A Troop, 1st Parachute Squadron RE led by Captain Gerald Sims, were to drop at 22:20, around 30 minutes before the main force, and act as a *coup de main* party to capture the Primosole Bridge by 23:40. One platoon from T Company, along with a section of five engineers, would immediately race off from DZ1 towards the bridge and assault it. They would parachute with their weapons on the man and not stop on the ground to gather any containers. They were to navigate along a pre-defined track to a position on the riverbank 220 yards (200m) west of the bridge. From here they would then move along the riverbank to assault the northern end of the bridge. The engineers would get to work to dismantle any demolition charges on the bridge. The remainder of T Company would collect some of the heavier weapons dropped onto DZ1 and quickly follow behind to reinforce the bridge or support the assault.

The R Company platoon would likewise race from DZ2 along with their five engineers and capture the southern end of the bridge without waiting for support. If all went to plan, both ends of the bridge would be assaulted simultaneously and reinforced by T Company to produce not only the delivery of the prize of the bridge but also of a strong force of some 150 men in position to defend the bridgehead. T Company would then be held as a counter-attacking reserve to defend against any enemy attacks to the north or south of the bridge. The responsibility for prisoners of war for the brigade had also fallen to T Company, 1 Para. They were to form two prisoner cages to the north of the bridge, one of officers and one for men. Any refugees were to be told to stay off the roads to keep them clear for the expected relieving forces approaching from the south.

Twenty minutes after the *coup de main* group was dropped, the remainder of 1 Para, along with Brigade HQ and No.4 Field Ambulance, would begin parachuting, both north and south of the Simeto, and make straight for the bridge by 00:40. Two members of the intelligence platoon were to drop with each company and set up white lights and mine tape to guide the soldiers towards the bridge. Stragglers' posts were also set up as additional RVs on the drop zones. R Company would approach from the south to support the southern end of the bridge, which should have already been captured by the *coup de main* platoon of R Company. They would then consolidate the southern end of the bridge and dominate the roads leading towards the 2 Para positions further south. One platoon from S Company was to push one kilometre northwards along the main highway and set up a road block by stringing together Hawkins grenades. They would then expect to be relieved by the arrival of 3 Para around midnight, when they would then move back to the bridgehead to rejoin S Company and act as further reinforcements. Meanwhile the bulk of S Company were expected to push through T Company at the bridge and form a defensive screen north of the bridge, taking two Vickers machine-gun teams and four PIAT teams from Support Company with them to face the main threat of the enemy approaching from Catania. The mortars were to be sighted once they reached the bridge and start recording likely targets on the ground.

S Company's secondary task was to assault the bridge if it was still in enemy hands. If the bridge had been destroyed, then they were to begin patrolling to the west of the bridge for suitable fording points so that the advancing land forces had at least have an infantry crossing point when they arrived to continue the advance towards Catania. This task of finding a fording point across the Simeto would prove invaluable to 1 Para's Commanding Officer Pearson in the latter stages of the battle.

Johnny Frost's 2 Para, along with Brigade Headquarters, the engineers and medics, would parachute onto DZ3 on the south of the bridge in the area of the Gornalunga Canal and the main highway. They would be jumping 30 minutes after the *coup de main* party, between 22:40 and 23:28.[6] Their task would be to cover the southern approaches by seizing the high ground to the south of the bridge which consisted of three hills code-named Johnny I, II and III. The battalion had the furthest to travel from its drop zone and the most complicated objectives of the brigade and as such its deadline to be in place was later than the other battalions at 04:00.

The three features were expected to be defended by a platoon-size formation of Italian troops from the 213rd Coastal Division. Once the enemy had been driven from the hills or captured, 2 Para were then expected to dig in and provide a screening force against the anticipated counter-attack on the bridge from the direction of Syracuse and Augusta. The high ground, once the heavy weapons had been dragged up the hills and bedded in, should then be tasked to provide a fire support base and observation platform from which to break up any counter-attacks, approaching from either the north or south. The Mortar Platoon were to bed in their mortars on the south-east of Johnny I and be prepared to provide all-round defensive and offensive fire. The Machine-Gun Platoon was to fan out across the Johnny I summit and also provide all-round defensive fire. In addition to its own firepower, Captain Vere Hodge of the Royal Artillery was attached to the 2nd Battalion as a naval bombardment detachment and was ready to call in naval firepower from his own dedicated cruiser waiting out at sea.

If time allowed, 2 Para was then to 'act vigorously southwards to assist the advance of 13 Corps'.[7] Lt Colonel Frost remembers:

> I was very happy with the task given to 2 Para... Brigadier Lathbury's orders had been crystal-clear and I felt therefore that there was no doubt in anyone's mind about what was to be done. Our dropping-zone was clear of and beyond those allotted to the rest of the brigade and our pilots should have no difficulty in finding the right run-in and landmarks in the shape of the river, the road and the bridge itself. After dropping and assembling we had a ready-made, unmistakeable axis to our objective in the shape firstly of a bund (a high bank), south of the river, and thence the main road to the 'Johnny' features.[8]

John Frost planned to assemble the bulk of 2 Para and tab to their objectives, stopping short of each one, before assaulting it in force. In case of being dispersed during the drop, he additionally tasked Lieutenant Tony Hitch's platoon to assault and capture Johnny II on their own if they were assembled prior to the battalion being ready to move off the drop zone. Frost planned to locate the bulk of his battalion on Johnny I, the central feature of the three Johnny hills, as this was the most strategically important of the three, as it gave over-watch positions on the main road leading from the south towards the bridge.

Meanwhile, E. C. Yeldham's 3 Para would drop onto DZ4, 1 kilometre north of the bridge along with No.3 Section Field Ambulance. Dropping in the first wave of the brigade at 22:25 would be a fighting patrol of two platoons sent to attack and neutralise an enemy anti-aircraft battery consisting of four 88mm guns to the north-east of the drop zone. With these guns neutralised, the rest of the battalion would jump 30 minutes later into a less hostile anti-aircraft screen and then deploy between two loops in the Simeto and straddling Highway 114 to cover the approaches from the direction of Catania, with a target time of achieving this by 01:35. This would involve the battalion forming an anchor point on its drop zone and pushing itself out into a straight line due east. It should have been the simplest of the objectives of the three battalions but would likely face the fiercest resistance once the enemy responded to the airborne landings after the initial element of surprise had worn off. They were then to patrol northwards towards Catania and break-up any counter-attacks heading towards the bridgehead. The main threats to the operation were clearing the Italian troops from the bridgehead area, defending the area from German counter-attacks from the north and dealing with any potential Axis forces inadvertently withdrawing from the land invasion and trying to cross the Primosole Bridge to escape northwards.

The paras weren't expected to be able to call immediately on any Allied air support as they would be thinly spread in the Sicilian skies supporting other elements of the invasion. Until airfields could be established on the Sicilian ground, Allied planes still had to base themselves at Malta or Africa. In contrast, the German Luftwaffe and Italian Regia Aeronautica were based around the Gerbini airfields south of Mount Etna. They therefore had a much longer operating flight window than their Allied counterparts. The Gerbini airfields lay only 10 miles (16km) from the Primosole Bridge and so the chance of low-flying sorties by marauding enemy planes was a high possibility.

Lathbury and his Brigade HQ were to land on DZ2 and then establish their base at a pre-defined farm building at the top centre of the drop zone near the banks of the river. They would wait here to manage the initial stages of the objectives being taken and the creation of the bridgehead and then move towards the bridge to take command from there at a later stage that night. Attached to Brigade HQ was a further naval bombardment detachment (NBD) officer, Captain Bolland, and also two forward observation officers (FOOs) whose job would be to call in the artillery of the advancing ground forces of XIII Corps.

The brigade engineers' tasks were to disarm any demolition charges on the bridge, begin to lay minefields to the approaches of the bridge and scout the riverbanks for fordable points in case the bridge was demolished before it could be secured. They would then revert to a defensive reserve around the bridge.

The medics were to move as part of Brigade Headquarters as far as the bridge and then divert to a pre-identified farmhouse at the base of Johnny I and establish the main dressing station (MDS). Due to the anticipated number of casualties, a section of the 16th (Parachute) Field Ambulance commanded by Lieutenant Colonel Wheatley would also drop with the brigade. Each battalion would have a supporting team of medical troops including a doctor and 16 other ranks. The headquarters element of the 16th (Parachute) Field Ambulance, consisting of two surgical teams and No.4 Section, would be co-located with Brigade Headquarters. Casualties from the south side of the bridgehead would be treated here aswell. No.3 section were to parachute on DZ4 with 3 Para and then set up an advanced dressing station (ADS) at the north of the bridge to deal with casualties primarily from 1 and 3 Para. The more serious casualties from the ADS on the north of the bridge would be sent across

Four men prepare a model for Operation *Fustian* in the Briefing Tent. (Courtesy of Air Assault Museum)

to the MDS. This main dressing station, once established, would not be moved due to complexities of moving mass casualties. The medical staff would not only treat Allied troops but also were obliged under the Geneva Convention to treat enemy troops equally, prioritising the casualties based on the severity of their injuries and not the colour of their uniform. This mutual recognition of gentlemanly conduct even during the heat of battle would become apparent later for 16th (Parachute) Field Ambulance as they would be allowed to continue operating on casualties, as the Aid Post became trapped in No Man's Land. This comprehensive medical support would provide better treatment for the casualties and also free up the fighting men for the initial assault and counter-attacks.

At 01:00 the gliders would start bringing in the artillery and jeeps on two landing zones (LZs). LZ7 north of the river would be designated for the larger WACO gliders, carrying A Troop of the Airlanding Artillery who would fall under 3 Para's command, and was to be marked by green marking lights. LZ8 south of the river was to be marked with red marking lights and would be used for the Horsa gliders coming in to land at 01:10, carrying B Troop and one section of C Troop from the Airlanding Artillery, which would be supporting 2 Para. Once landed, the twelve 6-pounder guns would be towed by their jeeps to the positions of 2 and 3 Para who would be holding the perimeter and best placed to utilise the guns to fire up and down the highways and form an anti-tank defensive screen. Two guns would head to Brigade HQ and then onto the bridge to guard either end. Each gun would be landed with around 24 rounds and once delivered to their positions the accompanying jeeps would then be used to scour the drop zones and help recover any lost weapons containers and equipment. If any artillery pieces were lost during the glider landings, the first four guns to arrive at the bridge would be positioned at the north bridgehead, as this was where the main threat of enemy armour was expected. These artillery pieces would be increasingly important to supporting the survival of the bridgehead as the Allied planners had already confirmed that 'after arrival at the dropping zone and until withdrawal, it will not be possible to supply the Airborne Division by air'.[9] Just in case the paras needed any further confirmation of their isolation until they could be relieved, they were constantly reminded in the official orders of their need to be self-sufficient and hang on to their ground until the link-up forces could arrive.

Relief

The relieving force for both the paratroopers and commandos would be from the British XIII Corps, commanded by Lieutenant General Miles Dempsey. The ground forces of XIII Corps would then link up with the airborne forces and commandos the following morning. This rapid link-up was important as intelligence suggested that both Italian and elite German formations, including armoured units, were in the area and would likely advance on the bridge by daybreak the following morning from both Catania and Syracuse.

The paras were also briefed about No. 3 Commando who would be conducting a separate operation 8 miles (13km) away to the south of the Simeto River near Augusta. The commando unit were to conduct an amphibious landing from the sea, then assault and capture the Malati Bridge over the Leonardo River which lay only 4 miles (7km) to the south-west of the Primosole Bridge. Once both objectives were secure the paras and commandos were briefed to establish a link if possible.

The corps consisted of the 5th Infantry Division, 50th (Northumbrian) Infantry Division and the 4th Armoured Brigade. The armoured brigade, with three tank regiments, was equipped with the American-built Sherman M4 tank. Early on 13 July the commander of the 50th Division, Major-General Sidney Kirkman, was called to General Montgomery's headquarters. Here he was informed about the two missions by the 1st Parachute Brigade and No. 3 Commando, and the requirement for the bridges to be acquired intact. Montgomery's intention was for the 50th (Northumbrian) Infantry Division to lead the Eighth Army's advance and relieve the paratroopers and commandos. To assist General Kirkman in the task, Montgomery placed 4th Armoured Brigade under his command. Montgomery was insistent that he wanted the infantry division to relieve the parachute brigade early on 14 July. He urged Kirkman to 'go on with all possible speed'.[10] This would require the division to advance around 25 miles (40km) in 24 hours. The 50th Division would land on 10 July and by this time would have been fighting for three days non-stop. With the daily temperature commonly reaching 100F (38C) many of the men in the division were likely to be physically fatigued and suffering from heat exhaustion. The division's situation was not improved by a grave error of judgement by Montgomery. During the planning for the invasion, he had overestimated the strength of the German and Italian resistance to the Allied landings. The British Eighth Army consisted mainly of infantry, tanks and heavy weapons but was light on any form of mechanical transport, so any advance by the 50th Division would have to be conducted on foot. On top of this lack of transport, some of the few precious vehicles had been sunk, along with their transport ships, by the Luftwaffe before it could be landed on to Sicilian soil. The 50th Division comprised the 69th Infantry Brigade, the 168th Infantry Brigade and, leading the charge to relieve the paratroopers at Primosole Bridge, the 151st Brigade, consisting of the 6th, 8th and 9th Battalions of the Durham Light Infantry.

The successful relief of the bridge would inevitably rely on holding off any enemy attacks. It had been assessed that the main thrust from the enemy would originate from the ground forces based at Catania airfield, who on realising that the airfield was not the paras' objective, would send patrols to the bridge, followed by a larger attacking force. It was therefore assumed that the main enemy response would come from the north, using the highway or the riverbank to the north-east as an axis of advance. Enemy infantry and tanks were also known to be positioned in between the bridge and the southern beachheads from where they would be pushed backwards towards the Primosole Bridge as a means of retreat towards Catania. Therefore, it was assumed with the approach of friendly forces towards the bridge would also bring the tide of retreating enemy forces keen to get over the bridge.

The senior officers of the 1st Parachute Brigade who set about planning the airborne assault had the grim but necessary task of factoring an estimation of casualties into the plan. The need for this was two-fold, firstly to ensure that there would be enough manpower to capture and hold the objective and, secondly, to include sufficient medical units into the orbat. It was anticipated that casualties would amount to 450 men, of which one quarter were expected to be killed and three quarters wounded.

All soldiers were trained in dealing with battlefield casualties. Men were not expected to stop to help a casualty, they were expected to carry on with the assault and only stop to treat casualties in any lulls in the battle. Casualties were expected to drag themselves into cover and begin dressing their own wounds, known as self-help. Their comrades would then help with first aid and get the casualties into better cover or back to the first aid post. Medics attached to the battalion were embedded with the front-line troops. They would look to triage casualties and treat where they could or arrange for casualty to be evacuated (cas-evac'ed) back to the main dressing station (MDS) where a team of doctors were equipped to deal with serious casualties and perform operations if necessary.

Once the objectives were finally briefed to the men, it was down to the NCOs to pull together the fine-tuning of each individual action. The lessons learnt over the last few weeks on the *Cactus* exercises now came into focus and they would need to remember everything that they had picked up during training to use for real in battle. The exercises would provide exact information down to the smallest details such as which soldier would hold open barbed-wire fences for the rest of the section to pass through or who would be responsible for breaking down a particular door at a particular farm building. Even the type of foods to be consumed prior to the operation was covered. The soldiers were ordered to eat plenty of sugar, very little fat and drink plenty of water. Passwords were issued, to be used in the event of being challenged in the inevitable confusion after a night drop into enemy territory. The challenging password 'Desert Rats' was to be answered by 'Kill Italians.' This level of detail is essential in military operations, especially airborne operations where plans inevitably change and each man in turn needs to know both their own and their comrades' job in order to function as a team if and when the plan changes. Sicily would definitely soon live up to the old adage that no plan survives contact with the enemy, however, the plan was to go awry before the 1st Airborne Division had even left the hands of the friendly forces.

The briefing finished with the reading of a letter written by the 1st Airborne Division's commander, Major-General Hopkinson. 'For the first time in history British Airborne Troops are to carry out operations on a big scale in the van of the army.' This revealed to the paras that there were further operations planned for Sicily other than their own Operation *Fustian*. Hopkinson went on to say:

> To those of you not taking part in these first operations I would say: 'Be patient – your chance will come.' To all of you I say: 'Be steadfast in your determination to win. From the 1st Parachute Brigade you have inherited a great fighting tradition. It is yours to preserve. Your friends out here and at home are expecting great things. See to it that they are not disappointed. I don't think they will be. Towards your enemies be skilful and ruthless; towards the civilian population show consideration; towards your prisoners be human'.[11]

The die had now been cast: it was to be an operation based on the classic model of airborne operations, an objective to be seized at lightning speed then held in order that the conventional ground forces could continue their advance against the enemy. The parallels with the later operations in Normandy and Arnhem are all too clear.

CHAPTER FIVE

'Green Devils'

Whilst the paras were training in the heat of the desert for their anticipated operation against Hitler's Fortress Europe, their opponents were waiting for the next blow of the Allies' hammer to fall upon them.

The majority of the forces on the island of Sicily were Italian and commanded by General Guzzoni, with his headquarters based in the town of Enna, situated in the centre of the island. German forces were led by Lieutenant-General Hube commanding XIV Corps, comprising the elite Hermann Goering Panzer Division and the 15th Panzergrenadier Division. In the event of an invasion, the Axis plan called for the German panzer divisions to concentrate against Patton's less experienced Seventh Army, whilst employing a delaying strategy against Montgomery's Eighth Army's push up the eastern Sicilian coast. All together there were around 200,000 Italian and 32,000 German troops on the island.[1] The organisation of the defences saw the coast guarded by reserve Italian formations, the ports defended by regular Italian troops and four Italian and two German divisions held further inland as mobile reserves. Both of the German divisions were equipped with panzers and armoured vehicles but most of their transport was still arriving from the Italian mainland.

Opposing the airborne troops for Operation *Fustian* would be both Italian and German forces of varying strength and motivation. The Italians forming the bridge defence force were mainly engineer conscripts formed into local militias, supported by a few regular army units also in the area. The Italian Army forces in the vicinity of Primosole Bridge came from the 213th Coastal Division, commanded by General Carlo Gotti, consisting of the 135th Coastal Infantry Regiment, the 22nd Artillery Group of 12 batteries of artillery and the Catania Harbour Garrison. Coastal divisions were second-line formations, usually full of men in their forties and fifties, and were intended to perform labour or other second-line duties, such as laying minefields and constructing barbed-wire fences, not beating off attacks from elite paratroopers dropping out of the night sky. Recruited from the local population, their officers were mostly former officers who had retired but had been called up again. Their morale and motivation were low, not least because of their second-rate equipment and weapons. It had been intended to improve their armaments with equipment recently seized from the disbanded Vichy forces, after their poor showing for the Axis cause in North Africa. But when the Vichy arms did arrive in Sicily, many of the weapons were unserviceable due to vandalism or poor maintenance. Some of the accompanying ammunition was also of the wrong calibre and in other cases was not provided at all. The Italians, however, would not be on their own. They were to be supported by the elite German 1st Fallschirmjaeger Division.

After the German retreat and evacuation of North Africa in May 1943, the division was hurriedly resting and re-equipping its troops, placing them on standby to deal with any Allied invasion anywhere in the Mediterranean theatre of operations. The Fallschirmjaeger of 1st Fallschirmjaeger Division were quickly identified as being suitable as a quick reaction force and capable of being airlifted as a response to an Allied invasion. The division was refitting after its recent year-long tour of the Eastern Front and the fighting in sub-zero temperatures around Leningrad. The men were glad to be based in France but knew the peacefulness of their summer in France would soon come to an end as they would almost certainly be deployed soon back to the fighting in either the Russian or Mediterranean campaigns.

The division had been born out of the 7th Flieger Division, veterans of the operations in the Low Countries, Norway, Crete and Russia, campaigns that had seen the Germans perfect the use of paratroopers and airborne forces in the role of 'vertical envelopment', a military tactic still in its infancy at the beginning of World War II. The division would later go on to fight at Monte Cassino, in Normandy and around the Rhine, being deployed as a 'fire brigade' unit to bolster weak points in the front line. The division was under the command of General Kurt Student, the 'Conqueror of Crete', as part of his Fliegerkorps IX.

The 1st Fallschirmjaeger Division, commanded by General Heidrich, comprised Fallschirmjaeger Regiments 1, 3 and 4, each with three parachute infantry battalions. The division was further supported by Artillery Regiment No.1, Anti-Tank Battalion No.1, Engineer Battalion No.1, Signals Battalion No.1, Machine-Gun Battalion No.1 and Medical Battalion No.1.

The Fallschirmjaeger, like their British airborne counterparts, were an elite formation from their very inception with a distinct *esprit de corps*. General-Major Kurt Student, the first commander of the Fallschirmjaeger stated that 'the first thing to do is instil regimental spirit … this pride must stem from a comradeship which is wider and deeper than that of any other regiment or corps'.[2] The simple act of volunteering for parachute selection and training meant that the men were motivated to be there and took pride in their profession and unit. Joining a new and instantly elite formation was a massive factor in attracting the right calibre of men to the Fallschirmjaeger ranks. There were other perks to being part of an elite unit as Karl Baumer remembers, 'I had no great desire to become a paratrooper, but, being young, was susceptible to the blandishments of our officers who promised more pay, a special, elite status, and of course being a more glamorous unit, more girls!'[3] As well as gaining the heightened status of being a Fallschirmjaeger, the single act of volunteering for the armed forces in a militarised Nazi Germany was seen as a positive step for many volunteers. On their recruitment, trained soldiers, sailors and airmen had to swear an oath of allegiance to the Fuhrer. 'I swear by God this holy oath: I vow that I will render unconditional obedience to the Fuhrer of Germany and its people, Adolf Hitler, the Supreme Commander of the Armed Forces, and that, as a brave soldier, I will be prepared to stake my life for this oath at any time'.[4] This oath was fanatically adhered to by units such as the SS and men were only relieved of this oath on the death of Adolf Hitler at the climax of the war. The Fallschirmjaeger were not as politically motivated as the SS but instead were bound by the determination that came with upholding the standards of a newly formed elite fighting formation, a determination also demonstrated by their British airborne opponents later in the war. It took a special type of person to volunteer for the great unknown of military parachuting, as Colonel von der Heydte recalls. 'I liked the adventurers best. They had jumped easily into life and they found it worth living, whatever it brought along, provided that it did not become monotonous. Their heads were filled with nonsensical pranks, but also with good ideas. They were born parachutists'.[5] This same sense of adventure and more relaxed approach to regular military discipline, opting for a stronger focus on military fieldcraft and soldiering, was deemed more important for potential airborne recruits to aspire to than the regimented drill and discipline of the regular army.

The first German parachute training school, Fallschirmschule, was established in 1936 at Stendal in Saxony, 60 miles (100km) west of Berlin. The Fallschirmjaeger was at this stage still split along Heer and Luftwaffe tribal lines, unlike the British Parachute Regiment which was an army unit from the outset. Both arms of the German military trained at Stendal and completed the same military parachuting course. Eventually the Fallschirmjaeger paratroopers and the Army paratroopers were merged into a single unit as part of the Luftwaffe.

After 1940 a further two parachute training schools were established at Braunschweig in Brandenburg and Salzwedel in Saxony following the success of the airborne operations in support of Germany's Blitzkrieg campaigns.

The first part of parachute training was four weeks in duration and consisted of battlefield tactics and weapons training. The second four weeks of training then focussed on airborne training, beginning with teaching the future paratroopers how to pack their own parachute. The men were introduced to the RZ1 parachute (Ruckenpackung Zwangauslosung or 'rucksack packed to open') and given a flight in a Dornier Do 23, which for many was their first taste of flying. In contrast to their British counterparts, the parachutes were packed by the Fallschirmjaeger. Karl Baumer recalls, 'we were told that it was only right that we packed our own 'chutes as our lives depended on their being packed properly, therefore our lives were in

OUR HANDS! No other person would ever pack our parachutes'.[6] Further ground training saw the recruits graduate from practising how to land correctly by performing rolls on the ground through to exiting mock-up aircraft doors and landing into sand pits. Once the basic ground training was complete the men were deemed ready to take to the air for the real thing.

Now ready to jump with their newly packed parachutes, they needed to complete six jumps from different altitudes and in growing stick numbers to meet the qualifying criteria for the Fallschirmjaeger to earn their qualified parachutist's badge, the *Fallschirmschutzenabzeichen*. The badge itself comprised an oval wreath of laurel leaves encompassing a diving eagle atop a swastika, and was worn on the centre left of the chest. The trainee Fallschirmjaeger jumped from Ju52s, known to the men as Auntie Jus or Iron Annies. These planes could carry 16 paratroopers to a range of 808 miles (1300km) and had a low top speed of 305km/h (190mph) which meant that it could easily lower its speed to drop paratroopers onto a drop zone but also meant that it was vulnerable to air attack, despite being armed with two 7.92mm machine guns and one 13mm machine gun. Final training jumps were at an altitude of 360 feet (150m) to simulate a combat-jump altitude and reduce the time that they were vulnerable targets in the air. The men free-fell for the first

Mussolini and Hitler were prepared to use Sicily as a delaying tactic and a buffer zone to prevent the Italian mainland from being targeted next by the Allies.

150 feet (50m), at which point their static lines would automatically open their parachutes for them. They would then have a matter of seconds until they landed. Once qualified, all Fallschirmjaeger were expected to repeat the six jumps each year to stay 'in date' as a parachutist and receive their additional parachute pay of 75 Reich Marks per year.

As parachuting was still very much in its infancy, it was still a daunting experience for trainee paratroopers to take their first leap out of an aircraft and into the unknown. 'To jump out of a plane requires all of one's courage, it is such an unnatural thing to do, for everyone is immersed in the knowledge of certain death to fall from a great height. We relied on that little piece of rope and hook at one end and connected to the 'chute at the other. If anything went wrong we were dead'.[7] The Fallschirmjaeger's parachute was uniquely different to the British paratroopers. The steps leading into the aircraft required both hands to be able to pull themselves up, so the men were taught to have their static-line clenched in their teeth so as to keep their hands free to climb inside the plane. After climbing aboard the aircraft, the men took up their seats opposite each other on long bench seats. However, on exiting the aircraft, the RZ1 parachute canopy was attached to two 'D' rings behind the paratrooper's waist, requiring the men to dive head-first from the plane into a horizontal 'crucifix' position, known officially as a 'pike dive'. This allowed the parachute to deploy whilst the men were in a horizontal position. The shape of the rigging lines from the paratrooper's back up to the canopy formed an 'A' shape as opposed to the Allied parachutes which employed rigging lines from the paratrooper's shoulders up to the canopy, providing more steer to the parachute. The Luftwaffe aircrew actually employed a similar parachute to the Allies and didn't use the same style of parachute as the Fallschirmjaeger. If they were in a vertical position the pull of the parachute opening would send them into twists and make their descent very dangerous. They would then be suspended by the parachute from their centre of their backs, meaning the parachutes were unsteerable and oscillated much more in the air, visibility was poorer than the British paratroopers who were suspended from their shoulders and also landings became more hazardous as the Fallschirmjaeger would land on their fronts as opposed to their feet which would help cushion the landing to an extent.

Once their parachuting skills were perfected, it was then on to weapons training. The Fallschirmjaeger of 1st Division were well equipped with a mixture of standard German Army-issue small arms such as the 7.92mm bolt-action Mauser 98 carbine and then the updated Kar 98K rifles initially. Each man carried the standard Wehrmacht-issue 60 rounds but the airborne troops developed an additional carrying case for their webbing to house a further 120 rounds.

However, German airborne forces jumped with their weapons stowed in a weapons canister (*waffenhalter*). In the early years of the war, the containers came in three different sizes with the smaller containers used for heavier items and the larger containers for bulky but lighter kit. After operaions in Crete in 1941, all containers were built to a single specification of 4.6m (15ft) long by 0.4m (16in) in diameter able to carry a payload of 118kg (260lb). The containers had a built-in corrugated iron 'shock absorber', which would crush on impact with the ground and protect the contents of the container. On average it would require 14 containers to transport the weapons of a platoon of 43 men. The ideal situation was that weapons would be claimed by their rightful owner once on the ground but each soldier was cross-trained to use whichever weapon they found available in the canister. The containers were broken down and the weapons distributed on the ground but for supporting loads, such as mortar rounds and other heavier kit, the containers came complete with carrying handles and a set of built-in wheels.

Later, as equipping parachute troops evolved, the Fallschirmjaeger were armed with more practical weapons such as the Erma 9mm MP40 sub-machine gun, known to the Allies as the *Schmeisser*. The Fallschirmjaeger carried a higher proportion than Wehrmacht units of the 9mm MP40 sub-machine gun as they were better suited to be carried by a parachuting soldier than the longer standard rifles. The men also carried a pistol as a standard sidearm, usually the 9mm Luger or 7.65mm Sauer Model 38H pistol.

The Fallschirmjaeger 42 assault rifle (FG42) was adapted specifically for airborne operations, giving the lightly armed paratroopers a weapon that could be easily parachuted in the weapon canisters but also provided a light machine gun on the ground. NCOs usually carried this weapon and carried six 32-round magazines on their webbing. The weapon was produced in fairly small numbers due to its complexity and was not be issued in time for the Sicilian campaign.

Heavy weapons were provided in the form of the MG34 machine gun, and the later MG42, in the tripod-mounted sustained-fire role, which were also more commonly used as section fire support weapons in the standard bipod role. The gunner would carry 50 rounds and the spare barrels for the machine whilst his number two on the gun would carry the remaining 500 rounds for the gun and be responsible for feeding the gun as it fired. The barrel needed changing after every 250 rounds to prevent over-heating. As the MG34 could fire up to 900 rounds per minute and the MG42 1,200–1,500 rounds per minute, several spare barrels were carried by the machine-gun team in leather barrel bags on their backs. Further ammunition would be split down and carried by the remainder of the platoon as the machine gun was considered a section weapon, with responsibility for its firing and maintenance falling to the entire platoon. The muzzle velocity of the MG34 was 755 metres per second and increasing to 822mps for the MG42, often meaning that the unfortunate enemy on the receiving end of its firepower were often unaware of what was about to hit them. The machine gun had a range of 1,000m in the bipod role or 3,400m when mounted on its tripod.

Similar to the British paras, the Fallschirmjaeger had a cut-down 8.8cm mortar known as the *kurzer* (short) *Granatwerfer 42*. This valuable weapon could fire high explosive rounds out to a range of 1,100m (3,660 feet). Anti-tank capability was provided by the 'throwaway' *Panzerfaust,* which fired a 15cm hollow-charge and was steadied in flight by tail-fins which unfolded after it was fired, and the RPzB 54, which was similar to the American bazooka system and could be reloaded and reused, proving to be a very effective tank killer. Mines were also carried by the men. The Teller mine was an anti-tank mine weighing 8kg and was usually buried 2–4 inches below the ground. Containing 5.5kg of TNT or Amatol explosive, it could easily destroy most Allied vehicles and armour. The Teller mine was also magnetic, allowing multiple mines to be attached together in order to destroy larger targets such as tanks. The smaller 'S' anti-personnel mine was lighter at 4kg. Once activated it would spring up to waist height and then explode, sending around 300 steel ball bearings out to a lethal radius of up to 25m.

Clothing was a pioneering factor of the German airborne forces, with many other nationalities following the German developments. The helmet of the Fallschirmjaeger was the standard Wehrmacht *Stalhelme* (steel helmet) but with the protruding rim cut down to prevent the air flow from lifting the parachutist's head by the chin-strap and also to prevent the sharp edge of the rim from damaging the rigging lines of the parachute. A stronger chin-strap was added which fastened at the side of the head as opposed to a single clip underneath the chin, helping to ensure the helmet was not lifted off the paratrooper's head as he exited the aircraft into the slipstream.

Other distinctive features of Fallschirmjaeger dress were the jump smock, with the later British Denison smock mirroring its design, which was normally worn over the pale-blue issue trousers of the Luftwaffe, however baggier sand-coloured trousers were issued in the North African and Italian campaigns. Trousers had a pocket for the Fallschirmjaeger-issue *kappmesser* (gravity knife) whose internal blade could be swung one-handed into action by pressing a lever and holding the knife upside-down so that the blade fell into place by gravity alone. Due to the length of time it took to remove the parachute harness, men often cut their way out of their harness. Leather gloves were also uniquely worn by the Fallschirmjaeger to prevent lacerations from rigging lines when the parachute opened. Built-in elbow pads were added to the jump smock and removable knee pads were worn for parachuting but often discarded once the men had landed. Silk neck-ties were commonly worn around the neck, with some units adopting a standard colour such as dark blue with white polka dots by the 5th Fallschirmjaeger Regiment. Standard-issue leather boots were adapted for the Fallschirmjaeger by removing the metal hob-nailed soles and replacing them with leather soles to aid grip when they were in the back of an aircraft waiting to jump. Side-lacing was introduced to help prevent twisted ankles on landing but it was discovered, similar to the British realisation, that this innovation did not have a marked effect on the casualty rate so was phased out and standard front-laced boots were re-introduced.

The men' personal kit was carried in webbing similar to that worn by their British counterparts but suspended from the back. The Fallschirmjaeger's kit consisted of a water bottle, canteen, sleeping sheet and gas mask in its container. This was then supplemented by their fighting kit with a bayonet, pistol, knife and stick grenades. Stick grenades were often tucked into the waist band next to the pistol holster which was worn on the left side of the waist. Over the top of their webbing specially designed bandoliers were issued to the Fallschirmjaeger which consisted of 12 pouches able to carry 100 rounds of rifle ammunition. Later variants of the bandolier would be introduced to accommodate magazines for the FG42 assault rifle.

The Fallschirmjaeger had a more diverse range of war-fighting experience as they had served in the early airborne operations of the Low Countries in 1940 but also fought hard in Crete and as infantry in defensive positions in Russia. Lessons learned, particularly from Crete, were immediately acted upon and improved their fighting ability. The quick-release buckle of the RZ1 parachute harness was updated with the RZ3 version so that it could be disengaged in only 10 seconds and from a prone position. Previously, the mechanism took a full 80 seconds to release and could only be done from a standing position, meaning many Fallschirmjaeger were killed while trying to release themselves from their parachutes and get into the fight on Crete. The men were also practised in firing from their parachutes and dropping grenades during their descent in case they were landing onto enemy-occupied drop zones again, as they had in Crete.

Their command structure was similar to the British Paras except that officers had to serve an 'apprenticeship' as an NCO before finishing their officer training and also the Fallschirmjaeger were keen to promote NCOs from the ranks to become officers. Therefore, a wealth of hard-won tactical experience was combined with the strategic thinking borne out of the officer training to create very experienced and disciplined leaders in the ranks of the Fallschirmjaeger formations. Time and again throughout their battle experiences the Fallschirmjaeger either acted on their own initiative or by hand signals and orders, between individuals and without officers needing to be present, to carry the fight to their enemy. Their communications relied on either land-lines to field telephones or by VHF radio sets which only worked on line of sight only. This meant it was essential that the Fallschirmjaeger could think on their feet and manoeuvre their smaller units on the battlefield as they saw fit. The fog of war often bogs attacks down but small groups of Fallschirmjaeger securing local objectives, once repeated along the entire front line, led to many success stories on the battlefield.

After the heavy losses on Crete, Student was summoned to meet Hitler on 19 August 1941 for a debrief on the operation. Student was keen for the Fallschirmjaeger to again be deployed to capture Malta or Cyprus and came prepared to state his case. Hitler cut him short however. 'General Student, I believe that the days of the paratrooper are over. They have no surprise value any more'.[8] With that short statement, the future of the German paratroopers was put into jeopardy just as the Allies were emulating their success and building their own airborne forces. The Fallschirmjaeger's capability to fight hard when they were on the ground meant that they would now be used as elite infantry rather than parachuted *en masse* into operations. However, their ability to rapidly redeploy now meant that they were put on standby for operations in the Mediterranean theatre of operations. In contrast to the German way of thinking on the future of airborne forces at this time, the Allies were building up their own forces after experiencing at first hand the Fallschirmjaeger's effectiveness at seizing static enemy positions and holding them until ground forces could arrive. It led Churchill to increase the size of the Parachute Regiment by nine times its pre-Crete strength.[9] British and German paratroopers were now proving their effectiveness when correctly deployed on the battlefield and they would soon face each other again after their initial blooding of each other in North Africa. Both sets of troops were coiled springs waiting for their deployment into battle. They didn't have long to wait, the invasion of Sicily was soon to be underway.

CHAPTER SIX

'*Husky* is let off the leash'

Airborne Landings

The invasion of Sicily began on the night of 9/10 July with a two-pronged airborne attack, by both British and American airborne troops, followed by seaborne landings the following morning along the south-east coast of the island.

The British air assault, Operation *Ladbroke*, was led by 1st Airlanding Brigade in a mass glider-borne attack to capture the Ponte Grande bridge over the River Anapo, thus securing the route for the advancing ground forces into Syracuse. The attack was spearheaded by the pathfinders from 21st Independent Parachute Company, who were to mark the landing zones for the gliders' landing zones. As the sun was setting on the evening of 9 July, the men of the 1st Parachute Brigade looked on jealously as their glider-borne colleagues emplaned ready for their part in the invasion of Hitler's Fortress Europe. The glider-borne men of the 1st Airlanding Brigade were fully kitted up for their action at Ponte Grande. The huge glider formation began taking off at 18:42 precisely from the airfields around Kairouan from which the 1st Parachute Brigade hoped to make their own journey towards the battlefield shortly.

All eyes were turned skyward as the tug aircraft fired up their engines and began pulling the glider armada into the air. The air fleet took off in stages, each flight of aircraft one minute apart and circling the airstrip until the entire sky-train was airborne at 20:20 and circling above the North African landscape, before heading east towards the first RV of the flight path. Instead of riding into battle on horse-back, these modern air-cavalry were now set to enter the battle in the back of a Horsa.

The formation consisted of 144 troop-carrying Horsa gliders towed by RAF Halifax bombers and heavier equipment in Waco gliders being towed by American C-47 Dakotas. The lead glider was being flown by the commanding officer of the Glider Pilot Regiment, Lieutenant Colonel George Chatterton, who had onboard Brigadier Philip Hicks, commanding officer of the 1st Airlanding Brigade.

Once assembled, the air armada dropped down to a low altitude of only 200–500 feet (60–150m) for most of the journey to their landing zones. The straight-line distance from Kairouan to Sicily was 250 miles (400km) but the flight path was a dog leg heading over the Kuriate Islands and then turning northwards at Delimara Point on Malta, lengthening the total flight path to 450 miles (720km). The 1st Parachute Brigade would follow the same route only a few days later. As they approached Malta, they could clearly make out the six searchlights pointing skywards as a guiding beacon and were met by patrols of Spitfires providing additional defensive cover. The majority of the formation at this stage was relatively intact with only a few stragglers heading back to base with technical difficulties.

As they steered northwards for Sicily, the British formation veered to the right of the flight path and the American aircraft veered to the left of the flight path. This allowed for the two separate formations to head for the designated landing and drop zones more easily once they approached the Sicilian coastline.

As they neared Cape Passero on the south-eastern coast of Sicily, strong winds began to blow them off course. The lead aircraft, recognising this error, abruptly turned to regain the flight path and at this stage some of the less experienced pilots began to lose formation. Aircraft were now over-taking each other and having to fly at different altitudes to avoid collisions.

The intended casting-off height for the gliders was pre-arranged at an altitude of 1800 feet (600m) and at a distance of 1.8 miles (3km) out at sea in order to avoid Italian coastal flak. The only communication between the glider and its tug aircraft was via a wire co-located on the tug rope. Communication via this wire was difficult due to the background noise and in some cases didn't work at all. The men in the back of the gliders therefore had no control over their casting-off point or didn't know exactly when it would be. The decision to cast-off was meant to be a mutual decision by the glider pilots and the tug pilots and should have been visually signalled in the event of the intercom wire not working.

As the air armada flew over the Allied invasion fleet and approached the coast around Syracuse It began taking enemy flak, which added to the growing confusion and broke up the formations further. At this point, around 22:30 and more than 1.8 miles (3km) from the coast still, some of the tug pilots released their gliders and headed for home. Many of these gliders were destined to end up ditching in the sea, having neither the height nor the distance to reach land, let alone their intended landing zones.

As one after the other, the gliders began to land in the sea, the wooden-built Horsas did provide a certain level of buoyancy and remained afloat. The two door doors aft of the cockpit on both port and starboard enabled the men to escape the interior and as the wings of the Horsa were mounted on the top of the airframe, in many cases the men were able to clamber onto the wings and await rescue.

The metal-constricted Wacos also began to ditch into the sea. Carrying heavy weapons and jeeps, they proved too heavy to float and quickly sank into the depths of the Mediterranean Sea.

Lieutenant-Colonel Chatterton did manage to release his lead glider, before being automatically let loose by his towing plane's pilot. After flying through a dust-cloud he was unable to see the shoreline and ended up ditching in the sea too. He was pulled from the cockpit and took his place in the water holding on to the glider wings, where he met Brigadier Hicks and the brigade-major. Hicks turned to his brigade-major and declared in an understated manner, 'All is not well, Bill'.[1] Two of most senior officers of Operation *Ladboke* were now in the Mediterranean Sea and out of action. Chatterton and some of the other survivors were soon picked by up a passing SAS dinghy and the airborne soldiers spent the remainder of the day going into action with the SAS troops taking out coastal Italian strongpoints. Hicks went on to land on Sicily and led a composite group in capturing a coastal battery. He was awarded the DSO for his actions. Hicks later participated in Operation *Market Garden* and temporarily took command of 1st Airborne Division when Major-General Urquhart was cut off and surrounded by German forces in Arnhem for 24 hours.

Not far behind Chatterton's glider was that of Major-General Hopkinson. He was soon to follow Chatterton into the water when his glider also came down short of the Sicilian coastline. Hopkinson was plucked from the sea later that morning by HMS *Keren,* as Admiral Lord Ashbourne recalls, 'I saw a body floating in the sea, almost alongside and evidently alive. I told the captain of the *Keren* to pick him up. A few minutes later a dripping soldier arrived on the bridge. He turned out to be Major-General G. F. Hopkinson commanding 1st Airborne Division. The last time I had seen him was in 1922 when I had rowed in the same boat with him at Cambridge University'.[2] Hopkinson was landed ashore later that day and eventually caught up with his headquarters. Only two months later near Taranto in Italy though, whilst directing 4th Parachute Brigade's advance on Castellaneta, Hopkinson was granted the unfortunate distinction of being the only British airborne general to be killed in action during the war.

The circumstances around the fiasco of the delivery of the airborne forces to the Sicilian battlefield was lamented by Admiral Cunningham. 'It does, therefore, appear more necessary that airborne troops should be considered as a useful auxiliary rather than as a governing factor'.[3] His sentiments were representative of the scepticism felt about the fairly inauspicious performance of airborne troops to date. The fighting spirit of the men had been proven in North Africa and would again be displayed in Sicily, but the coordination and effort required to deliver them accurately to battle was proving more than it's worth in the minds of several senior commanders in the Allied ranks.

Of the 144 gliders that set out for Sicily that night, seven had to turn back for technical reasons. A further 72 would land in the sea with only 44 landing within a ten-mile radius of their intended landing zone. One glider actually landed on the main airfield on Malta and the troops disembarked from the glider upon landing and rushed out expecting to get into action. They were promptly told by an RAF officer that they were in fact in Malta and to push their glider off the runway as it was preventing any other planes from taking off or landing. Only four gliders out of the total air fleet of 144 gliders actually made it intact onto the landing zones.[4] In stark contrast to these appalling statistics, every single Halifax and Dakota tug plane made it safely back to Kairouan.

The air armada had also been supported by Hurricanes equipped with cannons, rather than the standard machine guns, so that they could strafe any searchlights on the ground to aid the arrival of the slow-moving gliders. Further air support in the form of a diversionary bombing raid by a squadron of Wellington bombers was directed against Syracuse and Catania ports. In addition, from H-50 until H+15 motor torpedo boats neared the coastline and laid down a smokescreen to hide the approaching gliders from ground fire. The idea of submarines to surface and flash lights skywards to guide in the air fleet was discarded due to the difficulty in accurately positioning the submarines.[5] Despite these extra measures, the gliders were still hopelessly inaccurate because they were cast off far too far out to sea.

Only one glider, flown by Staff Sergeant Galpin, carrying a platoon of the 2nd Battalion of the South Staffordshire Regiment led by Lieutenant Lawrence Withers, landed on the correct landing zone. As Withers extracted himself from the glider and began to form his men up, the lead glider of the *coup de main* group carrying the company commander, Major Ballinger, flown by Captain Denholm also came in to land. The sight of other gliders must have buoyed the spirits of the men already on the ground but Denholm's glider overshot the landing zone and skidded into the riverbank as it took incoming tracer fire, in turn igniting a Bangalore torpedo inside the glider with the resulting explosion killing all onboard. If Withers and his men had any doubts as to their predicament as the lucky few safely on the ground, it quickly became apparent that they would not be getting much support from the rest of the 1st Airlanding Brigade in their objective of capturing the Ponte Grande. Therefore, Withers set off for the bridge with the few men that he had with him. He gave a quick 'orders' group on stopping short of the bridge. He and five other men would swim across the river and attack the pillbox guarding the northern approach. Simultaneously, the remainder of the platoon would attack the south of the bridge. The Italians from the 121st Coastal Infantry Regiment were taken completely by surprise, with only some sporadic small-arms fire being wildly returned. Within minutes the bridge was secured and the Italian prisoners rounding up and locked in a blockhouse on the northern side of the river. Demolition charges on the bridge were then located and dropped into the river. One platoon of men had now achieved the stated objective for a whole brigade. Reinforcements were now needed to fend off the expected counter-attack, however, one third of the brigade was now missing in the drop and only one in fifteen of the brigade would take part in operations around the Ponte Grande.

By daybreak the glider force was up to a strength of eight officers and 65 men, with only a 2-inch mortar for fire support. The Italian troops had created a perimeter around the bridgehead, thus preventing any further airborne reinforcements from reaching the bridge. The Italians began engaging the defenders at 04:00. Withers checked his watch and could hear the seaborne invasion bombardment beginning. He only had to hold the bridge until 07:30 when he expected to be relieved as planned by the 5th Division driving up from Cassibile only 7 miles (11km) away.

However, despite light resistance from some Italians who were clinging on to the area around the bridge since its capture, further Italians arrived in strength at 11:30 with armoured and heavy weapon support. The fighting then raged on with the British resisting overwhelming odds until 15:30 when the remaining 15 men were captured. However, they were liberated only half an hour later by the advancing Northampton Regiment approaching from the beach landings. As the prisoners spotted an approaching British captain they waved and shouted for him to make a run for it. Instead the officer took cover behind a tree and fired a single shot from his pistol at the lead Italian guard. The guard was hit between the eyes and was immediately killed. A second guard was then killed by the officer. As two

Fully laden paratroopers of 101st Airborne Division board their C-47 Dakota. (Battlefield Historian Ltd @ battlefieldhistorian.com BHC 000390)

guards began to move forward to return fire with their rifles they were overpowered by the prisoners and killed. The captured rifles were then put to use against the remaining guards who promptly surrendered. The prisoners now took their captors as captives. The bridge was subsequently overrun by the 5th Battalion of the Royal Scots Fusiliers and was back in Allied hands only half an hour after being lost to the Italians. Despite the bridge being taken and secured, the airborne forces had had to fight for much longer than expected with reduced numbers and the ground forces had arrived too late to relieve them. This pattern was to be tragically repeated across the later airborne operations of the Sicilian campaign, and indeed of the war.

Casualties of the 1st Airlanding Brigade were 490: 61 KIA on land, 133 wounded, 44 missing and 252 drowned. The Glider Pilot Regiment lost 14 killed, 29 wounded and 58 missing. After the fiasco, the British and Americans were confined to their respective camps in Africa to prevent trouble brewing between the British troops and their American pilots.

Meanwhile, the American airborne operations were the first combat jumps undertaken by the 82nd 'All American' Airborne Division. The division would be jumping over two consecutive nights on 11 and 12 July, due to the aircraft shortage caused by many of the American transport aircraft being used in the British attack on the Ponte Grande. The first American paratroopers to jump would be from the 505th Regimental Combat Team, led by Colonel James Gavin. He had flown in a reconnaissance mission over Sicily in an RAF Beaufighter based in Malta to get an idea of the ground a few days before the planned jump. Gavin's men would be transported by 266 Dakotas onto four drop zones around Gela to secure airfields and high ground inland from the beaches that would host Patton's seaborne landings the next morning.

The next night would see the arrival of the Colonel Reuben Tucker's 504th Regimental Combat Team to further add to the numbers on the ground and maintain the inland bridgehead for Patton's advance. The glider-borne element of the division, the 325th Glider Infantry, would have to be landed by sea, as their consignment of gliders had been given over to the British 1st Airlanding Brigade for their assault on the Ponte Grande. British forces, particularly the airborne forces, were viewed as more battle hardened by the top brass and therefore gained priority in being assigned transport aircraft to deploy on the battlefield.

Sicily was to be the division's first operational jump. For many, it was also to be their first night jump. Unlike their British counterparts, the American paratroopers did not have to complete a night jump to earn their 'wings'. The Americans would also not be employing pathfinders or beacons to mark their drop zones in order to maintain operational security until the last possible moment. This would prove, therefore, to be a learning experience for the entire American airborne apparatus. The 82nd were keen to finally get the chance to prove themselves in battle after all their training. They had volunteered for an elite unit and considered themselves superior to their 'straight leg' infantry colleagues, who in turn referred the paratroopers as 'bent legs'. The American infantry had already been blooded in Africa and now the paratroopers were keen to make their debut in the war.

The scaled-down plan of the 82nd Airborne Division was put into practice when they took off from Kairouan around 18:00 on 11 July. As Gavin waited in his Dakota he was passed a message from a member of the airfield's weather station with regards to the wind speed over the objective, 'thirty-five miles an hour, blowing west to east'.[6] Although the plan was not changed, at least Gavin knew to expect a dispersed drop and potentially many injuries from hard landings. Training jumps would usually be cancelled if winds were over 15mph during the day and 9mph at night. This was operational now, however, and the jump would be going ahead no matter the wind speed.

As the American air armada passed over Malta on its way to Sicily, watching below on the ground was Eisenhower. He rubbed together the seven lucky coins that he kept in his pocket as the armada passed overhead on its way to combat.

As the formation neared Sicily it experienced a combination of anti-aircraft fire and strong winds and the formation became dispersed. The anti-aircraft fire accounted for eight Dakotas being shot down. A further three became lost and returned to base with their paratroopers still onboard. As for the men of Gavin's regiment that managed to land on Sicily, the bulk of them were dropped 25 miles (40km) from their drop zone. Only around 200 men were assembled at the designated rendezvous point. The rest of the 82nd were spread all over south-east Sicily, with some unfortunate paratroopers ending up in the sea after jumping as commanded on the green light, only to find out that they were still over the sea. Some 23 of the Dakotas managed to drop their paratroopers 60 miles (100km) away near Noto in the British sector.[7] The ability of the paratroopers to capture strategic objectives by using speed and surprise was essentially rendered irrelevant by their being delivered far from their targets and so widely scattered. However, one result of the confused drop, was the confusion also handed to the enemy's intelligence picture with mass reports of paratroopers landing all over southern Sicily.

The American paratroopers made their way towards the sounds of the battle raging in the distance, stopping to sever communications and ambush enemy units as they progressed. Four days later only two thirds of the American paratroopers had found their units again. Although the Allied plan was dealt a blow by the missing paratroopers, it certainly added to the confusion experienced by the Axis forces as the whole of southern Sicily from Gela to Syracuse appeared to be one large drop zone. The scene was now set for the arrival of the seaborne troops.

Seaborne Landings

The seaborne element of the Sicily invasion was launched by Admiral Cunningham with the simplistic but straight-forward order to the invasion fleet – 'Carry out

Operation *Husky*.[8] With this order, the amphibious force set off from various ports in North Africa headed for Sicily.

At around 01:45 General Guzzoni was informed of enemy activity on the landing beaches. Reports of airborne landings were obvious indicators for a possible invasion at dawn. He notified both the Italian XII and XVII Corps who were defending the south-east coast to be alert for a seaborne invasion. The coastal divisions didn't have much time to prepare themselves for battle, as the landings began only an hour later.

The strong winds that had hampered the airborne operations also made matters difficult for the amphibious landings. The Italian defenders questioned the ability of the Allies to land in such high seas but they soon sighted the massive naval armada that was fast approaching the shore. The armada was heading for the 26 main beaches spread along 105 miles (169km) of the southern and eastern coastline of the island, between the town of Licata in the west and Cassibile in the east. Operation *Husky*

From the deck of a Coast Guard manned transport, a Coast Guard photographer captured these shots of an American cargo ship hit by German dive bombers in an air raid on a convoy during the Invasion of Sicily. Fire, started by bombs dropped amidships, spread rapidly to the ship's munitions supply, which exploded to form dangerous though picturesque patterns across the Mediterranean. (Battlefield Historian Ltd @ battlefieldhistorian.com BHC 003039)

constituted the largest amphibious operation of World War II in terms of the size of the landing zone and the number of divisions put ashore on the first day.

The first troops ashore at around 03:00 were the Special Forces and commandos. Enemy batteries at Cassibile and Capo Murro di Porco were the objectives of No. 3 Commando and Lt-Col 'Paddy' Mayne's Special Raiding Squadron respectively. At Pachino, the most westerly of the beaches in the British sector, the Canadian 1st Division came ashore 45 minutes behind schedule at 05:30 with its flanks secured by No. 40 and 41 Royal Marine Commandos. The Canadians had sailed directly from England and straight into the invasion of Sicily without incident but on approaching the coast some of the larger landing craft ran aground on submerged sand bars, leading them to despatch their troop-laden DUKW amphibious landing vehicles earlier than planned. This extra distance to shore delayed the troops landing but the DUKWs managed to drive straight up the beach and disembark their troops into the protection of the sand dunes. In the face of almost no opposition, the Canadian 2nd Brigade landed on the right flank and the Hastings and Prince Edward Regiment landed on the left flank and began moving inland. By 06:45, the divisional commander, Major-General Simonds, had signalled the XXX Corps commander, Lieutenant General Leese, to confirm all of the initial objectives had been secured. By lunchtime the tanks and artillery of the division were being landed to allow the push inland and the link-up with the airborne forces at Ponte Grande to begin.

Leese's other divisions were faring much the same. The 51st Division was landing to the immediate right of the Canadians near the town of Maucini. They had sailed directly from ports in Africa for Sicily, arriving on the beaches at 02:45 as planned. They similarly had an uneventful landing and by mid-morning were pushing their way inland, taking the town of Pachino and linking up with the Canadians on their left flank.

To the north of the 51st Division, the 231st Brigade, led by Brigadier Roy Urquhart of later Arnhem fame whilst leading the 1st Airborne Division, came ashore to provide a link between the 51st and 50th Divisions, the latter of which was landing near Avola. The 231st Brigade, known as the Malta Brigade after spending much of the war based on the fortress island, would encounter the Napoli Division that morning in their first real fight against the enemy. The Italian defence relied on the inferior coastal troops exacting a price on the seaborne landings and attempted to delay the inland Allied push. The better-trained and equipped divisions were held in reserve further inland and brought forward to deal with enemy thrusts inland. Accordingly, the 231st Brigade had got ashore fairly easily against only light resistance and was well prepared later in the day for the expected counter-attack of the Napoli Division led by its R35 tanks. The 231st Brigade met the Italian advance with their own tanks and dug-in anti-tank guns, leading to a short, sharp artillery and tank duel, leaving the Napoli Division to retreat with heavy losses.

The 50th Division was meanwhile landing around Avola, spearheaded by the 151st Brigade, containing the 6th, 8th and 9th Battalions of the Durham Light Infantry, who would later be tasked with pushing towards Primosole Bridge as a relieving force for the 1st Parachute Brigade. The small Landing Craft Assault (LCAs) containing the men of the Durham Light Infantry had been lowered into their boats 12 miles out to sea instead of the planned 7 miles (11km). As a result, the boats began landing individually and spread all along their designated beach, instead of as a concentrated force. The defenders from the Italian 206th Coastal Division luckily did not put up much resistance as the landing troops began heading inland from wherever they had happened to land. Troops from the 6th Durhams headed for Avola train station and linked up with unexpected units along the way, including American paratroopers and units from the British 5th Division that had landed off course yet further north up the coast. To the north-east of Avola the 9th Durham Light Infantry were also hitting the beaches, 90 minutes later than scheduled and similarly scattered upon landing. However, by late morning they were reorganised and heading for their objective of Avola, with their support battalion, the 8th, close behind.

To the north of Avola were the landing beaches of the 5th Division around the town of Cassibile. The 5th Division was the most travelled division of the British Army during World War II. It began the war in France as part of the British Expeditionary Force, later to be evacuated at Dunkirk. Its brigades then served in Norway before heading out to India via Madagascar. Then division was then transferred back to the Middle East via Persia, Iraq and Syria. It then began training in Egypt for the Sicily invasion and onto Italy, before finally serving in the last months of the war in Germany. At Sicily, the division landed an hour later than scheduled on their beaches but by 05:00, the beach was declared cleared and the town of Cassibile was captured by 10:00.

Montgomery was adamant that Syracuse should be captured on D+1 of the invasion and the 2nd Royal Scots Fusiliers headed on foot for the port of Syracuse, to link up with the men of the 1st Airlanding Brigade. Without finding any expected Allied or locally-sourced transport on route, the battalion had to move slowly, halting to clear each known enemy position, instead of outflanking the positions and moving towards the Ponte Grande at full speed. The lack of urgency was a sign of things to come for the airborne troops. The infantry seemed in no apparent rush to relieve the airborne troops at the Ponte Grande, believing that a whole airborne brigade was located there. Instead a mere platoon was fighting for its very survival against overwhelming odds. This was to be a pattern that was to be repeated continually throughout the war as ground forces failed to relieve the lightly armed paratroopers in good time.

Scattered airborne troops from the 1st Airlanding Brigade now attached themselves to the column making its way to the Ponte Grande, urging them on to relieve their comrades.

From his headquarters in Malta Montgomery now began to see a clear picture of the landings. The opposition seemed to be lighter than expected and he was conscious of the need to relieve the 1st Airlanding Brigade and secure Syracuse. He sent a message to Dempsey to 'operate with great energy towards Syracuse'.[9] This message from the Eighth Army commander failed to impress itself upon the sluggish advance that was unfolding on the ground.

The troops landing on the American beaches to the west of the British beaches were similarly meeting light resistance but they began to meet the Axis main mobile

Gen Montgomery tours the British beachhead on the day after the assault landings. Monty is riding in Maj Gen Wimberley's personal DUKW as his own transport was late arriving and was yet to be unloaded. British 51st Highland Divisions formation sign, a prominent combined 'HD' can be seen on the front of the vehicle near the drivers position. (Battlefield Historian Ltd @ battlefieldhistorian. com BHC 003039)

reserves as they moved inland. In Major General Terry Allen's US 1st Infantry Division sector at Gela, the inland areas were supposed to have been captured and held by the 82nd Airborne Division. Due to their scattered drop, there was a gap in the Allied lines which allowed the development of a division-sized Italian thrust towards the landing beaches. Italian infantry from the Livorno Division, supported by tanks from the Niscemi Armoured Combat Group, squeezed the Gela beachhead until naval gunfire was brought down to break up the attacks. The Livorno Division, comprised mainly of Italian conscript troops, repeated the attack only two days later, this time supported by the panzers of the Hermann Goering Panzer Division but again they were repulsed by recently arrived tanks and artillery on the ground, and also by naval gunfire from the invasion fleet anchored offshore.

The US 3rd Division had managed to land and capture the port of Licata early on the morning of D+1. This meant that supplies could be landed directly into the small port and enabled the necessary logistics to support the Allies' push northwards across the island.

The surprise and the sheer size of the Allied invasion force, coupled with the air campaign to destroy the German and Italian air forces based in Sicily prior to the invasion, led to less enemy air activity on D+1 than anticipated. However, with such a vast array of targets anchored offshore, and with the advantage of operating from airfields on the island, the enemy planes soon made an appearance. German Ju-87 Stukas and Ju 88s, along with Italian Stukas, known as *Picchiatello*, and Savoia-Marchetti SM79 torpedo-bombers began to take a toll on Allied shipping. Among the ships sunk were the Indian hospital ship *Talamba* and the USS *Maddox*, as well as numerous other supply vessels.

Following the success of getting the five Allied divisions ashore on D-Day, the Allies now needed to push inland and exploit their initial success and surprise. Alexander wanted the Allies to establish a coordinated line from the American-held Licata in the west to a British advance on Syracuse and Catania in the east. Once this baseline was established, the two Allied armies could then hook round both sides of Mount Etna to clear the rest of the island, capturing key ports along the way. The ultimate prize on Sicily was still Messina. It was the closest point to Italy and getting there would effectively put the cork in the bottle of the Axis forces' retreat back to the mainland.

Syracuse was taken on 10 July largely unopposed by the Italian defenders. However, the Axis forces were now beginning to recover from their initial shock at the speed of the Allied landings and were beginning to counter the landings. Syracuse was seen as an obvious key port. The German commander Schmalz led his battle group, supported by Italian tanks, against the British in Syracuse. They managed to break the front line, held by the Wiltshire Regiment, and penetrated as far as the suburbs of the city before being halted by British artillery and tank fire. Despite the capture of the port, it had been sabotaged and damaged by the Italian garrison before they retreated, however, and it wasn't until it had been cleared by minesweepers and shore clearance parties on the 11th that convoys could enter the harbour with the first convoy, MWS37, arriving on 13 July.

Augusta was proving a more difficult port to capture though as the Italian defenders there were putting up a fight. The Royal Navy closed in to bombard the port but, after taking heavy return fire from coastal batteries, withdrew. Paddy Mayne's Special Raiding Squadron was again called upon to take the port of Augusta under the cover of a naval bombardment led by three destroyers. Under heavy fire, the SRS managed to land and managed to secure the port after overcoming several machine-gun posts. Mayne was awarded one of his four DSOs for this action. The Royal Navy now had control over most of the eastern coastline of Sicily. The remaining Axis vessels were either bottled up in ports, headed for Italy or attempting lone attacks on the mass Allied armada. Despite this massive amount of firepower lying offshore and only a few miles away from advancing Allied troops inshore, the lack of reliable communications meant that only a day after Augusta was taken, the men of 1st Parachute Brigade fighting at Primosole Bridge only once managed to contact an Allied naval vessel to call in ship-to-shore fire support.

US forces landing on D Day on beach at Gela, to begin their Sicilian Campaign (Operation *Husky*). (Battlefield Historian Ltd @ battlefieldhistorian.com BHC 003018)

Early on 13 July, Paddy Mayne's small force was relieved by the British 5th Division to complete the capture of Augusta. On their inland flank, Major-General Sidney Kirkman's British 50th Division were pushing north towards Lentini, the last town before crossing the Simeto and advancing on Catania. They now began meeting the Italian and German divisions that had been held inland as a reserve. The initial speedy progress out from the beachheads was slowly being checked as, for the first time, the Allies started to reach prepared defensive positions, held by troops just waiting for the Allies to come within range of their sights.

Further inland, the British 51st (Highland) Division were moving towards the slopes of Mount Etna to prepare to take the towns of Palazzolo and Vizzini. Meanwhile the Canadian 1st Division had secured Pachino airfield in the south-east corner of the island. This allowed Allied aircraft to begin basing themselves on Sicily for the first time, giving much-needed air support to the ground troops. With this objective secure, the Canadians headed for the hill-top town of Ragusa and to link up with the Americans.

Back in the American sector, the failure of the airborne troops to capture a protective belt of land ahead of the beachhead meant that the Axis forces were free to constantly probe the defensive screen and endanger the whole American beachhead. Patton, therefore, ordered his reserve parachute troops from the 504th Parachute Infantry Regiment, under Colonel Reuben Tucker, of the US 82nd Airborne Division to parachute into Sicily in order to reinforce the beachhead perimeter by capturing transport links further inland, preventing the enemy from advancing.

That night, the 144 Douglas C-47 transports carrying Tucker's paratroopers arrived over the Sicilian coast passing above the Allied fleet just as an Axis air raid was finishing. The first few planes flew over the fleet without incident. Suddenly, one gunner on one Allied ship opened fire on the Dakotas. In unison, the Allied fleet joined in and a wall of anti-aircraft fire raced up into the sky. Immediately, Dakotas full of Americans were exploding and being shot down. Entire sticks of paratroopers starting exiting over the sea to escape the inevitable shooting down of their aircraft; and some paratroopers floating down, having escaped their fiery planes, were shot in their harnesses as they descended. As quickly as the firing began, the naval officers began to order cease-fires as they realised they were butchering their own men.

The 52nd Troop Carrier Wing lost 23 of 144 C-47s to friendly fire; there were 318 casualties with 83 dead. Thirty-seven aircraft were damaged, while eight returned to base without dropping their parachutists. One paratrooper ironically noted that, 'evidently the only safe place for us over Sicily tonight is over enemy territory!'[10] The friendly-fire disaster would have far-reaching consequences. Not only had it led to the deaths of so many paratroopers, it had also significantly reduced Patton's intended use of the paratroopers to protect his beachhead. Commanders were furious as reports began to surface of the disaster.

General Ridgway, commander of the 82nd Airborne Division, was ready and waiting for the returning Dakotas in Africa and witnessed the shot-up remains of the air armada. He even saw some paratroopers still sitting in their seats where they had been shot dead by their own side. Eisenhower was also receiving reports of the friendly-fire slaughter and informed Patton to instigate a report immediately. In only a matter of hours, Patton duly submitted his initial findings to which Eisenhower responded:

> If the cited report is true, the incident could have been occasioned only by inexcusable carelessness and negligence on the part of someone. You will institute within our command an immediate and exhaustive investigation into the allegation with a view to finding responsibility. Report of pertinent facts is desired and if the persons found responsible are serving in your command, I want a statement of the disciplinary action taken by you. This will be expedited![11]

With the 1st Parachute Brigade due to drop in the next few days, and with all of the airborne operations carried out in Sicily so far being scattered or attracting friendly fire, the Allies needed to quickly identify and fix just where their airborne operations were currently failing before another disaster was experienced.

The supporting glider assault by Colonel Harry Lewis's 325th Glider Infantry Regiment, part of the 82nd Airborne Division, then waiting in North Africa to airland the division's heavy weapons and reinforcements, was cancelled by Ridgway, 'in view of the unfortunate incident last night.'

Despite the failing of the two American airborne operations, the ground troops were making steady progress. The US 1st Infantry Division took Ponte Olivo on 12 July and continued north, while the 45th Infantry Division on the right flank had linked up with the Canadians at Ragusa, after taking Comiso airfield. On the extreme left of the American flank, the 3rd Infantry Division pushed inland from Licata, quickly increasing its bridgehead as it reached Argento, 25 miles (40km) along the coast and moving 20 miles (32km) inland to Canicatti.

The success in the advances by both the British and American armies now threatened to spill into an insubordinate race to Messina by Alexander's main commanders, Patton and Montgomery. Montgomery felt that the east of the island was the quickest route to Messina with key ports along the way, leaving the Americans to clear the less strategically important western side of the island in slower time.

Patton believed that the harder fight would be on the east coast, therefore he should push on to Palermo and put pressure on the enemy by then hooking east towards Messina. With only limited resources, Alexander could only support one of the advances.

Montgomery now lobbied Alexander for his plan to be approved. He proposed a single main thrust towards Catania and then onto Messina, with a supporting thrust inland towards the base of Mount Etna. In order to complete this inland hook, he needed Alexander to approve the redrawing of the army boundary between the British and American armies and the subsequent re-routing of the Americans off their main highway, instead giving control of the road to Montgomery's forces.

In the initial stages of the invasion, British XIII Corps was tasked with capturing the ports of Syracuse and Augusta as quickly as possible to allow supplies to be brought onto the island and sustain the advance. The main road from these ports to Messina passed through the city of Catania at the foot of Mount Etna. The base of this bottleneck could therefore be fairly easily defended by the Axis forces, allowing them to despatch troops south along the coastal road to intervene in XIII Corps' advance on the ports. It was therefore decided to insert the 1st Airborne Division to capture the Primosole Bridge between Augusta and Catania, in turn blocking any Axis advance and also allowing the Allied advance to press on over the bridge and northwards, preventing a strong defensive position building up around Catania and also over-running the Axis airfields situated there. Operation *Fustian* was now born and would lead to the arrival of 1st Parachute Brigade onto the battlefield in Sicily in what was to be the largest attempted airborne operation so far.

The British airborne targets of Ponte Grande had been captured by the 1st Airlanding Brigade. The operation planed for the 2nd Parachute Brigade was now cancelled as ground forces had already secured the target. Meanwhile, news of the initial events of the invasion was filtering back to the men of the 1st Parachute Brigade waiting to get in on the action from their airfields in North Africa.

With Kesselring now in charge on the ground in Sicily, he created a plan to effectively concede the western half of the island to the Americans with a series of rearguard actions to slow them down. The main focus of the Axis defence would now

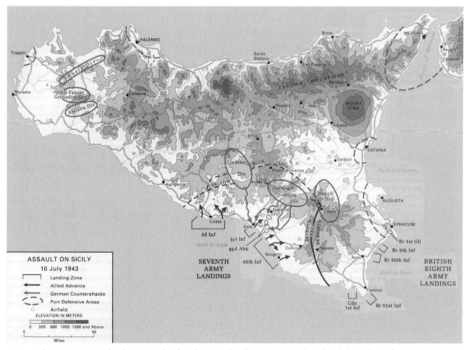

Operation *Husky* showing the landing and subsequent push inland by Allied forces.

be the narrower eastern half of the island. Kesselring acknowledged that he could not now hope to hold on to Sicily but instead use a few carefully chosen defensive lines to form a fighting retreat back to Messina and then Italy. His plan was to use the Catania Plain below Mount Etna as a bottleneck to halt the British advance with a series of defensive lines. This would allow Axis forces on the western part of the island to begin moving back towards Messina for evacuation to the Italian mainland. Sicily was now to be used a defensive exercise by the Axis to perfect their delaying tactics by using minimal troops to inflict maximum casualties and delays on the Allies. The first of these defensive lines to be established was around the Simeto River. The Fallschirmjaeger were to parachute into the area of the Primosole Bridge and begin the process of acting as a filter to allow German and Italian forces to withdraw through them, whilst concurrently fighting off any Allied attacks. The Fallschirmjaeger's role was to begin slowing the Allied advance, causing it to lose momentum as it then hit the main defensive 'Etna' line further north towards Catania. The early speed of the Allied landings and advances was now to be checked on Kesselring's ground of choice. The first line of defence would run inland from Catania to Etna, designated the Hauptkampflinie. Whilst Schmalz's battle group slowed the British advance south of Catania, Kesselring planned to use this delay in the Allies' advance to rush in reinforcements to Sicily. The Fallschirmjaeger were now tasked to deploy to Sicily and halt the Allied advance across the island.

CHAPTER SEVEN

'Storming Eagles'

At the time of the Allied Sicilian invasion, the 1st Fallschirmjaeger Division, along with the remainder of *Flieger Korps IX*, was based at Flers near Avignon in France, refitting after serving on the Eastern Front. Immediately on hearing news of the invasion, Kurt Student, began lobbying the German High Command (OKW) for the involvement of his Fallschirmjaeger. Hermann Goering was also keen for the Fallschirmjaeger to be deployed and support his hard-pressed Hermann Goering Panzer Division, which was bearing the brunt of the British offensive on the island. Both Student's and Goering's appeals were initially brushed aside as it was preferred that armoured panzer units should instead be deployed to Sicily. The invasion of Sicily occurred at a critical point for Nazi Germany though. Only five days previously, it had launched Operation *Citadel* as part of the battle of Kursk. As such, panzer divisions that had been earmarked for the defence of Sicily and Italy were now engaged on the Eastern Front under massive Red Army pressure and could not be spared.

Hitler once again had to turn to the rapidly deployable Fallschirmjaeger and on 11 July Heidrich was summoned to the Italian Southern Command at Frascati in Italy to be briefed by Field Marshal Kesselring. He was ordered to mobilise his division and start sending the men to Sicily without delay. Before Heidrich had even left Avignon for Italy he had pre-empted the move to Sicily and ordered 3 Fallschirmjaeger Regiment, supported by 1st Machine Gun Battalion, 1st Engineer Battalion, 1st (Radio) Company from the 1st Signals Battalion and an anti-tank battery to also emplane, and follow him to Italy, ready for further onward deployment.

The 3rd Fallschirmjaeger Regiment was under the command of the popular Oberstleutnant Ludwig Heilmann, known as 'King Ludwig' to his men. He had already served in Poland and France with the 21st Infantry Regiment before volunteering for the Fallschirmjaeger and then fighting in Crete. Heidrich had directly telephoned Heilman from Rome and told him that 'you will personally reconnoitre the landing zone. The Field Marshal (Kesselring) will provide you with a swift combat aircraft. Start at 05:00. Conduct yourself according to the situation. We ourselves don't know what's going on over there, Good luck'.[1] The deployment plan of the

Fallschirmjaeger called for the 3rd Fallschirmjaeger Regiment to parachute near Catania and move towards Lentini to support the Hermann Goering Panzer Division.

The second wave would see the machine gun battalion and signals company landed at Catania airfield and move south towards the Primosole Bridge and hold the ground to the south of the bridge to prevent the German troops from being cut off by the advancing Allies.

The third wave, consisting of the engineer battalion and anti-tank battery, would then parachute around Primosole Bridge. The air transport would then return to Avignon and begin bringing in 4th Fallschirmjaeger Regiment. Due to the Luftwaffe's limited capacity to airlift men in such large numbers, 1st Fallschirmjaeger Regiment would be transported to Naples by train and then ferried across to Sicily to join the fight. It was this quick thinking and decisive action that meant an entire Fallschirmjaeger Regiment managed to sneak into the Primosole Bridge area without Allied intelligence even noticing.

Back at Avignon, and the nearby Tarascon airfield, a small armada of Ju52s and Heinkel 111 bombers, serving as transport aircraft, were hurriedly assembled from airfields all over France and Italy in order to provide enough capacity to airlift the Fallschirmjaeger to Naples and then onwards to Sicily when the order came. DFS Gotha 230 gliders would also be used to bring in the Fallschirmjaeger. The Deutsche Forschungsanstalt fur Segelflug (German Institute for Glider Research), or 'DFS' for short, had their pre-war glider project taken over by the Nazis and

A Fallschirmjaeger adopts the distinctive 'crucifix' position when jumping from a Junkers JU52 aircraft. (Courtesy of Air Assault Museum)

turned their high-altitude meteorological gliders into a weapon of war. Glider clubs were common in Germany, and they were established as a basis for training and recruiting boys into the Luftwaffe at a later stage, some of whom were now in the ranks of the Fallschirmjaeger. The DFS 230 was developed to carry ten troops and, like the American Waco glider, had a steel frame covered by stretched canvas. The glider was fitted with machine guns to give it the ability to counter ground-to-air fire on its descent. The larger Goethe 242 gliders could airland 21 troops. Later Gigant Me-231 gliders were also employed as transport gliders and were motorised with six engines and, renamed the Me-323, were used to airland troops to the battlefield, particularly in Russia. Earlier in the war, the division was supported by its own dedicated air fleet, under Transport Wing 30, but the war had led to a lack of aircraft and planes were flown in from all parts of the Axis empire to provide the lift capability to airland and parachute the Fallschirmjaeger into Sicily.

Each time the Fallschirmjaeger went into battle, they could see that the German war machine was less well able to support them as it had done during the Blitzkrieg campaigns at the start of the war. The Allies would have both air and naval superiority and the momentum on the ground would also be with the Allies as they could dictate the time and place from where they would attack Hitler's Fortress Europe. Importantly, Fallschirmjaeger morale was high and they believed that they could win any battle that they were thrown into but many of them were now questioning if Germany could win the overall war itself.

Accordingly on 11 July, an advance party from 1st Fallschirmjaeger Divisional HQ was sent to Sicily to select suitable landing grounds for the Fallschirmjaeger. The three-man advance party, consisting of Hauptmanns Specht and Stangenberg and led by Oberst Heilmann, flew directly from Avignon to Sicily to select the drop zones. Landing in the midst of an air raid at Fiumicino airfield near Catania, with Spitfires circling overhead, their pilot had to weave in and out of the valleys around Mount Etna to avoid detection and managed to land just as the Allied bombers and their fighter escort were leaving. Heilmann described the landing as a 'work of art'[2] as the pilot weaved like an infantryman on their approach to the airfield with its fresh bomb craters. After their adventurous landing at Catania, Heilmann and Stangenberg were then rapidly transported south of Primosole Bridge, taking cover from Allied air attacks on the way, where they quickly selected a drop zone for 3 Fallschirmjaeger Regiment to parachute onto that same night. Once they had checked the map coordinates they moved to the area of the bridge near Statione di Passe-Martino and telephoned Heidrich with the proposed drop zone details. Heidrich agreed the drop zone and gave Heilmann the green light to signal his regiment to head for Sicily and begin parachuting in. Meanwhile, Sprecht had gone into Catania and had begun requisitioning transport. He then led this new-found column of vehicles towards the drop zone just as the lead aircraft of the Fallschirmjaeger approached.

Sitting facing each other in the fuselages of their Ju52s and Heinkel 111s, the men's parachutes on their backs pushed them to the edge of their seats. In the back of the planes the Fallschirmjaeger were singing along to their adopted anthem, *Rot Scheint die Sonne* ('Red Shines the Sun') with particular aplomb:

> When Germany is in danger there is only one thing for us;
> To fight, to conquer and assume we shall die
> From our aircraft, my friend, there is no return!

The singing was interrupted around 30 minutes before jumping as the senior officer or NCO in each plane would shout the order *'Fertigmachen!'* (Get ready). The Fallschirmjaeger would then stand up and hook up their static lines before checking both their own and their comrade's kit. With five minutes to go, the second order would be shouted amidst the noise and mass of men and equipment fighting for space, *'Fertig zum sprung!'* (Get ready to jump). The first man would inch his way into the door and hold onto the metal bars at the side of the door, ready to launch himself into the sky. As they neared the drop zone, the Boschhorns inside the plane would begin to sound off and accompanied with shouts of *'Gehen Sie! Geh, geh, geh'* (Go, go, go), they would dispatch themselves straight from the doors of their transport aircraft.

Major-General Richard Heidrich, Commander 1st Parachute Division (left), was quick to deploy his Fallschirmjaeger to Sicily. (Battlefield Historian Ltd @ battlefieldhistorian.com BHC 000400)

The ease by which the 3 Fallschirmjaeger Regiment landed in Sicily was in stark contrast to the later drop by the British paras. The Heinkel formation flew in daylight without fighter escort and was narrowly missed by a group of American P-38 fighters that was returning to its bases due to lack of fuel. The sight of the Heinkels and Ju52s would no doubt have been radioed back to Allied intelligence but the cargo of the planes was unknown and so the secrecy of the German deployment was maintained.

As the air armada came into view in the distance fires were lit on the ground to mark the beginning and end of the drop zone, with the pilots simply aiming to drop their parachutists between the two lines of fire. This was a simple but effective method of marking a drop zone, especially as they were approaching the drop zone in daylight and not under Allied air or ground attack. At 18:15, as the German commander in Sicily, General Kesselring, watched from the ground, the 1,400 men of 3 Fallschirmjaeger Regiment were dropped by over one hundred Heinkel He-111s onto the drop zone into moderate winds and with no ground fire. The timing of the jump had been carefully planned to coincide with the window when Allied planes headed back to base for the day at around 18:00 and didn't reappear again until daylight hours the next day.

With the exception of a few light casualties from heavy landings, the men moved off in an organised fashion towards their pre-selected defensive positions. What a difference a day would make for the 1st Parachute Brigade.

The Fallschirmjaeger hastily formed up in only 45 minutes, boarded the waiting trucks and moved south towards Lentini as a blocking force for the oncoming Allied land forces. Heilmann himself was at Schmalz's headquarters in Carlentini at 20:00 and ready to place his regiment at the disposal of Battle Group Schmalz. Schmalz immediately sent Heilmann's 2nd Battalion to reinforce the overlap between his battle group and the Hermann Goering Panzer Division. The remainder of Heilmann's force was sent to help defend the coast between Carlentini and the sea. The Fallschirmjaeger were now in their allotted positions to face the Allied ground offensive. However, they weren't expecting an airborne operation right on top of them.

The next evening, further elements of the division were scheduled to airland at Catania airfield in the second Fallschirmjaeger wave. The 1st Fallschirmjaeger Machine Gun Battalion commanded by Major Werner Schmidt, a former Berlin policeman,[3] had landed overnight at Pompigliano airfield near Naples where the air formation was forming up ready for the flight the next morning to Catania. Here the men had their first glance of the Me-231 Gigant glider that would be used to land the division's anti-tank units of 1st Fallschirmjaeger Anti-tank Battalion and 1st Fallschirmjaeger Artillery Battalion. The air formation of Me-231 Gigant gliders and troop-carrying Heinkels left Naples for Catania early the next morning, 13 July, and landed at Catania during an Allied air raid by American B-17 Flying Fortresses, losing two of the Me-231 Gigant gliders and their cargoes of anti-tank guns and men to the falling Allied bombs. Two of the Gigants had also crashed on take-off back in

France and a further two were lost over the sea *en route* to Italy. The Fallschirmjaeger Division was now drastically short of its own anti-tank defences but it still had the support of armour and artillery from the Hermann Goering Panzer Division with which it would link up with around Lentini after landing.

Major Schmidt was in one of the first planes to land at Catania. Upon landing he quickly ordered the men to form up south of the airfield in case of a second Allied air raid.

Leutnant Poppel had landed earlier at Catania airfield at 08:14 and could see the two burning German Gigant aircraft. He realised that this would be a big blow in terms of men and anti-tank weapons so early in the campaign. As he landed, a lorry drove by and Luftwaffe ground crew hurriedly dashed out to meet them on the concrete runway, explaining that Allied fighters had just strafed the airfield and had destroyed two German aircraft for the loss of one of their own. The newly-arrived Fallschirmjaeger immediately threw their kit on to the lorry, bade the He-111 aircrew who had delivered them safely to Catania farewell and then made their way 5 miles (8km) to the south of the airfield to join up with the rest of Major Schmidt's formation.

Here he handed over command to Hauptmann Otto Laun, whilst he headed for Heilmann's command post in Carlentini. Whilst Schmidt moved on to Heilmann's headquarters, he had delegated the command of his troops to Captain Laun and told him to move the battalion just south of the Primosole Bridge and start digging in, ready for the arrival of further Fallschirmjaeger engineer reinforcements who were parachuting into Sicily that night.

Laun took his men in vehicles south on Highway 114 and over the Primosole Bridge. Once over the bridge, he placed his battalion in an orange grove just below the hill designated Johnny II by the British. The Fallschirmjaeger had unwittingly placed themselves on ground overlooking the area designated as DZ2 by the incoming 1st Parachute Brigade. As they set up their machine guns for the night, the Fallschirmjaeger had no idea of the destruction that they would be able to bring onto the 1st Parachute Brigade's air assault in only a matter of hours.

The men, experienced and well trained, now swiftly moved into battle preparation. They quickly dragged their weapons containers and other equipment under the cover of trees and made sure their 'ground sign' was camouflaged from aerial observation. As Poppel remembers, 'everyone's encamped under the olive trees, cleaning weapons and equipment, doing a fry-up or just basking in the sun. The whole farmstead is now excellently camouflaged, with no indication of any military presence'.[4] Once they had got themselves into defensive positions and checked their weapons, as per the Fallschirmjaeger rule of 'first my weapon and then myself', the men began to carry out their own personal admin such as cooking, eating, washing and sleeping. As the British liked to brew up their tea, the Germans liked to brew up coffee. Due to shortages of coffee back in Germany the men were issued with ersatz coffee, known to the men as 'nigger sweat', which was made from acorns. Accompanying the coffee would be a slice of 'Old Man', or tinned meat. As the men settled into their normal routine, Schmidt arrived at Heilmann's headquarters for a further briefing based on the latest intelligence reports available.

After being shown into the operations room, Heilmann briefed Schmidt on the current situation and warned him that 'something is bound to happen tonight. The enemy will try to sneak through to the Catania plain, and to do so he'll send in more troops – either by sea or by air. If he manages to land them in our rear and dig in, we're cut off for sure. So your battalion will remain south of Catania. Hold the bridge over the Simeto and put one company between there and the sea.[5] Heilmann's appreciation of the Allied thinking was spot on. If the Allies landed to the rear of the Fallschirmjaeger division, then Schmidt's battalion would have to hold the bridge in order for the remainder of the division to withdraw north of the Simeto River back towards Catania. Armed with this intelligence, Schmidt returned to find his machine gun battalion already constructing defensive positions 2,000 yards (1,800m) south of the bridge in order to allow withdrawing Axis forces to filter through them.

The Green Devils, however, were not expecting another encounter with their Red Devil adversaries so soon after North Africa. Likewise, the Red Devils were not expecting their Green Devil counterparts to even be in Sicily. Both sets of Devils were about to have a rude awakening.

CHAPTER EIGHT

'Death from Above'

After the problems of the first two airborne operations in Sicily, the RAF advisor assigned to the 1st Airborne Division suggested that the American C-47 pilots adopt the bomber-stream formation employed by the RAF instead of their normal 'v' formation. The bomber-stream formation entailed the aircraft flying in pairs one behind the other with one-minute intervals between each pair of aircraft. This suggestion was dismissed by the American pilots of US 51st Wing, who were mostly pre-war airline pilots, not least because their training had not included any instruction in night-time navigation and the inexperienced crews relied heavily on following the aircraft in front of them.

The men of the 1st Parachute Brigade had had a grandstand view of the air fleet of the 1st Airlanding Brigade flying over their camp for a full hour between 18:00 and 19:00 on 9 July. They knew that their Airlanding colleagues had gone into action and were worried that the whole campaign could be over before they had a chance to get involved. However, rumours had been circulating for the past few days of a less than smooth drop and high casualties experienced by the 1st Airlanding Brigade. Evidence of the intensity of the ground-to-air fire was seen in the holes torn in the airframes of the returning aircraft and by the faces of the shell-shocked aircrew leaving their cockpits after their night's work.

On the evening prior to *Fustian*, the men of the 1st Parachute Brigade had also sat and watched their comrades from 2nd Parachute Brigade walk out to their convoy of trucks to ferry them to the airfields 20 miles (32km) to the south to take part in Operation *Glutton*, their assault on Augusta. *Glutton* had already been postponed by 24 hours before it was cancelled on the second attempt the next evening. Montgomery's land forces had already captured the town and port of Augusta. News was spreading fast as to the successful and fast advance of the troops on the ground in Sicily. The 1st Parachute Brigade were now itching to get their operation underway. They knew that the fate of their 2nd Parachute Brigade colleagues could await them, putting all their training in the heat of the desert over the last few weeks to waste.

The cancellation of Operation *Glutton* did render one major benefit to the 1st Parachute Brigade as it freed up additional tug aircraft. This meant that the men of D Troop of the Airlanding Artillery could also be glider-landed into the battle, adding some much needed extra 6-pounders to the anti-tank defences.

The order to emplane and begin *Fustian* came through on the afternoon of 12 July. However, at 16:00[1] the operation was postponed for 24 hours. The men had gone through the whole process of orders groups, checking their kit and then putting all of their equipment and parachutes on their shoulders and walking in single file over to their allocated truck, marked with a chalk number, which corresponded to their plane number. The convoy had made its way through the dust of the desert and out to the airfields, only to be told an hour after emplaning that the operation was postponed and that they were to return to base and await further orders for the possibility of repeating the operation the next evening. Enforced rest was ordered on the night before an operation and, as a result, the men were ordered to their beds at 22:00, with a later than usual reveille of 07:30 the following morning.

The men of the 1st Parachute Brigade spent the day of 13 July by their beds, apprehensively waiting to receive the order to go into battle. Most men just sat around in their uniforms with their weapons to hand, waiting for someone to tell them what was going on. They were without any information, as the officers were still waiting for confirmation from Montgomery's headquarters for authority to launch the operation. The men now had mixed feelings. Many wanted to get on with the operation and stop all the uncertainty by just sitting around and waiting. Others already felt that the operation would be cancelled anyway and just wanted the order to stand down so that they could unpack their kit and go back to their daily business. Both the battle-hardened veterans and yet-to-be-blooded replacements were anxious at the lack of news. Some would have packed and repacked their kit, constantly adding in or taking out small pieces of kit to waste a few moments waiting time and burn some nervous energy.

The kit for the operation had already been set out in express orders. The men were to wear their airborne smocks over their denim trousers and Angola shirts, with all seams in their clothing to be powdered beforehand with anti-louse powder. 'This dress will be strictly adhered to and no variations will be permitted'.[2] They were to take their red berets for ease of ground- and air-to-ground recognition. Also, for recognition by the approaching relieving forces, the paras were to take a luminous metal strip per man and a two-foot by four-foot red flag with a white star in the centre per platoon. In reality these were packed in the containers and invariably lost in the drop, leaving the men to rely on their trusted maroon berets as a recognition signal to friendly forces. The men each took a small washing and shaving kit and they were also to take face veils to prevent mosquito bites, as well as take four Mepacrine anti-malarial tablets and Mark II Anti-mosquito cream. The cream was to be applied with two layers and then massaged into the skin for one minute every hour. After eight hours another two layers of cream were to be added. The artillerymen were also ordered to take their gym shoes in their packs, presumably they thought that they would find some time to relax once their job during *Fustian* was complete. All troops left behind their respirators but took an entrenching tool each. These would prove invaluable for scraping a hole out of the hard Sicilian soil in order to provide a basic level of cover from fire.

The men were also instructed on what food and water they would be carrying into battle: 24-hour ration packs including two hard-boiled eggs, two tins of cheese, one tin of dripping, chewing gum, three bars of raisin chocolate, two packs of sweet biscuits, six dry biscuits and a pack of boiled sweets. Additionally, they would carry a Tommy cooker and tea-making kit.

They would carry one water bottle (with two sterilising tablets added) and a further 3-gallon water container dropped with each platoon. Two and a half pints of water per man was also carried in the plane to be drunk prior to parachuting into Sicily. The men were instructed not to drink any local milk or eat local fruit and vegetables. The men were instructed that in the event of a man becoming a casualty, his food and water ration was to be left on him so that he could be fed at the aid post.

At 13:45 the men were roused from their slumbers and were ordered to board the lorries once again. As the men boarded the trucks, the battalion signals officers synchronised watches with their fellow officers, to then in turn pass on the correct time to their NCOs and men. Once everyone was on board at 14:30, the convoy of trucks repeated the one-hour drive to the six airfields. Upon arriving at the airstrips, the trucks drove over to the aircraft with the corresponding chalk number on its fuselage. The hastily repaired damage rendered to the aircraft by anti-aircraft fire could be clearly seen by the paratroopers and testified to the rumours of heavy fighting over Sicily. Weapons containers were attached to the aircraft first and then heavier equipment loaded into the fuselage. Two additional containers for each platoon were also packed onto the aircraft. One contained additional weapons including a spare Sten gun, four rifles and 16 extra grenades. The second container carried spare ammunition in the form of 250 extra .303 rounds for the rifles and Bren guns and 1,250 additional 9mm rounds for the Sten guns. Once the kit was loaded on to the planes, the men could spend some free time catching some sun or keeping under the wings in the shade. Once again there was nothing for the men to do but sit and wait for news.

Eighteen hours after the previous night's cancellation, the brigade-major, David Hunter, was waiting in the operations room for the signal to come through that their operation was to be given the green light. After hours of anxious waiting the message came over the radio at 18:30 in clear: 'MARSTON tonight'. It was the coded phrase needed to set the largest airborne operation of the Allied war effort so far into motion. Hunter ran the short distance to Brigadier Lathbury's brigade headquarters tent and excitedly announced that the coded phrase, 'MARSTON tonight' had arrived from Tac HQ. Lathbury immediately called in the three battalion commanders for a final briefing, shook each of them by the hand and then set off for his nominated Albemarle which would take him and his brigade headquarters to their drop zone.

Word now began filtering down to the men that the operation was definitely on for tonight. The three battalion commanders had called in their officers to brief them that the 'Go' signal had been given. The sudden appearance of an impromptu gathering of officers quickly led the men to believe that something at last was being decided either way. Next the officers moved over to their respective companies and platoons and began to deliver the news that it really was 'MARSTON tonight'. The relief felt by the men that the operation was finally confirmed was palpable. It gave them the opportunity to fully focus once again on the job at hand and their individual roles in the upcoming night's work. There was still an air of concern that the operation would be given a last-minute reprieve and a few sceptics refused to believe that the operation was going ahead until their planes were in the air and heading towards enemy territory.

At 18:30 a hot meal was provided to the men at the airfield and they were given further rations to have on the plane before they jumped. Each plane was given a Thermos flask of tea, one sandwich per man and chewing gum.[3]

Next the men helped each other clamber aboard the Dakotas. Weighed down by kit, the men would be pushed up the narrow ladder leading into the fuselage and pulled from above by other members of the unit as they reached the top. Once inside the confines of the drab green interior, the men found their seat among the bucket seats set into the benches in the order they were to jump. They put their kit bags between their legs and began to make themselves as comfortable as they could. Some men kept their maroon berets on until the last minute and then stuffed them down their smocks, whilst others moved into battle-ready mode swiftly and donned their airborne helmets. Officers had their binoculars around their necks and again stuffed them into the front of their smocks, all in preparation for being 'ready for anything' when they hit the ground. The atmosphere was tinged with the nervousness felt by all men on the eve of battle. There was a sense of confidence radiating from the men, however, as they knew they were well trained and experienced and they were looking forward to entering the battlefield once again to prove themselves as an elite fighting unit.

The first aircraft took off at 19:01 from Airfield C and by 19:23 all 24 aircraft at this particular airfield were airborne and on their way. The same pattern was repeated at each of the other five airfields with an average time of a 30-minute window in which to have all aircraft up in the sky and circling into formation before heading east over the Mediterranean and towards the target. There was a three-quarter-moon giving a good degree of illumination on a clear and mainly cloudless evening. The flight to Sicily was shaping up to be a straight-forward task.

There were only a few minor mishaps on the ground for such a large fleet of planes. One Dakota at Airfield B suffered a puncture on the runway but this only took eight minutes to repair before it was sent on its way. At Airfield C one plane wouldn't start and its paratroopers had to quickly emplane to a waiting spare aircraft

Weapons packed into an airborne container and protected with hay. Many were lost during the drop. (Courtesy of Air Assault Museum)

before they too were soon on their way. Two planes from Airfield D returned soon after take-off. One plane-load of paras managed to change into a serviceable aircraft and take off again but two hours behind schedule, whereas the second plane returned with a damaged engine and was grounded.

John Frost had total confidence in the aircraft carrying him into battle that night:

> We had had such excellent relationships with the Americans that one felt nothing could go wrong. The weather was perfect and at 19:30 the battalion began to take off. 'A' Company and part of battalion Headquarters were being flown by one of the best squadrons. This squadron had always managed to drop us accurately on the exercises that we had done before, and their commander was confident that he could do likewise in Sicily. Our flight went exactly according to plan. Later I learned that some of the other squadrons had flown over the Navy and been fired upon... We, however, saw none of this.[4]

John Frost's confidence in the success of the upcoming operation was also reflected by Montgomery, declaring from his caravan headquarters 20 miles (32km) south of Catania on the morning of the jump that 'I shall be in Catania tonight.'[5] Montgomery had moved his headquarters and staff from Malta to Syracuse soon after the invasion to be able to have a clearer idea of events unfolding on the ground in Sicily.

By 20:00 a total of 133 paratroop aircraft and 16 tug-glider combinations were airborne and heading for Sicily at an altitude of only 100 feet (30m) above sea level. This air armada was carrying the 1,856 men of the 1st Parachute Brigade and comprised 105 Douglas C-47 Skytrains belonging to the 51st Troop Carrier Wing, 51 each from the 60th and 62nd Troop Carrier Groups, while the 64th Troop Carrier Group supplied the other three aircraft. No.38 Wing RAF supplied 11 Albemarles. Following behind the parachutists were the glider-borne formations, piloted again by No.38 Wing RAF, consisting of 12 Albemarles and seven Halifaxes, towing 11 Horsa gliders and eight WACO CG-4A gliders. The gliders cargo consisted of 77 men of the 1st (Airlanding) Anti-Tank Battery, Royal Artillery together with their twelve 6-pounder anti-tank guns and their 18 jeeps. Three of the aircraft failed to get airborne due to mechanical difficulties on the airstrip at Kairouan, otherwise the armada proceeded to on its way with few problems encountered. The loss of aircraft during Operation *Ladbroke* a few days earlier meant that there were not enough of the more powerful four-engined Halifaxes to tow all of the heavier Horsa gliders.

Paratroopers in the fuselage of a Dakota, awaiting the order to stand up and prepare to jump. (Courtesy of Air Assault Museum)

As a result of the mistrust of the American pilots' navigational abilities, developed following the operations already undertaken over Sicily, it was decided that RAF planes must be used instead. Additional Albemarles were therefore released by the RAF to tow the remaining Horsas. As the two-engined Albemarles would have to be at full throttle to keep up with the four-engined Halifaxes, the Horsas being towed by the Albemarles had their wheel-based undercarriages wired up so that they could be jettisoned to reduce weight if required. These gliders would then have to land on their skids rather than wheels.

The aircraft's flight path took them from North Africa, around the south-eastern corner of Malta as a reference point and then up the eastern coast of Sicily to a point 10 miles (16km) east of Cape Passero, then due north to a point 10 miles east of the Simeto river before turning due west towards the drop zones. The route was measured so that the leading aircraft arrived at their drop zones at 22:20. Unlike *Ladbroke*, when Hurricanes attacked the searchlights and Wellingtons provided bombing diversions and dropped dummy paratroopers, there were no supporting air attacks for the *Fustian* force.

The men in the back of the aircraft knew that their flight time would be 2.5–3.5 hours in duration. This gave them all some time prior to the jump to spend on their own 'admin' as they wished. Some were lost in their own thoughts, thinking of friends and family back home or what they were going to do after the war was over. Some would be looking out of the small square Perspex windows to see if they could make out any features on the ground and track their progress. Some would simply sleep for the entire journey, as they didn't know when they would next have the luxury of sleeping. Others would talk or get involved in sing-a-longs to waste some time and boost morale. Others would be struggling with air sickness and simply be wishing away the minutes until they could jump out of that plane and get their feet on solid ground again, regardless of what would be facing them.

As the Dakotas made their way across the Mediterranean Sea that night they were buffeted by side winds and moving up and down as they experienced thermals in the air. This process would chip away at the men more prone to air sickness and all too often some of the men would have to call for the onboard bucket. Apart from the embarrassment and traditional leg-pulling that would result, the person being sick would also be bringing up their last meal, thus weakening themselves and wasting precious rations. Finally, the smell of vomit would add to the already uncomfortable interior of the Dakota. Many of the paras that night would have far preferred to hurry up and get to grips with the enemy than spend another second squashed in the back of a glider or aeroplane. They would have begun to mentally go through their personal and team drills, from exiting the aircraft correctly to their upcoming job once on the objective, whether that was to clear demolition charges or to provide cover for others who were to rush across the Primosole Bridge.

Two Dakotas operating over Sicily during Operation *Husky*.

The constant humming of the noise of the engines meant the men had to shout in the back of the aircraft in order to talk. The drone of the engines would instantly disappear when they exited the aircraft into the, hopefully, silent Sicilian night air. The men would also be either too hot or too cold. Some men would sit by the exit door and have a constant or intermittent draft blowing straight at them whilst others would be further down the aircraft sweating from the heat created by being fully kitted up and in close proximity to the other men in the confines of a small aircraft.

Whatever the men's thoughts and discomfort, as they neared the Sicilian coast their mentality would have automatically changed to that of the professional paratrooper. With one hour to go before the jump, the men would be told to 'Stand up and hook up' – their signal to begin to stand up from their seats and hook up their static lines to the onboard steel cable. The men started to check and re-check their kit, as well as each other's kit, as part of a 'buddy-buddy' system. They checked every pouch, pocket and piece of equipment, starting from the top down, to make sure it was securely fastened and that they would not lose any kit as they jumped from the plane. Chinstraps were always pulled extra tight to avoid the embarrassment of helmets disappearing in the slipstream as they left the aircraft. Their weapon systems, the men's lifeline once on the ground, would also be additionally checked to ensure that they were secure. Last but not least the men would check that their parachutes were securely fastened.

The men would be parachuting from the rear door of the plane and would pass underneath the tail of the plane as they fell. They were therefore stood up and facing the rear of the aircraft in the opposite direction that it was flying. Beginning at the rear of the stick, each man would then 'sound off for equipment check'. The rear man would smack the man in front's shoulder and shout his jumping order number and 'ok'. This process would be repeated all along the line until the front man would receive the final smack on the shoulder and declare to the dispatcher – 'One ok, stick ok'. The men were now checked and ready to jump. Most of them probably didn't want to jump from the plane in the next few minutes but each knew that the quickest way to get their feet back on solid ground was to jump out of the plane when told to do so. The men would have felt vulnerable in the slow-moving aircraft: 'There is something especially disturbing about being shot at from below – one's body seems so much more vital when attacked from that direction'.[6] These elite troops knew the run-in to the drop-zones could be the most dangerous part of the whole mission and they were potentially about to be attacked by a faceless, inferior enemy many miles away in the dark of the Sicilian countryside with a 'cheap shot' of anti-aircraft

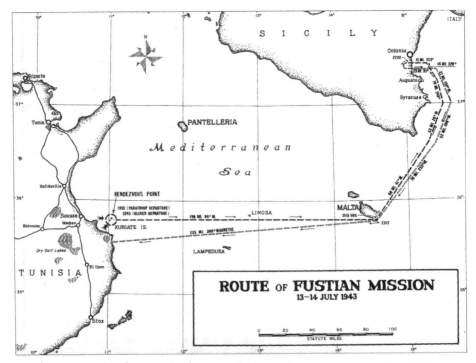

The air route taken from North Africa to Sicily during Operation *Fustian*. (TNA KEW)

fire before they could fight back, and they wanted to be able to demonstrate their superiority and get down on the ground and prove themselves.

'Action Stations' was called by the dispatcher as the planes neared the Sicilian coastline. The first man now moved into the doorway and the rest of the stick shuffled down the plane slightly. The man in the door would be scanning the black sea outside and waiting for the outline of the Sicilian coastline to come into view. He would then have the advantage of surveying the ground that he was about to jump into and try and orientate himself to any landmarks to aid navigation when he landed on the ground behind enemy lines. He would also be able to look out across the sky and see other planes from the air armada, and determine enemy anti-aircraft fire and any friendly casualties being incurred. The men further down the stick would be propping themselves up against the walls of the fuselage for a bit of extra support under the weight of their kit. The men would stay in these positions while they waited for the '2-minute' warning signalled by the red jump light coming on. For *Fustian*, the two-minute warning was reduced to only 15 seconds. Further information would have been passed by the aircrew to the waiting paratroopers, such as wind speed, so that they could be prepared for a heavy landing in high winds. The only signal they would get after the red light was automatic. The pilot would lastly hit the green switch button from his cockpit, accompanied by screams of 'Go, go, go!', the men would start moving forward and tumbling out of the aircraft.

When the planes arrived off the coast of Sicily they were meant to stay 10 miles (16km) offshore until reaching the Simeto River, where they would then turn to the west and begin heading inland. All went well until 33 aircraft neared the Sicilian coastline and flew over the Allied fleet in error. The result was that the aircraft were greeted by friendly-anti-aircraft fire from the Allied naval vessels below, who were on alert after being warned of an impending Luftwaffe raid. Two aircraft collided in the confusion and crashed into the Mediterranean Sea below. Dakotas 102 and 103, carrying 3 Para men, also collided but managed to get back to their airfields in Africa. A further two planes were shot down and nine were badly damaged, forcing them to head back towards the North African coast with their cargoes of paratroopers, which now included multiple casualties. Fifty-five pilots reported their planes being hit by anti-aircraft fire, both enemy and friendly, that night. Four planes, carrying the bulk of T Company 1 Para, were ordered to turn back by their squadron leader at the first barrage of flak.

The friendly barrage put up into the night sky by the Allied fleet also served to notify the Italians onshore that Allied aircraft, or even Axis aircraft, were on their way towards them. They soon recognised the silhouettes of the Dakota aircraft and waited for the planes to pass out of range of their own Allied naval guns first, as they were already inflicting damage on behalf of the enemy gunners. The aircraft then came within range of the waiting guns of the Italian coastal defences.

The standard German and Italian flak gun, the 20mm *Flakvierling* 38, was a four-barrelled weapon system with a firing rate of 1,800 rounds per minute up to an altitude of 2,200 metres, putting the airborne armada well within its killing field. The firepower that these weapon systems could pump into the night sky was enough to scatter the inexperienced pilots out of the formations without even hitting any aircraft.

Many planes were hit though. Dakota 42, carrying half of the Headquarters of 2 Para, including RSM Oliver, was shot down and crashed into the sea. Another nine Dakotas were claimed by the Italian gunners with numerous more planes being shot up. The paratroopers in the back of the aircraft didn't even have the option to begin jumping yet, as they were still over the sea. Without the Italians receiving warning from the Allied naval fire the lead aircraft may well have been able to reach the drop zones unmolested by ground fire and drop many more men, much closer to their intended target, potentially changing the course of the battle.

Gordon Mitchell of 1 Para remembers the reaction of the dispatcher onboard his Dakota to encountering flak for the first time: 'He put on his steel helmet and grabbed a Tommy gun, which he fired out of the open door. He seemed to think we were being attacked by fighters!'[7] The inexperience of the anti-aircraft gunners on the ships was also equally obvious, 'some of which mistook cargo racks on the aircraft bellies for torpedoes'.[8] The trigger-happy nature of the naval anti-aircraft gunners, coupled with the nervousness of the Dakota pilots, would prove to be a potent mix. The Dakota pilots were not armed and did not have any armour plating on their aircraft. They also did not have rubber self-sealing fuel tanks which led to many not wanting to take unnecessary risks with their aircraft by flying through what seemed a wall of flak. Only two months before the invasion most of these pilots had been employed in roles such as freight carrying, courier work and general transport duties,[9] they were not trained and experienced combat-tested pilots.

Enemy flak accounted for the leading tug and glider combination carrying Major Lander, commander of the Pathfinders. The tug aircraft was shot down and exploded in flames, pulling its glider with it. Lander had only hitched a ride as a passenger to see the accuracy of the work done on the ground by his men, in turn guiding in his own glider to the pathfinder-marked landing zone.

Finally, the paratroopers were over land and were able to start descending from the carnage of the skies back down to Earth again. The men in the back of the planes, except for the lead men of the chalk who had a view of the outside world near the door, had no idea of the scene outside their planes. They were willing the plane on to its drop zone, or just anywhere over Sicily at that point, so that they could get away from being inside their slow-moving targets.

Individual pilots were making their own decisions in the sky now, with a lack of cohesion from the air armada. The tight formations had broken up even before they had sighted the Sicilian coast. The planes took off in all directions and many missed their targets. Dakota 68 headed back to Africa with the pilot declaring that he 'wouldn't release the men unless they were over the dz, as they would be of little value'. The paratroopers hooked up and ready to jump in the back of the planes begged to differ, all they wanted to was to get on the ground and into the fray. Dakota 83's pilot, ferrying men of 3 Para, ordered the aircraft abandoned after one of its containers carrying ammunition was hit by flak and exploded. He threw four dead and two wounded paratroopers out of the plane before jumping himself. Dakota 90 was carrying men from the Royal Engineers when it was hit by flak. The pilot was wounded. The co-pilot had never dropped paratroopers before and decided to return to base with all the paratroopers still onboard. Dakota 96 similarly was hit by flak. Fire from four or five merchant ships killed its co-pilot and wounded the pilot. The pilot then managed to fly the plane back to Malta and landed successfully with its 3 Para men still onboard.

The planes were meant to reach a drop speed of 100–120mph and an altitude of 450–600 ft (137–183m), allowing the paratroopers to exit the aircraft at one-second intervals. This was to limit the dispersal of the troops and also to reduce the amount of time the vulnerable paratroopers were suspended in mid-air facing enemy fire. The average jump time spent in the air would only be around 20–30 seconds.

For the last few moments before the jump, the adrenalin would have been pumping furiously inside each man. Each man was focus solely on jumping out of the door only a few metres away in the side of an aeroplane. For some men, the emotional toll of parachuting was so great that they would be physically and mentally drained by the time they hit the ground. They then had to pick themselves up and fight a battle against an enemy prepared and greater in numbers. Their only goal at this moment was to get out of the aircraft in an orderly manner without either themselves blocking the men behind them or another man in front of them blocking their path, either delaying their exit so that they were dropped miles off course or worse weren't able to jump in time and returned to base on the aircraft.

When the men were being thrown around in the back of the aircraft it was difficult enough for them to regain their footing with the amount of equipment that they were wearing. The men's parachutes had been fitted with a longer strop (9 feet 9 inches) especially to be used for the Dakotas, as the men were now standing upright to parachute rather than sitting on the floor when they had previously jumped through a hole in the floor of the Whitley bombers. The strops were hooked up to the inboard static line running the length of the aircraft and these strops also added to the obstacles for the men. They couldn't jump unless their strops were cleared and so it was essential that any entanglements had to be cleared prior to jumping but this took precious seconds to achieve. Once they had managed to disentangle themselves from each other some planes had already passed the drop zone leading men to jump late, and so be dispersed well away from the drop zone and remainder of their stick, or even worse to sit back down again as the Dakota headed back to North Africa.

The men at the rear of the aircraft would not be able to see the green light and would just start moving as the front of the line began to jump. They might have been able to hear shouts of 'Go, go, go!' from the jump door and see the static line cable start to bounce up and down as the static lines of the men already jumping were gripping the cable as the parachutes began to open outside in the Sicilian night sky. Only as they shuffled closer to the exit door would they hear the slipstream outside and begin to see the ground below. As they each came to jump they would push their static line out of the way towards the dispatcher and with a jump, usually accompanied by a push in the back from the dispatcher to make sure that they would definitely get out of the door, they would feel their stomachs drop as they began freefalling. They would free fall for around three seconds until the static line yanked the parachute from its bag and began catching the wind and deploying. Whilst freefalling each paratrooper was meant to shout out the drill of 'One thousand, two thousand, three thousand, check canopy' as a means of measuring roughly four seconds in the air before checking that their parachute had deployed correctly. In reality, most men simply clenched their teeth, jumped and waited for the pull of the canopy opening.

The men didn't have reserve parachutes, if their main parachute didn't open, there wasn't too much that they could do about it, as the RAF instructors liked to joke during their parachute training, 'if the parachute doesn't open, just bring it back and we'll give you a new one.' As the paratroopers left the plane, the noise and buffeting of the slipstream would have suddenly given way to a pull on the back as the parachute deployed and the paratrooper then began to swing in his harness and experience the sudden silence as the roar of the aircraft engine faded into the night sky and he became momentarily alone in the Sicilian night sky.

Corporal Stan Brown of the Pathfinders was No.1 in the door of the Dakota behind Pearson's plane. As the first man in the door he had a view over the leading planes of the formation as they neared the Sicilian coastline and began to take anti-aircraft fire for the first time:

> As we approached the island we were met with what appeared to me to be a solid wall of anti-aircraft fire…The tracers formed the most remarkable display of fireworks I have ever seen. It seemed to me that it would be quite impossible to pass through. The pilot must have had similar thoughts because we did a violent bank and headed towards the sea. The performance was repeated many times over the next hour. I could hear the rattling of shrapnel on the fuselage and 'stick' behind me were being thrown all over the plane.[10]

Vic Coxen, Officer Commanding R Company 1 Para, remembers, 'I was looking out of the window and saw the river; came back and hooked up. At that moment the aircraft banked and went out to sea again. I unhooked and went forward and asked what was the matter. The pilot said we were ten minutes early. I said, 'That doesn't matter a bugger, they know we're here – they're already firing at us. Get in!'[11] Coxen's Dakota eventually dropped the men too low and too fast, with the result that some men were injured, including Coxen's batman who broke both of his legs. On getting their stick organised on the ground and dealing with the casualties,

Coxen then realised that they had been dropped 17 miles (27km) south of their intended DZ.[12] Coxen led his stick north-east towards the bridge but overshot and ended up attacking an Italian coastal battery and taking 70 prisoners at dawn after the drop. He released the prisoners to avoid them following his group and then belatedly made his way to the Primosole Bridgehead, arriving in 2 Para's positions on Johnny I later that night.

Lance Corporal Osborne of 1 Para Anti-Tank Platoon recalled how 'it was just like jumping into an inferno, the countryside for miles was ablaze, tracer bullets were coming up at us from enemy machine guns on the ground.'[13] On landing he found the anti-tank weapons container had crashed to the ground when its parachute failed to open, rendering all the weapons unserviceable. He was armed with only two grenades. He set off with his section towards the objective and managed to find another weapons container, from which he armed his group with rifles and a Bren gun. The initial barrage of flak had caused the lead planes to start manoeuvring in the night sky as they tried to avoid the ground-to-air fire.

The pilots were now keen to dodge the flak on their run-in to the drop zones and dump their cargo of paratroopers as quickly as possible and return to base. The planes were meant to slow down from their cruising speed to 120 knots per hour to allow a lower slipstream for the men to jump into. As Pathfinder Joe Smith remembers 'There was no attempt to throttle back and on exit my kitbag was literally torn from my leg'.[14] The pilots were feeling justified in simply getting their plane somewhere over Sicily and then let the paratroopers in the rear of the aircraft choose when to jump.

Dakota 25, carrying men of R Company 1 Para, experienced flak over the drop zone and began to take evasive action. The unexpected manoeuvring as the men began to jump into battle caused No.6 in the stick to become entangled in his strop and hold up the remainder of the stick. After the entanglement was cleared and the men started jumping again, their parachutes began opening early inside the aircraft as the static line cable had been damaged. The men dropped 5.5 miles (9km) north of DZ2. Dakota 26, also carrying men from R Company 1 Para, was next in formation after Dakota 25 and dropped its men 5 miles (8km) south of DZ2, creating a spread of half of R Company over 10 miles (16km). This highlights the scattering of the air formation on encountering enemy flak and clearly explains the dispersal of troops on the ground.

The dispersal of the parachutists from the drop should have been minimised with the pathfinders being dropped first and lighting up the drop zones for the following planes carry the bulk of the brigade. However, pathfinders, such as Sergeant Joe Smith and Corporal Brown on Pearson's Dakota, were still in the air waiting to jump when other planes caught them up in the confusion and their paratroopers were jumping before the pathfinders. The plan was that the Eureka sets carried by the pathfinders would have communicated with the Rebecca sets on the leading planes. The Eureka sets on the ground would be backed up by flares on the ground but with the amount of tracer fire and burning haystacks these signals would have been lost. The gliders were not equipped with Rebecca sets so they had to guide themselves onto their landing zones by using the bridge, the Johnny features and Simeto River as landmarks on the ground. Joe Smith landed only with a broken Glim lamp after his kitbag was lost on jumping from the Dakota to mark Landing Zone 8 for the gliders. He had to twist the bulb on the Glim lamp in an attempt to send out a Morse code signal for any gliders looking for the landing zone. When gliders began to land around him he then made his way to the bridge unarmed as he had lost his Sten gun in the jump.

The 3rd Battalion drop zone of DZ4 was the responsibility of pathfinders Sergeant Seal and Lance Corporal Crighton. They flew in the same plane as Major Coxen, OC of A Company 1 Para, but were dropped 8 miles (13km) off the drop zone and at an altitude of only 200 feet (60m) which knocked both men unconscious upon landing. They had lost all of their kit during the jump and had to fall in with a passing 3 Para patrol and move off to the bridge. The remaining pair of pathfinders, Lieutenant Spivey and Lance Corporal Price never managed to parachute as their plane headed home after one attempt to run through the flak. The failure to deliver the pathfinders on time and accurately would later have severe consequences as the incoming gliders were fully expecting their landing zones to be identifiable by the new Eureka beacons and failing that, a landing strip marked out with coloured lights and flares. The glider pilots were to be left disappointed when they arrived; they would have to navigate from the 'moonlight maps' and from memory of the maps in the briefing rooms back in Africa to try and find the correct spot to put down their gliders and precious cargo.

Some of the inexperienced pilots now refused to go any further into the flak and tracer fire as Alastair Pearson now experienced for himself. His plane suddenly began performing a smart about turn, which woke Pearson from his sleep. He moved forward to the cockpit to see what was happening and found the pilot in the grip of fear, with his co-pilot sobbing with his head in his hands.

'What the hell do you think you're playing at?' he roared.

The pilot clenched his teeth: 'I'm not prepared to go in,' he said. A large and terrible oath drowned out the noise of the engines.

'And I,' bellowed Pearson, 'am not prepared to go back.'

Pearson then took out his revolver and pointed it at the sobbing co-pilot.

'Well, I'd better start off by shooting you, then perhaps it will encourage him,' he said, referring to the pilot. 'And I'll shoot you too, if necessary, because I've got a perfectly good pilot sitting in the back.' The pilot Pearson referred to was an ex-RAF pilot who had been court-martialled several years before for dangerous flying.[15]

The pilot, realising he would have to follow orders, abruptly pointed the aircraft once again in the direction of the drop zone and headed through the flak. Pearson buckled himself back into his parachute, just in time for his stick to start jumping.

Being the stick commander, Pearson had to dispatch the bulk of his stick before taking his turn to jump towards the back of the stick.

Also onboard Pearson's Dakota was Sergeant Joe Smith from the pathfinders. 'I was jumping number 6 or 8 … and Colonel Pearson was a couple of places behind me'.[16]

The Dakota pilots were trained to angle their aircraft's nose towards the ground, in turn raising the tail above the exiting parachutists. However, this resulted in Pearson's plane losing altitude as the men jumped. Pearson, who had jumped number 10 in the stick, was the last man from the plane to land relatively unscathed. The men jumping behind him, at numbers 11 to 20, were all killed or seriously injured from jumping at too low an altitude.[17] On the ground, Pearson took off the protective strapping that he had bandaged his knees with, put his pipe in his mouth and a revolver into the waistband of his trousers, and promptly marched towards the bridge.

Captain Gammon MC of 1 Para had a similar experience to Pearson, his battalion commander. The crew chief of his Dakota informed him that they would be jumping 30 minutes earlier than scheduled. Gammon was unconvinced that the green light to jump could be approaching already but as he moved into the door to make out any landmarks on the ground he saw 'white in the moonlight, a large replica of the models and photographs we had studied during our briefing, pillboxes, wire, and even a soldier standing in the roadway'.[18] The flight was going smoothly when suddenly the plane started taking evasive action from enemy ground fire. Gammon jumped into the night air to give the rest of the stick behind him the opportunity to get out of the aircraft before it was hit by anti-aircraft fire. As he floated down to earth he witnessed all the signs of a night-time airborne drop. Tracer fire was approaching from the ground striking the planes and paratroopers in mid-air, burning vegetation and buildings on the ground were mesmerising him until he soon noticed the fast approaching 'ground-rush' as the floor seemed to rise up rapidly to meet him. He braced himself for landing, keeping the feet and knees tighter and remaining 'tight'. The temptation for all paratroopers was to 'reach for the ground', causing the legs to come apart and incur injuries as a result. Gammon had a decent landing and after taking a deep breath and releasing himself from his harness, he sat up and took a look around his new surroundings, finding himself with only his batman in attendance and with no sight of the weapons containers. He only met up with other men from his plane a few days after the battle on the hospital ship sailing back to Africa. Their plane had dropped the men following Gammon into the Sicilian night at too low an altitude and many suffered broken limbs, heading straight into German captivity or having to wait for rescue. As Gammon was leaving the drop zone he met up with Lieutenant J. Helingoe and proceeded towards the bridge.

Lance Corporal Coster of 1 Para had had a soft landing on a haystack in the vicinity of the bridge. Upon landing, six Italian soldiers emerged from the haystack and disappeared into the night: 'they ran like hares'.[19] He might have become an instant prisoner, or worse if he had had the misfortune to land on top of German troops.

Major Arnold of the 1st Anti-Tank Battery was parachuting into battle from Dakota 113 ahead of his glider-borne troops and their guns. He was meant to head straight for the bridge and scout the ground ready to await his glider-borne 6-pounders as they came in to land. Instead, he was dropped 4 miles (6.4km) south of the bridge. As so often is the case for airborne troops, command was instantly assumed by lower-ranking officers and soldiers in order to maintain the momentum of the operation. In this case, Second Lieutenant Clapham was the first artillery officer to arrive at the bridgehead and he began the task of over-seeing the establishment of an artillery defensive line.

Also onboard Arnold's plane was a group of six pigeons, brought in to improve communications. Pigeons were shipped from England to North Africa specifically for the Sicily invasion. On arrival however, it was discovered that they had not been trained to fly over the sea and therefore 18 new pigeons were purchased in Africa as replacements. Six were sent on *Ladbroke* but lost when their glider was shot down into the sea. The remaining 12 were passed to 2 Para Brigade but then inherited by 1 Para Brigade for *Fustian*. Six of the pigeons were taken on *Fustian* and dropped from a specialist container. However, as the men were dropped so far from the bridge and with masses of other kit to carry, it was decided to release the pigeons early and concentrate on just getting the men to the bridge.

Brigade Commander Lathbury also jumped at low altitude like the bulk of his men. Lathbury recalled that the pilot veered just before the men jumped and this resulted in the stick being dropped 'on the high ground overlooking Catania Plain, some three miles south from the right place. [The pilot's] reading of the five hundred feet on the altimeter represented only just over two hundred feet above this high ground. It was only just high enough, but I could not have cared less at the time'.[20]

Major A. Young, of the 16th Parachute Field Ambulance, suffered a heavy landing and broke both of his legs. In the darkness two medics from his stick managed to locate him and began to assess his injuries. As they were doing this, 50 Italian soldiers approached and promptly surrendered to the three parachute medics. The medics struck a deal with the Italians that in return for their surrender being accepted, they would carry Major Young to the Primosole Bridge whilst the other two medics hurried on ahead to the bridge.

Despite the machine-gun fire and flak whizzing through the air, once out of the aircraft the paratroopers would have been feeling relief that they had not been shot while still in the aircraft and that their parachute had worked correctly. They would then have scanned the night sky for other parachutists. The new longer strops on the parachutes caused many burns to the arms of the falling paratroopers as it pulled the parachute from the bag for deployment. Some paratroopers immediately had to deal with more important parachuting issues though. The most common issue was that of twisted rigging lines caused by a poor exit from the aircraft meaning that the parachutist was set spinning in the slipstream causing their rigging lines to twist and reducing control over the parachute. They would need to perform high kicks in mid-air to spin themselves out of these twists before carrying on with their normal parachuting drills. Some men would have twists all the way until they hit the ground, causing heavier landings and potential injury. However, without any parachuting issues the parachutist would then steer into his own clear airspace and he would then begin to try and assess his drift in relation to the ground. There was a steady wind blowing 14 mph from the north-west-north direction, which made parachuting conditions difficult in the night conditions. Training jumps were cancelled if the wind was over 7mph. Finally, if the paratrooper had time, he would have tried to orientate himself to the ground whilst he had the advantage of a decent view.

A previously unknown factor which affected parachuting had been recognised on previous jumps in North Africa, namely that the air was thinner in the North African desert than it had been for training jumps in England. The men jumping in North Africa, therefore, had a nasty surprise of falling more quickly in the thinner air and therefore experiencing heavier landings. The air in Sicily was forecast to be nearer to the parachuting conditions of Africa than Europe but not quite so severe. At least the men were aware of the possibility this time around.

As the men floated down to earth, they scanned the horizon and ground below them for any landmarks that could be picked out in order to give a better sense of direction once on the ground. The landmarks, however, were few and far between in Sicily at night. Some men were dropped close enough to their intended drop zones to be able to pick out the silver ribbon of the Simeto River or Gornalunga Canal and therefore be sure of their position. Others were dropped away from the drop zones and in such a haphazard fashion that by the time they had felt their parachutes open, they were almost immediately hitting the ground.

On nearing the ground, the men would release their kit to allow it to swing below them and not injure them on landing. However, a lot of men would have realised that their kit had been ripped away from them in the slipstream as they had jumped.

As it was a night jump, the horizon would have 'disappeared' once the men were at tree-top level. This added to the feeling of 'ground-rush' and the sense that all of the sudden, after seemingly floating in the air, they were approaching the ground at an alarming rate. This meant that, unlike a day jump, the paratroopers couldn't easily pick out the ground and would have had to brace early for landing. The men would tuck their chins down onto their chests, pull in the elbows to their sides and most importantly keep their feet and knees together with their legs slightly bent in order to absorb the impact of landing with as much cushioning as possible. Landings could be from any direction depending on the angle that the men were approaching the ground and so they would turn their feet sideways onto their direction of drift to allow for a sideways land to cushion the fall and prevent their body being twisted on landing. Some would be facing the ground as it approached them and would perform a forward roll to help cushion the landing. Others would be approaching the ground backwards and have to attempt a backwards roll. In a lot of cases the men simply closed their eyes, adopted the landing position and accepted whatever landing that was coming their way. Once on the ground the men would let out a sigh of relief, check for injuries and then twist and push their parachute release button to get out of their parachute harness. The men pulled in their kit, if still attached to their kit-ropes, and then started making their way to the RV point, hoping to pick up some kit, weapons and comrades on the way.

All the men on the ground were told to look for long green flashes on a torch to direct them to the brigade RV point. Lieutenant Golden, second-in-command of the Brigade Signals Section, was to jump No.1 in the door from plane 106 and head to the RV and start sending out his signals with a torch to help organise the men in the dark. However, the navigator was blinded by searchlights on the run-in and dropped the men 4 miles (6.4km) south of DZ2, 40 minutes late. Dakota 106 then had the misfortune to be shot down over the sea as it made its turn for home. The crew managed to bale out and were picked by a passing Allied vessel.[21]

Once on the ground the men quickly had to adjust to the night. Night vision would start to kick-in soon after landing as the men's eyes adapted to the night time. However, with the amount of fires and flares in the area, as soon as they looked at bright light their night vision would be reduced. Some men would have been staring at fires burning on the ground as they descended and had their night vision compromised as a result.

Some of these fires on the ground would have been started by stray tracer rounds setting haystacks alight but also by the Fallschirmjaeger, who had marked their drop zones in a far more rudimentary fashion just hours earlier. They simply lit a beacon at each end of a drop zone and the pilots would drop the men between the two points.

The men now tuned their ears to even the slightest sound to ascertain whether it was friendly or a threat. The Sicilian night was filled by a chorus of croaking frogs which continued until daylight, long after the sound of firing and aircraft had died down. Commanders began to make out silhouettes in the dark and see other men landing nearby. They quickly rallied the men and checked their maps to orientate themselves to the ground and fix their position in order to head out towards the bridge. Some officers and NCOs would have their men huddle round them to provide cover against their torches as they attempted to read their maps. Many officers and NCOs used the American Usalite hooded torches rather than the British standard-issue torches, as the 90-degree angle of the torch and its coloured lenses were better for reading maps at night whilst shielding the light from the enemy. A two-minute map check could prove crucial in saving groups of men heading off into the Sicilian night in the wrong direction.

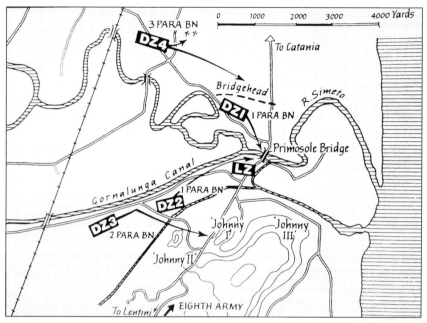

Drop zones for Operation *Fustian*

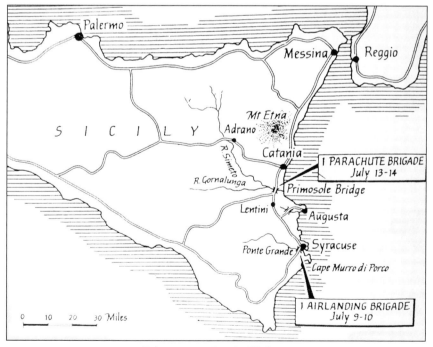

Airborne operations in *Husky*

The men would be whispering in the dark as they came to another figure moving around. The official challenge of 'Desert Rats', replied with the password 'Kill Italians' was invariably followed up by the men whispering their name and unit to each other as they got closer in the dark. After confirming their identities, small ad-hoc groups agreed to stick together until they could find their own units at the bridgehead. As the men began to form up on the ground, they all recognised that they needed to make best use of the darkness and confusion to make their way to their targets before the enemy could understand their objectives and begin counter-attacking. As the men made their way through the chill of the night they were constantly interrupted by flares lighting up the night sky, instinctively forcing them to hit the ground to avoid being illuminated for the enemy to see. Silhouettes moved and disappeared as the individuals and stragglers moved around the Sicilian countryside, causing an air of extra vigilance as the men scanned the darkness as they went about their night's work.

Some men even bumped into their Fallschirmjaeger opponents in the gloom. One paratrooper assembling his machine gun from a container was approached by a grey-smocked figure who asked him in German: "Have you seen my Schmeisser?' He said 'Nein' and then shot him'.[22]

As they headed through the darkness they would be looking out for comrades on the ground and also those still falling from the sky. Unlike previous operational jumps in North Africa, the men did not have to recover their parachutes for future jumps and race against the local Arabs who were equally intent in securing the parachute silk and other air-dropped supplies for themselves. The ground they were landing on was generally farmland and grazing fields with fairly hard sun-baked stony ground providing their fair share of hard landings. Some fields had been recently ploughed, allowing for some slightly better cushioned landings.

Robert Smith of the Field Ambulance landed on the ground but then looked up at the following planes. 'As I lay on the ground a plane was hit in the under-belly and I saw a pinpoint of flame almost simultaneously as she exploded'.[23] This highlights the suddenness of the potential disaster for the waiting paratroopers. They waited with extraordinary discipline to be given the green light before jumping but some never had the chance to make it out of the door and to safety, despite being hooked up and ready to jump. As the planes dropped their paratroopers or headed for home, the men who made it through the wall of flak and had landed in Sicily began to take stock of what had happened in the skies over Sicily that night.

The final result was that out of the starting 133 aircraft only 39 dropped their troops on or within half a mile of their drop zones, 48 more dropped them more than 1.5 miles (2.5km) away and 17 returned to base with some troops still on board. A further 12 were unable to reach or find their drop zones at all. A total of 11 parachute aircraft were shot down. Less than 20 per cent of the brigade was dropped according to plan and nearly 30 per cent, through no fault of their own, returned to base without dropping.[24] The furthest off course were some groups from 3 Para and the Royal

Engineers who landed 12 miles (19km) to the south of the bridge, while another four aircraft dropped their sticks on the slopes of Mount Etna 20 miles (32km) to the north. Twelve officers and 283 other ranks, out of a total of 1,856 all ranks that left North Africa, were available for the battle for which they were intended. The missing 1,561 troops of the brigade would be sorely missed in the next phase of the operation.

Meanwhile back at the airfields the rear-echelon headquarters and the RAF eagerly awaited the return of the planes so that they could begin to piece together the intelligence picture of how the drop had gone. The first planes began to appear in the night sky above Airfield C at 23:40 and were cleared to land. They had flown out at 500 feet (150m) to maintain an element of surprise for the enemy but without being weighed down by their cargoes of paratroopers and coming back at a higher altitude of 1,000–3,000 feet (300–900m), they were expected to cover the return leg of the flight much quicker. Of the 24 planes that had left that evening from Airfield C, 20 were carrying men of 2 Para and 4 were carrying men of 3 Para. Ten of the planes that now returned finished taxiing along the runway and came to a halt. As their doors opened and ladders were lowered down, entire sticks of paratroopers began to emerge down the steps. The sight of planeload after planeload of returning paratroopers invoked a sense of dread amongst the waiting personnel. A further two planes returned with part of their sticks. This meant that at least a third of the men of 2 Para had not managed to even get into action and that was before the other planes began landing at the other airfields. The jumpmasters and pilots from each plane were immediately hustled over to the ops tent and told to point out either exactly where they had dropped their sticks or asked why they hadn't dropped their sticks. This information was vital in understanding just what was happening on the ground over in Sicily and was immediately fed up to headquarters. As further planes began to land back at the other airfields the same pattern was being repeated.[25]

AIRFIELD	Time of return	Full stick not dropped	Part stick not dropped
A	00:43–03:00	3	6
B	00:45–02:47	7	6
C	23:40–01:29	10	2
D	00:30–03:27	4	3
E	00:59–04:02	-	-
F	01:30–10:00	1	-

The table above shows that 25 full sticks and 17 part sticks returned to base. Once this information was pulled together by analysts at headquarters it was immediately apparent that at least 500 men had not even jumped over Sicily. Damage to aircraft and de-briefs from the aircrew were revealing that both enemy and friendly flak had caused the air armada to be dispersed. Pilots from 51st Troop Carrier Wing had been ordered not to display any lights on their aircraft during the operation. On coming under fire from the Allied fleet some pilots quickly put their lights on to highlight that they were friendly aircraft. In some cases, this stopped the incoming fire but in other cases it merely attracted an even greater weight of fire.

The top brass were now able to make a fairly educated guess that the airborne troops on the ground were widely scattered and already under attack from enemy ground forces. They held out hope that the aggressive paratrooper spirit would yet play out and that the bridge could be captured but holding it against superior forces whilst XIII Corps advanced was becoming a tough ask for 1st Parachute Brigade.

The result of the drop was that 2 Para were dropped largely intact and on time, this allowed them to form up better and move off the drop zone quicker than the other battalions. 1 Para was widely dispersed but 3 Para had had a disastrous drop. They had been dropped in the wrong place and at the wrong time, effectively taking one third of the brigade's fighting strength off the battlefield before the fighting had even started. Again, as in training jumps, the small number of aircraft that managed to correctly drop their troops on time and on target highlights that such a reduced fraction of the brigade was where it needed to be to on landing. However, the men showed enough initiative and devotion to duty to put this behind them and start tabbing towards the bridge to join the fight.

The only positive of such a dispersed drop was that it sowed fear and confusion into the enemy as scattered drops didn't immediately make it clear just what the objectives of these paratroopers were. Many reports of isolated firefights were sent to German and Italian headquarters that night with varying degrees of accuracy as to just what numbers of British paras they were facing and where exactly they were heading. This gave the British time to move towards their objectives whilst the enemy forces held firm and played the waiting game. The Primosole Bridge, however, was an obvious objective and the Italian garrison were stood-to and expecting enemy troops to approach in the not too distant future.

The lightly armed paratroopers would also be calling on the artillery support of the Eighth Army and the Royal Navy anchored offshore. However, both of the FOOs failed to arrive on the ground. One returned to base as their aircraft had not dropped any parachutists and the other was killed when their glider was shot down. Of the two naval bombardment detachments (NBDs), only Captain Vere Hodge managed to parachute in the correct area. Captain Bolland manged to parachute but landed miles from the objective and would not arrive at the bridge in time to direct any fire. Each naval bombardment officer had been allocated a dedicated cruiser offshore from which to call in fire. So now, with the loss of both FOOs and an NBD they had lost three quarters of their heavy artillery support.[26]

Not only were the men scattered across south-eastern Sicily but so too was their supporting equipment. Of the 428 containers loaded onto the Dakotas only 291 were dropped over Sicily, and only 147 of these were recovered. One hundred and nineteen containers were still attached to the aircraft when they landed back at base in North Africa with a further 18 lost on the planes that were shot down.[27] In addition only around a quarter of the trolleys and panniers to ferry equipment around on the battlefield were recovered, thus reducing the airborne soldiers' mobility and flexibility.

The brigade had been practising a 2,000-yard dash to the bridge in the North African desert as part of their fitness regime prior to Sicily. However, once on the ground, few men were within the expected 2-kilometre radius of the target and had now faced a tough night-time march through enemy territory.

The flak gunners had had a fairly easy time in locating the approaching paratroopers' Dakotas. Out of the gloom of the night sky, there now came the sound of the louder rumble of heavy bombers. It was now the turn of the gliders to brave the flak and make their silent arrival.

CHAPTER NINE

'Silent Arrivals'

As the Dakotas were taking off with their paratroopers towards Sicily, the glider formation began to take to the air. The gliders were lined up behind their tug aircraft, attached by nylon tow ropes. The engines from the tug aircraft began to kick up the desert dust and, once the take-off started, the glider was pulled through the dust cloud with almost zero visibility until they became airborne and managed to start flying into clear air. The tug aircraft resorted to turning on Aldis lamps in the rear gun turret to guide the glider pilots through the haze on take-off and prevent any crashes before they had even manged to leave the runway.

Crashes did unfortunately happen though. The first glider casualties occurred on take-off, when two aircraft towing WACO gliders crashed. Further losses were incurred soon after the gliders were airborne, with one of the Horsa gliders being released early by its towing aircraft and crashing into the sea.

Visibility for the glider pilots during the flight was limited to the small lights on the wing tips of the tug aircraft and the glowing heat from the rear exhausts. Other than these small indications of light, the glider pilots were effectively blind until they reached land and be able to hopefully start picking out landmarks on the ground.

By the time the gliders arrived at their landing zones, two hours had lapsed since the parachute landings had started. When they did finally arrive over Sicily, the element of surprise had been well and truly lost. In the resulting confusion, four gliders were shot down by the coastal anti-aircraft batteries. Of the eight WACOs carrying the bulk of B Troop RA, glider 115 had crash-landed on take-off back in North Africa with glider 118 cast off near M'saken by its tug aircraft due to handling issues. Glider 116 did manage to reach Sicily but was shot up by anti-aircraft fire and came to rest on the edge of Catania airfield, where it received further bursts of machine-gun fire. The men on board, led by Sergeant Shelswell, couldn't offload the 6-pounder but managed to remove the firing mechanism before making their way to the bridge and eventually manning a captured enemy 88mm gun later that day.

The remaining five Waco gliders were released near to the landing zones but, after taking fire, all crash-landed some way away from their intended target sites. Gliders

117, 118A, 118B and 118C all managed to land but heavy damage on landing meant that all four were unable to offload their jeeps and guns. Lastly, glider 114 was still missing, presumed shot down. The bulk of the equipment carried by the WACOs was now either captured by the enemy or jammed inside the fuselages. Where possible, the troops began the task of hacking open the gliders with axes to try and free the equipment and get it to the bridge where it was needed.

The Horsas didn't fare much better than the WACOs. The first Horsa in the formation, chalk number 119, was piloted by Lieutenant Greggs and Sergeant Beddows and was carrying men of A Troop RHA. It was released without warning by its tug aircraft more than 2 miles (3.2km) out to sea and at a high altitude of 2,500 feet (750m) meaning it would struggle to get down to land even in the sea without stalling in mid-air. The glider and its entire crew were lost at sea.

As well as contending with enemy fire, unknown to the glider pilots, intelligence had failed to spot that there was a line of telegraph poles running alongside the main road, which further added to the difficulties of the glider landing operations that night. These accidental defences were encountered again in Normandy, with the use of cut-down telegraph poles being dug into suspected landing zones, known as 'Rommel's asparagus'. Some skilled pilots actually used the poles to catch their wings and help the glider slow down on landing.

Horsa glider being loaded with a jeep. (Courtesy of Air Assault Museum)

As the paratroopers were heading off to their targets from the drop zones, straight overhead they heard the swooshing sound of the first gliders beginning to land the anti-tank troops and their 6-pounders. Captain Gammon of 1 Para witnessed the second of the gliders make its approach, break into two on landing on the lip of the riverbank, with the rear half of the fuselage slipping into the river with all its men and equipment, he recalls, 'I thanked God that I went to battle by parachute and not by glider'.[1]

It was found in previous exercises that 80 per cent of glider troops suffered airsickness and as a result all the men were issued with tablets of Hyoscine to combat this. This drug was effective in 50 per cent of cases but still didn't ease the tension caused by the impending landing in enemy territory.[2]

Horsa 120, carrying men from B Troop, managed to circle over the objective area after accurate flying by its tug under fire. Squadron Leader Peter Davis was piloting the Albemarle towing Lieutenant Bill Barrie in Horsa 120 and he remembers 'target area one raging battle, never seen such a sight, fires, flares, flak of all sorts, searchlights – only needed Mount Etna to blow off to make it complete. Felt sorry for Bill Barrie. We escaped with a lot of loud bangs and one small hole under the wing. Do not like being fired at on tow'.[3] This highlights that the RAF pilots made a determined effort to get their gliders over their intended landing zones but they were also keen to get out of the firing line and back to Africa. The flak damage to Davis' Albemarle may well have been why the tow rope to Barrie's Horsa suddenly broke, releasing him at 1,600 feet (500m) at 01:07 and led to him landing 5 miles (8km) west of the bridge. However, it was a good landing, and in less than three hours the 6-pounder was unloaded and being towed by its jeep to the bridge, where it would soon be much needed.

Not every tug and glider combination was so lucky. Horsa 121, also carrying men from B Troop, was shot down along with its tug on the run-in to the landing zone.

Horsa 122 managed to reach LZ7 but was riddled with machine-gun fire from the ground causing it to veer off course and land north-east of Lentini. The undercarriage became jammed during the rough landing. All crew were instructed to use axes to cut the glider's tail off if the unloading ramp was jammed and if that didn't work then they were to use the Cordtex nets. Attempts to blow the rear of the glider off using a Cordtex net resulted in leaked fuel from the jeep inside the glider catching fire with the entire glider rapidly engulfed in flames and destroyed. After the Sicilian campaign, it was clear that the Cordtex nets would result in most gliders being totally destroyed by the resulting fire and the practice was rarely used in future operations.

Horsa 123 was released at only 500 feet (150m) at 01:20 but managed to make a soft landing 7 miles (11km) to the south of the bridge and also managed to free its jeep and gun in only 30 minutes, which was soon heading to the bridgehead, dug-in and ready for action.

WACO glider showing its front fuslegae lifted to allow for loading. (Courtesy of Air Assault Museum)

Horsa 124 was late taking off from Africa due to a broken rope. The men onboard eagerly watched the ground crew attach another rope just in time for them to take off as planned. Their joy was short-lived however as they received incoming flak on the approach towards the coastline and asked their tug pilot to circle them out to sea for 30 minutes so that they could treat the wounded and then re-prepare themselves for battle. After 30 minutes, they informed their tug pilot that they were ready to go back into the storm of fire and be cast off. The glider was released at 700 feet (210m) and managed to land successfully, bringing another all-important 6-pounder into the fight.

For Horsa 125 it was a story of what might have been. The tug for glider 129 accidently took off without towing its glider. Meanwhile, tug 125 instead took glider 129 which ended up being the most accurate to land of the entire glider fleet. Tug 129 landed back at the airfield and was hooked up to glider 125 but the tow rope broke on take-off and damaged the glider, meaning the gun crew from D Troop never even made it into the air that night.

Horsa 126 was piloted by Sergeant Protheroe and Staff Sergeant Kerr and their tug pilot was Flight Lieutenant Tommy Grant, who had towed the glider of Staff Sergeant Galpin to the Ponte Grande Bridge only three days before. Their glider was released over LZ8 at 00:45 and landed intact at the south end of the bridge. As it came to a halt, it started taking enemy fire from the south-west pillbox at the end

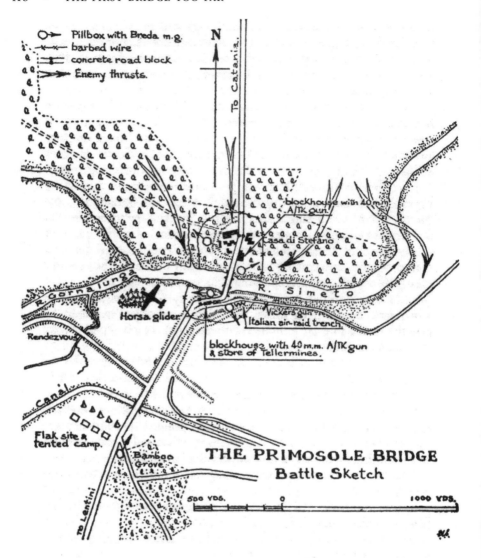

A sketch map showing the ground at the bridgehead. (Courtesy of Gordon Stainforth)

of the bridge. The gun crew and Protheroe managed to scramble to the riverbank for cover. After the bridge was taken they returned to the glider and its gun was unloaded in one hour, which the two pilots would later help man during the battle.

Horsa 127's Halifax tug was blasted out of the sky by flak as it was making a second pass over the battlefield. The glider was carrying the Battery HQ. The suddenness of its tug being shot down and lighting up the night sky meant that the glider pilots had to make an immediate landing which resulted in them crashing north-east of Lentini into a riverbank and incurring casualties of four killed and three further casualties.

Horsa 128 was piloted by Sergeant Mackenzie and Lieutenant Wachli. The flight over to Sicily was remembered by Sergeant Mackenzie as going according to plan until the landing. 'Our tug pilots took us into exactly the spot where we needed to be. We could at this stage see the bridge and the shape of the river'.[4] However, as they were released at 500 feet (150m) over LZ8, and with the confusion of fire and lights on the ground, they overshot their landing zone and skidded into the river, crashing into the northern bank and four of the men in the fuselage were killed. The two pilots were badly injured when they were thrown through the Perspex cockpit windows and out onto the riverbank. Its gun and jeep could not be salvaged.

Horsa 129 (Stainforth and Lathbury would later walk past this glider and saw the men breaking up the fuselage with axes) had the most accurate landing of the entire glider fleet, coming into land only 500 yards (450m) of the southern end of the bridge, after clipping the top of the bridge itself. Staff Sergeant White, piloting Horsa 129, later commented that they did not need the pathfinders to mark the landing zones with their marker beacons, as the tracer and lights from explosions were illuminating the landing zones better. He arrived over the target 27 minutes late and circled around the bridge through the upcoming fire. He managed to land on target on LZ8 just 100 metres from the bridge and with no casualties. The jeep and 6-pounder were unloaded under the supervision of Lieutenant Clapham, albeit slowly as they had become wedged into the glider frame on landing, and positioned by the bridge facing to the south. Along with the 6-pounder delivered by Lieutenant Thomas' Horsa 123, which had landed in a ravine 7 miles (11km) further south, these two guns provided the backbone of the artillery defence of the bridge over the next 24 hours of battle.[5] Clapham's commander, Major Arnold, had been dropped by parachute 4 miles (6.4km) south-west of the drop zone during the night and, instead of acting as the recce party for the artillery and siting the guns at the bridgehead, he wouldn't arrive at the bridge until later that morning

Of the total glider force of 16, only four gliders managed to land relatively unscathed, all the others being caught by the Fallschirmjaeger machine-gun fire and destroyed on their landing approaches. Six crashed into the sea and a further six crashed on landing. The four intact gliders had been carrying three of the 6-pounder anti-tank guns, which were now readily incorporated into the bridgehead defences, along with the glider-borne troops and their pilots. The sudden arrival of such a vast airborne fleet now lost its element of surprise for Operation *Fustian* and in response it had stirred up a hornet's nest, led by the Fallschirmjaeger.

CHAPTER TEN

'Hornet's Nest'

The Fallschirmjaeger jump into Sicily was to be one of the last parachute jumps for them after Crete. They were only to jump into combat once more after Sicily and that was during the Battle of the Bulge in December 1944. For the British paratroopers it was to be only a preliminary jump ahead of even bigger airborne operations ahead of them over the next twenty months. The battle experience of the Fallschirmjaeger would soon come to the fore as over the last three years many of the men in its units had served from the Blitzkrieg days through Russia and then North Africa. Along the way they had managed to bring new recruits in to the regiments and had had time to blood many of them on the battlefield. The British paras were also now battle-tested but many of the replacements were approaching Sicily and about to enter into their first taste of battle. The shock of battle would be felt more keenly by the raw British recruits more than the experienced German troops. For the British paras who had just experienced their first 'hot' drop zones, it seemed like the enemy had been waiting for them to arrive, they could not have known that the Germans had also sent paratroops to reinforce their ground troops.

The Fallschirmjaeger Machine Gun Battalion had been warned that the Fallschirmjaeger Engineer Battalion, commanded by Hauptmann von Bultzingslowen would be parachuting into the Catania area that night to reinforce the perimeter. On first seeing paratroopers descending from the night sky, there was no immediate alarm. They had not expected their comrades to jump so far south which caused some of the Fallschirmjaeger to criticise the pilots for dropping their comrades off course. As one Fallschirmjaeger noted, there was no thought of a British airborne landing 'when we heard aircraft flying low overhead. We guessed that these were transports and then we were aware that gliders were swooping down and that men were falling from the sky. That these were the expected Para Engineers was the first thought of all of us. Even after the troops had landed their identity was still not clear. The error was excusable. Both we and the Tommies wore the same style of overalls and our helmets were almost identical. It was the whistles and the shouted orders that first alerted us…'[1]

Martin Poppel was awakened from his slumber by the sound of the approaching aircraft. He too expected this to be the reinforcements in the shape of the engineer battalion arriving. Poppel remembers:

> … at 22:00 hours aircraft suddenly appear overhead and our own sentries are shouting 'German paratroopers!' We know that reinforcements should be landing or making a drop sometime. But shit! shit! – when the signal flares light up the eerie darkness – we see yellow and red parachutes. In an instant we all realise what's going on! British airborne troops overhead![2]

The Fallschirmjaeger now experienced the sense of dread that they normally invoked in their enemies: they were shaken by the uncertainty of just how many British paratroopers were dropping and what support they had brought to attack on their own positions, especially as they had had no real time with which to recce anything more than their immediate vicinity due to their lack of motorised transport. However, being battle-hardened and experienced troops, they knew all too well about the chaos of an airborne landing in the dark and they quickly realised that they had a brief window of opportunity to anticipate the main objective of this airborne operation. By questioning what their own role would be if they were dropped around the Primosole area, they readily assumed that it must be an attempt to gain the high ground and hold the Primosole Bridge for the advancing Allied ground troops.

The Fallschirmjaeger on the ground turned their heads towards the night sky and strained their eyes to try and pick out the sounds or shapes of the silhouetted air armada. The fires burning on the ground, the anti-aircraft fire on the sky and the distant searchlights all served to help both illuminate and silhouette the aircraft above. Although they were expecting their own Ju52s and Heinkel 111s to arrive with the engineer battalion, they didn't recognise the sound of the German engines that they were so accustomed to. These planes had not only a different sound but the lower-flying planes could be picked out as the distinctive shapes of Dakotas. The aircraft recognition lessons now proved their value as they distinguished enemy aircraft from friendly aircraft in the skies above them.

The Fallschirmjaeger readily opened fire on the transport aircraft, as they were legitimate targets. The parachuting men of the 1st Parachute Brigade were not targeted, however, as they parachuted down to the ground, as their Fallschirmjaeger opponents respected their fellow airborne soldiers. Many of the landing British paras were allowed to get themselves out of their harnesses and out of the trees, or wherever else they had the misfortune to land, before surrendering. These acts of chivalry would not be extended to the glider troops coming in to land a few hours later.

Those men of the 1st Parachute Brigade that landed on the southern drop zone were well within range of the 1st Fallschirmjaeger Machine Gun Battalion. After managing to escape the machine-gun fire aimed at their aircraft, some were captured as they landed on top of the Fallschirmjaeger positions. About 100 paras became prisoners of war as soon as they had touched Sicilian soil. Some managed to escape however. Private

The German view of the Paras descending. (Battlefield Historian Ltd @ battlefieldhistorian.com BHC 007023)

Stemp of 2 Para was taken prisoner by Fallschirmjaeger as soon as he landed. Within minutes though he had made a run for it and found some weapons on the drop zone. He eventually managed to reach the 2 Para positions and fought throughout the day in the defence of the Johnny Hills, earning himself a Military Medal for his actions.

During the planning phase of Operation *Fustian*, the 1st Parachute Brigade had estimated that the main threats to the operation were clearing the Italian troops from the bridgehead area, defending the area from German counter-attacks from the north and dealing with any potential Axis forces inadvertently withdrawing from the land invasion and trying to cross the Primosole Bridge to escape northwards. They were not expecting the elite Fallschirmjaeger to be anywhere near the target area, let alone to be dug in and ready to defend the drop zones. The rude awakening for the British paras was now being realised. Instead of being dropped accurately as entire units with all their kit, utilising the cover of darkness to capture their objective against light Italian opposition and to re-organise themselves ready for any counter-attacks at daybreak, they now found themselves being shot out of the sky, dispersed in much fewer numbers than planned on the ground, without weapons and facing determined counter-attacks from elite German Fallschirmjaeger who were already orientated to the ground. For the paras that were now managing to land in the Sicilian darkness, an extremely daunting night's work lay in front of them.

The men of the 1st Machine Gun Battalion had positioned themselves directly on the intended flight path of the incoming Dakotas and Horsas. They had a clear line of sight at the approaching aircraft and their machine guns were already trained in an easterly direction. As the Fallschirmjaeger guns began to open up, they found their range and targets very quickly. 'Our fellows behind the machine guns are shooting like supermen. Four big American transport planes, Douglas type, crash to the ground in flames, and three gliders are set on fire'.[3] British paratroopers were now landing in the midst of the Fallschirmjaeger positions and either had a brief opportunity to provide some covering fire to prevent the Germans firing at the aircraft or were quickly captured as soon as they landed. Many paratroopers landed with no weapons giving them no options, but some did manage to fight back and inflict casualties on the Germans. Krassa from Poppel's companie was shot in the lower left leg but, after being patched, up continued to fire at the Allied air armada with his machine gun.

The first prisoners were brought in to the German lines as the planes continued to arrive to deliver more paratroopers to the fight. Poppel was surprised at the standards of the paratroopers as he saw them for the first time in Sicily. He believed they were lower quality than British troops he had faced on the battlefield previously:

> I talk to lots of Tommies, mostly men of my own age. They're certainly not eager to fight, and their equipment looks fairly pathetic. The uniform resembles our motor vehicle combinations, though the camouflaging of the steel helmet looks useful, and their footwear is generally old and worn out. The guns look pathetic, reminding us of Russian weapons. Simply knocked together, the muzzle sight consisting of just an emergency sighting bar. Their parachute rations aren't what we remember from Crete either, and are in no way comparable with our own. The only things we savour are the wonderful chocolate and – of course – the cigarettes.
>
> They're well in advance of us in one area though and that's the fact that they all have their own sanitary and medical equipment with them. Each man has three 1cc ampoules of morphine, water disinfectant, Atebrin [anti-malarial drug] and even anti-mosquito ointment. A fantastic pack, and small and handy to boot.
>
> Physically they are medium-sized, good-looking fellows, some of whom have already fought in Africa while others are direct from Britain. In my opinion their spirit is none too good. They tend to surrender as soon as they face the slightest resistance, in a way that none of our men would have done. They reckon that Mr Churchill is a good man, but not a model or example to follow. And they're not as sure as victory as they were on Crete in 1941.
>
> Their whole weaponry, ammunition and machines, comes mainly from America, and their rations from the States of that nation. All in all I get the impression that these troops are somewhat different to the ones we faced in 1941. They have deteriorated in every respect.[4]

Poppel's initial thoughts of the British prisoners didn't respect the fact that they had just run a gauntlet of anti-aircraft fire, been dropped on the wrong drop zones and had lost all of their kit. They hadn't had the chance to fight back and give a good account of themselves. The real battle for the Fallschirmjaeger against an organised British paratrooper force was yet to come.

Poppel may well have fought seasoned professional soldiers in Crete and expected every British para to be equally seasoned. Despite the tough training of 1st Parachute

The skies filled with parachutes was a rare sight in Sicily due to the dispersal of the air armada. (Battlefield Historian Ltd @ battlefieldhistorian.com BHC 000397)

Brigade's replacements, many of the paratroopers were going into action for the first time and, through fear or tactical naivety, may have submitted to captivity too easily in the eyes of veteran Fallschirmjaeger. The comparison of the men though, is in contrast to the hatred reserved for other enemies, such as the Russians. The criticism of weapons may well relate to the Sten gun the paras were carrying into battle. Certainly they were technically inferior to the MP40 Schmeisser, but this reflected a development by the Allies to mass-produce lightweight weapons for Special Forces soldiers such as the paratroopers. The British uniform was loosely based on the Fallschirmjaeger jump smock so it is interesting to see that Poppel wasn't too impressed by it. The technical development in personal medical equipment and medical care for the troops was noted with envy. The personal medical kit and the support of a parachute-dropped field ambulance unit, complete with a mobile operating theatre, no doubt helped prevent deaths and treat casualties better and quicker on the battlefield for the paratroopers as opposed to the Fallschirmjaeger, as attested to by the amount of casualties treated in the 16th (Parachute) Field Ambulance dressing station. It is also interesting that the Fallschirmjaeger liked the camouflage on the British airborne helmets, this is something that was later incorporated into Fallschirmjaeger uniforms, particularly later in the *bocage* of Normandy.

Major Bohmler later recalled the respect between the two foes and the esteem in which the Fallschirmjaeger held the British paratroopers. They were 'splendid fellows, each single one an athletic type. Now it was clear the British had airlanded and we were involved with "colleagues"'! Really a pity that one had to fight against such spirited types so similar to our German paratroopers, and who did not seem annoyed that they had been captured by their German 'brothers-in-arms'.[5] This shows that many veterans of North Africa had a mutual respect of their opponents' abilities on the battlefield which extended to chivalry on the battlefield.

Whilst the main crescendo of the parachute drop was dying down, with only the few remaining straggling Dakotas looking for their drop zones, the Halifax and Albemarle bombers could be seen in the moonlight and searchlights making their approaches. The combinations of bomber and their towed gliders were instantly recognised by the waiting Fallschirmjaeger as the support weapons coming in to support the paratroopers. They knew the value of shooting down these gliders before they could deliver their anti-tank cargoes to the front line. Once released from the bombers, the gliders became more difficult to spot as they circled silently overhead looking for their land zones. Due to their silent approach and low altitudes, they hoped to land before they attracted enemy fire. However, the Fallschirmjaeger had been on alert and firing at the Allied aircraft for the last few hours and they soon spotted the gliders approaching through the night sky. Once located, the Fallschirmjaeger machine gunners swept these slow-moving aircraft with fire, particularly tracer rounds, which quickly ignited the wooden frames of the Horsas.

For those gliders that managed to land, the men needed to move as far away as possible from the wreck of the glider as they represented the biggest target on the ground for the German troops to aim at. Once the paras and gliders had landed, they immediately melted away into the dark of the night, so it was much more efficient for the Axis forces to shoot down entire planeloads rather than to try and battle them once they were organised on the ground and able to fight back. For those paratroopers and glider-borne troops now on the ground, they had to quickly organise themselves and achieve what they had come to Sicily for.

CHAPTER ELEVEN

'Seizing the Objectives'

Seizing the Bridge

As the airborne armada criss-crossed the night sky, disgorging their paratroopers, releasing their gliders and dodging the constant flak, the men who had already landed on the ground were quickly collecting their weapons, forming into small groups and heading for the bridge and the Johnny hills. The charge for the bridge was led by Captain Rann of 1 Para, who had managed to round up some 50 men from both 1 and 3 Para on the drop zone. They had landed close to the northern end of the bridge and quickly formed up to march towards the target. Through the darkness, they began to briefly see the outlines of the bridge as it was momentarily lit up by explosions. The patrol made their way towards the bridge, weapons in their shoulders and scanning for signs of the enemy. By 01:30 and reckoning that they hadn't been spotted by the sentries, the group took cover in a ditch to observe the target and establish a quick pattern of life of any enemy troops there. After a few minutes it was clear that the bridge had not yet been assaulted and they could well be the only paras to have made it to the bridge so far. Rann surmised that the *coup de main* party was clearly behind schedule and probably dispersed due to the nature of the delivery of the troops. Whilst he kept 'eyes-on' the bridge, he instructed a seven-man recce party, under Lieutenant Lasenby from the Signals Platoon, to move forward, take a look at the bridge and report back the situation on the ground there. Whilst the recce of the target was taking place, Rann formed his group into three separate groups, an attack force, a covering force and a reserve force, and began briefing them on their roles for the upcoming attack on the bridge. The men waiting with Rann had a short period of time to check their kit and prepare themselves for battle, some for the first time.

After 15 minutes the recce party returned and Lasenby reported to Rann that the bridge had not been taken and all was quiet so far. Rann immediately briefed his men with a set of quick battle orders for a hasty attack on the bridge. The covering group lifted themselves up into firing positions on the lip of the ditch and prepared to take on any enemy that got in the way of Rann's assault force.

On Rann's signal, he then led the attack force over the bridge from the northern end. In one single upward motion the paras began sprinting towards the bridge, silently at first but then opening up with their war cry of 'Waho Mohammed' as they began firing at enemy positions as they closed on the enemy trenches and pillboxes at the northern end. With the Italian defenders caught by surprise, they surrendered or made a run for it. Rann expected to have to fight for the bridgehead and call his reserve force forward to make the dash over the bridge towards the southern end. With limited resistance from the enemy, he decided to keep the momentum of the attack going and shouted instructions for his assault force to keep charging over the bridge for the other end. The assault force moved along the length of the bridge before arriving at the southern end and again firing at enemy positions until all of the Italian garrison had either fled or surrendered. A Gammon bomb was thrown into one of the two pillboxes and resulted in 18 Italian soldiers emerging into the open to surrender. Both ends of the bridge had now been cleared.

On seeing Rann's assault force clear the southern end of the bridge, the reserve party also moved over the bridge to provide support. The covering group then moved on to the north end of the bridge so that now Rann's group were in firm control of both ends of the bridge.

The speed and surprise of the assault showed the offensive spirit of the paratrooper in action and led to a surprised enemy only managing to fire off a few wild shots before they were overwhelmed in less than three minutes of fighting.

Some 50 Italian prisoners were rounded up from the bridge area and moved to a farmhouse just past the northern end of the bridge, where they were to spend the remainder of the battle. 1 Para were now in firm possession of the bridge, with stragglers beginning to arrive from out of the dark all the time. There is nothing quite like the sound of gunfire to attract paras to a location quickly. By 03:30, enough men had arrived at the bridge to bolster Rann's force, and they began to send patrols out into the darkness to clear the area of enemy troops and guide in further stragglers from the drop zones towards the bridge.

Lasenby's patrol set about helping a crashed glider crew untangle themselves and their cargo from their glider 100 yards (90m) from the southern end of the bridge. Another patrol returned with a platoon of Italian engineers which added another 30 prisoners to the farmhouse. The Italians were now becoming a burden for the paratroopers as it took men to guard them and deal with the steady trickle of prisoners constantly approaching the bridgehead. Provost staff from the brigade were meant to deal with the prisoners but none of their number had managed to reach the bridge.

Another of Rann's patrols linked up with the advancing Lathbury. Whilst the main brigade objective was being seized, Brigadier Lathbury, starting out with just his batman, Private Lake, was making best possible speed to join his men at the bridge. The two men found a container on the drop zone and managed to arm themselves before moving on. The brigadier was not in communications with the rest of his brigade, or in fact with anyone except his own batman, as all the brigade headquarters wireless sets had been lost in the jump, with one landing in the Simeto River. On moving across the drop zone Lathbury began to pick out silhouettes of figures moving around in the dark and soon met Major David Hunter, the brigade-major, and some of the members of brigade headquarters at the designated brigade HQ RV point. Leaving the brigade-major to coordinate any stragglers, Lathbury organised the bulk of the men at the RV into a marching order and led them off towards their primary objective.

Lathbury and his party stopped 500 metres short of the bridge in a dried-up river bed. Lathbury remembers 'There were no sounds of fighting from the bridge and there appeared no reason to suppose that it had been captured'.[1] The sounds of fighting during Rann's assault to secure the bridge had been lost in the sheer volume of firing and explosions in the vicinity that night and the ambush of the first enemy convoy had already finished, leaving a halt in the firing at the bridge. This lulled Lathbury into thinking that the Italian garrison were still in place.

At 03:15, as the brigadier sent two men forward towards the bridge to ascertain the situation, Lieutenant-Colonel Johnny Frost of 2nd Parachute Battalion passed Lathbury's position. Frost was limping after a heavy landing in a ditch, when his left leg landed on the sun-baked bank and took most of the weight of his fall. Despite his injury, he was leading a column of around 40 members of 2 Para and was heading to the Johnny positions a further 1,200 metres to the south.

Frost, along with his battalion headquarters, had landed exactly on their target drop zone at 22:30. The lead planes had managed to get over their drop zones, drop their paratroopers and begin making their return journey to Kairouan before the enemy defences had really got sight of them. A tailwind behind the 2 Para planes had meant that they had arrived 20 minutes before any other formation, at 22:14, even before the *coup de main* party of 1 Para who had expected to be dropped first, and as a result had missed the friendly fire out to sea and then flown over the coastal defences before they were fully on alert. This was fortunate for the men of 2 Para as the Fallschirmjaeger, watching their drop but believing them to be fellow Fallschirmjaeger arriving, had held their fire. However 2 Para's second wave of paratroopers had been scattered in the drop. The Germans soon positively identified the second wave of troop-carrying planes as Dakotas, and the paratroopers exiting them as British paras. As they began to take heavier anti-aircraft fire they scattered their troops away from the drop zones as they attempted to evade the incoming fire poured at them from hidden positions on the ground. The Fallschirmjaeger Machine Gun Battalion alone would account for two gliders and three Dakotas shot down, with 82 prisoners from 1 Para taken that first night.[2] By the time it rallied near the drop zone it numbered only 170 of all ranks. Only A Company, commanded by Major Dickie Lonsdale, was able to muster most of its strength which had about

70 men and was soon joined by 20 men from the Signals Platoon. The rest of the group was made up of stragglers from the remainder of the battalion.

The battalion's adjutant, Captain Victor Dover, and the second-in-command, Major Johnnie Lane, were missing. They had both been onboard Dakota 42 along with half the medical team. In one of the more extreme cases of a scattered drop, Captain Dover and the rest of the stick had actually been dropped over the southern slopes of Mount Etna and by daybreak he had only managed to link up with only three other men. This number then dwindled down to just Dover and Corporal Wilson from Brigade Signals. On realising that he wouldn't be able to regain Allied lines with the number of German patrols in the area, let alone play a part in the operation to capture Primosole Bridge, he commanded his two-man group for 23 days behind enemy lines, attacking opportune targets and generally harassing the enemy. The group had to hide from German search parties, sustaining themselves only on water and apples that they found in the Sicilian countryside. Dover was later awarded the Military Cross for his actions and Corporal Wilson the Military Medal.

After gathering together his headquarters, Frost had begun to lead his group in the direction of the battalion RV point at a track junction by 22:40 and soon linked up with 50 men of A Company, led by Major Lonsdale, who were also making their way to the RV. Shortly after the brigade Signal Section, a medical section and some of 2 Para's Support Company also arrived at the RV point. Here two plane loads from C Company, under Major John Ross, joined the group as well as other stragglers appearing singly or in small groups. A head count was taken at 01:00 and the total number of 2 Para men stood at 112 all ranks. They decided to wait a further hour for the sound of the Dakotas to disappear and then reckoned that they had most of the men that were going to appear that night. Frost's group then made their way to the forming-up point just short of Johnny I 2 miles (3.2km) away at 02:00.

Frost's group had stopped short of the target at the forming-up point. As they looked back towards the drop zones they could see sporadic enemy shrapnel rounds and machine-gun fire being fired into the darkness of the drop zones. As Frost's group continued to form up they encountered the brigade Defence Platoon at 02:15 who were heading back towards the drop zone in the hope of finding some wireless sets in working order. They had been sent back by Brigadier Lathbury as it had already been noticed that communications were a problem and radios needed to be found as a priority. They also informed Frost that Lathbury was already moving up towards the bridge. Frost made off after Lathbury to have a quick 'O' group and decide their next moves.

After finding Lathbury near the bridge, Frost quickly spoke to his commander to confirm his intent to push on to the Johnny features. He then remembered to wish Lathbury a happy 37th birthday. As quickly as they appeared, Frost and the 2 Para column then disappeared into the night. Lathbury could now begin to see his plan come together. Despite a clearly scattered drop, Frost was still advancing to capture the Johnny hills, and Lathbury was just short of the bridge and preparing to seize the objective.

Focussing again on the bridge, he could see enemy convoys crossing the bridge in both directions, oblivious to the proximity of the paras. Lathbury's intention was to ambush one of these convoys on the bridge, thus capturing two prizes for the price of one assault. It was now 03:15 and Lathbury divided his force into four sections; one section was to cover whilst the other three sections advanced towards the bridge. However, as he neared the bridge from the south he heard voices speaking in English. A figure approached out of the darkness from the other side of the river. It was Yeldham's Intelligence Platoon sergeant who he had sent forward to brief Lathbury of the general situation, in particular, Yeldham's almost entirely missing 3 Para. He informed Lathbury that the 1st Battalion had just captured the bridge from the north bank but that the drop had widely dispersed both 1 and 3 Para.

In fact, 3 Para had suffered the most during the drop, being widely scattered without any bulk of the battalion being dropped accurately together or on time. Only one officer, Yeldham, and five men had succeeded in joining up with 1st Parachute Battalion at the Primosole Bridge by 01:30. Yeldham remembers jumping from

Twp paras prepare a PIAT for firing. It proved to be a deadly weapon in the defence of the bridge. (Courtesy of Air Assault Museum)

his plane: 'we float down into a world of searchlights, tracer bullets and burning corn stacks'.[3] He had landed only 10 minutes later than scheduled and not too far from the battalion RV point but when he got there, there was only himself and his batman, the RSM and his batman, one private and a sergeant from the Intelligence Platoon. They were met at the RV point by a solitary pathfinder who was waiting to light flares ready for the gliders to land. Yeldham had no choice but to wait at the RV point and try and organise his men into a fighting unit once they arrived. He finally met 20 men from 1 Para who were heading down the pre-arranged track towards the bridge. He let the 1 Para men proceed with a message that he would follow them towards the bridge in 30 minutes after gathering more 3 Para men.

Thirty minutes went by without a single member of 3 Para arriving at the battalion RV. Yeldham now realised that his battalion had been seriously dispersed and decided to make his way to the bridge in hopes of finding some of his battalion heading there also. On approaching the bridgehead, he sent a runner forward to make contact with Lathbury and relay the sorry tale of 3 Para's strength after the drop.

Lathbury immediately understood the consequences of the scattered drop. He sent the runner back to the bridge to inform the remnants of 1 and 3 Para to abandon their plans of a defensive screen a mile north of the bridge and instead draw closer to the bridge and defend it at all costs. Lathbury could now start piecing together the situation after the scattered drop. Instead of a cohesive brigade-size force on the ground he now had essentially two depleted and unsupported company-size groups on the ground with no artillery or communications, and they needed to face up to the reality that they had just parachuted on top of a battle-ready Fallschirmjaeger formation.

With the bridge secured and Frost setting out to capture the Johnny hills, Lathbury's list of objectives was being achieved, despite the fact that he now had far fewer men than anticipated with which to hold them. Lathbury then led his Headquarters group towards the bridge. On approaching the southern end of the bridge, Lathbury's column came across a group of artillerymen with axes chopping away at their Horsa glider (Clapham's glider 129) to try and recover their 6-pounder. The column passed on by and arrived at the southern end of the bridge just as a German convoy was ambushed on the northern approach to the bridge. Lathbury moved over to the north of the bridge to ascertain what the position was there and what the firing was all about, as the rest of the column began to clear away the defences left by the Italians.

As Lathbury came over the bridge he saw a green flare fired from a Verey pistol by Rann's group on the north side of the bridge, which was a pre-arranged signal to indicate the capture of the bridge. The capture of the south end of the bridge was to be signalled by firing red Verey pistol flares. However, Lathbury wrongly assumed that the signal showed that the ambush was over and that the convoy had been fully cleared. In fact two Italian trucks had become stranded in the middle of the bridge and hadn't yet been cleared by the paras. A number of grenades were thrown by an Italian soldier who had dismounted from one of the trucks which was towing an 88mm gun. Lathbury was wounded from shrapnel in his back and thighs. He immediately delegated command to Pearson, who had earlier arrived at the bridge from the north, to consolidate the bridgehead whilst Lathbury received first aid, including a 'large tot of whisky'. Whilst Lathbury was receiving treatment, at 03:30 Stainforth and his engineers were working their way over the structure of the bridge removing all signs of cabling and explosives. Lathbury now enquired as to the extent of securing the bridge from demolition. 'How long will it take you to get all this stuff off the bridge?' asked Lathbury.

'Only about a quarter of an hour, I think, sir.'

'OK. Get a move on, then. It must be finished by daylight' As Stainforth went to get on with the job in hand Lathbury further asked, 'How long will it take the Bosche to put it all back?'

'Not less than four hours for a bridge this size, I should say, sir,' replied Stainforth.[4]

This knowledge gave Lathbury an indication that even if he couldn't hold the bridge he should be able to deny the Germans and Italians access to the bridge in which for them to re-rig the bridge for demolition before the 50th Division were scheduled to arrive at around midday.

Pearson's first task was to ensure that the demolition charges attached to the bridge were removed. The engineers, led by Sapper Hall, had already discovered the explosives packed into the bridge's piers. Thirty sacks weighing 9 kilos filled with explosives were removed from the piers and thrown into the river below. Next the engineers tore down all the cabling running across the bridge. Some cabling was for telephone wires and lighting but with speed of the essence, the men simply chopped and pulled down any cables that they could find to ensure no wiring was missed that would enable the enemy to detonate any missed demolition charges. With this task achieved it ensured that, as a worst-case scenario, the bridge would have to be contested and could not be simply destroyed.

The men at the bridge needed urgent organising as well. As units and individual soldiers arrived at the perimeter they were challenged by the men already established as sentries. Once they had confirmed the password and advanced to be identified, they were then directed to where their units or position in the line would be. Men arriving carrying additional kit, such as mortar rounds, would be directed to the corresponding weapon in order to drop off the ammunition. With few heavy weapons arriving, any support weapon ammunition arriving was stored centrally by the quartermasters in an impromptu ammunition dump near the southern end of the bridge. The men staggering into the perimeter were more than happy to dump any specialist kit they had, thus relieving them of heavy loads and responsibility. The 1st Parachute Brigade had managed to employ local Arabs and their mules to help with some of the heavy lifting in North Africa. They weren't to have the same luxury in Sicily.

A sketch showing the engineers removing demolition charges from the bridge structure immediatley after its capture. (Courtesy of Gordon Stainforth)

First Contact from the North

The first contact with the enemy around the bridge came from the north and was directed against the hastily organised perimeter manned by the remnants of 1 and 3 Para. An Italian convoy, headed by a German armoured scout car, approached the bridge at 03:45 carrying ammunition and towing a 75mm artillery piece for use by their retreating comrades to the south. They had no idea that the bridge had been captured by British paratroopers only moments before and drove straight on to the bridge. The paras were fully alert to the presence of the enemy convoy and had prepared a perfect ambush with PIAT anti-tank weapons and machine guns. The paras trained their sights on the slowly moving convoy, picking out the blissfully unaware enemy as targets in their crosshairs, just waiting for the order to open fire and unleash a hailstorm of explosions and bullets.

The ambush would be triggered by the officer whispering into the ear of the PIAT man, 'Fire!' The first thing the Germans and Italians would know of the ambush would be the impact of an anti-tank rocket instantaneously destroying the lead vehicle in a ball of flame.

The lead scout car was only 50 metres away from the PIAT man, its silhouette growing larger and filling his crosshairs with each passing second, when finally, the order to fire was given. With a pull of the PIAT's trigger the rocket flew forward and covered the short distance to the target in the blink of an eye. It was a direct hit. The vehicle exploded, sending a ball of orange flame into the night sky and signalling the start of the ambush. The burning vehicle came to a flaming halt and blocked the road for the vehicles following behind. Two paras managed to pop up from their trenches and lob Gammon bombs at two of the trucks, destroying them as the grenades exploded with devastating force, setting the vehicles on fire. The first three vehicles had been destroyed by a combination of weapons in a brief but deadly skirmish as Lance Corporal Osborne described: 'One of the lads fired a paratroop anti-tank gun at the tank, and two Gammon bombs were thrown at the other two vehicles. These are deadly weapons and smashed them to bits'.[5] As the burning vehicles lit up the Sicilian night sky, the machine guns, which had been shadowing the convoy through their sights, now got to work. The Vickers, Brens and captured Bredas sprang into life against the illuminated convoy and started tearing into the soft-skinned vehicles with their rapid fire. The rear vehicles hastily drove off the road to turn around, heading straight back out of the firing line to report the presence of enemy troops at the bridge.

As the remains of the convoy drove off into the night back towards Catania, the paras emerged from their firing positions to inspect their work. Pathfinder Joe Smith managed to recover an Italian rifle from a destroyed scout car, which replaced his Sten gun lost the previous night during the jump. The 75mm artillery gun was found to be intact and unhooked from its destroyed vehicle. Under the instruction of Major Hunter, it was pushed towards the end of the bridge on the northern side, where it was left in position to cover the road heading north towards Catania, the expected direction of arrival of German reinforcements.

As well as providing some weapons and a morale boost for the paras, the ambush also served as a sound and light beacon for the paras still wandering the Sicilian countryside. The burning lorries, and the ammunition that they were carrying, were by now well alight and added an orange glow to the area around the north of the bridge. The paras moved back into their trenches to avoid being illuminated themselves to any prowling enemy and also to be down-wind from the smell of burning fuel and tyres hanging in the night air.

After salvaging the 75mm artillery gun, Major Hunter now took some members of the Brigade Defence Platoon, using one of the damaged but serviceable German trucks, towards the southern drop zones to scour them for kit that was lost during the jump, particularly radios, heavy weapons and ammunition. It also provided an opportunity to round up any stragglers or wounded men still roaming the Sicilian countryside.

As Hunter's drop zone party headed south, 2 Para's Liaison Officer arrived from Johnny I on a captured Italian motorcycle to deliver a situation report to Lathbury. He outlined that Johnny I was held by Frost's 2 Para and were dug-in on the summit. Johnny II had also been cleared but not held due to lack of numbers. At least Lathbury now knew, that despite the disaster of the parachute insertion, all of his brigade objectives had been taken. However, he had to ask himself, with the inevitable German counter-attacks, how long could his depleted units hold out.

To add to the confusion around the bridge, Italian prisoners were still being found hiding around the bridgehead, concealed in the groves and cellars of the farmhouses. Others voluntarily walked towards the bridge to surrender and end their war as peacefully as possible. They mainly included the locally conscripted coastal battery troops, along with an assortment of coast guards, police and air force men on leave. Importantly for the paras, these prisoners also brought their weapons and ammunition with them, which was gratefully received and re-allocated to men who had lost their weapons on the jump. The prisoners were marched over to a farmhouse on the north bank and locked up there throughout the remainder of the battle.

The leisurely milling around of Italian prisoners was soon put to an end with the appearance of the first combat enemy air activity. Soon after daybreak, no doubt given their targets by the earlier Feiseler Storch spotting plane, a sortie of Messerschmitts and Focke-Wulf 190s had approached from the north, down the valley, staying close to the ground to minimise their engine noise and therefore their approach. They appeared unexpectedly on the scene catching most men off guard. The speed of their arrival and their low altitude meant that they were upon the bridgehead before anyone had chance to react. Many of the men saw the planes only as they heard the guns beginning to strafe the bridgehead positions and watched as the ground was churned up by bursts of cannon and machine-gun fire. The men dived for cover as the planes fired their cannons and machine guns, tearing up the ground and kicking up clouds of dust. They homed in on the wireless mast of the sole working around by Brigade HQ. The Messerschmitts also focussed on the carcasses of the Horsa gliders lying in the vicinity of Landing Zone 1. A few men had taken cover behind the wooden gliders as the ground was so hard to dig into. Some equipment and casualties were also being extricated from the wreckage of the gliders also which provided the largest targets for the marauding German fighters. The men soon learnt to take their chances of digging-in away from the gliders despite the lack of natural cover. The lack of transport, heavy weapons and dug in positions of the lightly-armed paratroopers made a hard target for the fast-moving Luftwaffe fighters.

The planes flew low enough for the paras to gain a quick glance of the black Luftwaffe crosses as they flew past the bridge to the south and then disappeared in a loop back to Catania. Based on past experience gained in North Africa, John Frost had issued orders that aircraft were not to be engaged as their chances of downing an aeroplane were small and therefore a waste of precious ammunition. Instead, the paras relied on digging deep slit trenches and camouflaged them to avoid being hit. The Luftwaffe on this occasion were not engaged, partly due to the no-firing order but mainly due to the sheer speed of their arrival and disappearance. The planes, having completed their strafing run, then disappeared back to their airbase in Catania. It had been a wake-up call for the paras to remain alert. After the initial element of surprise gained by their parachuting into Sicily, the enemy now knew exactly where they were, and were coming to get them.

With daylight approaching, 120 men from 1 Para, with a few additions from other units, were holding the bridge. Not until 05:00 would any more men from 3 Para arrive. Captain Waddy had managed to round up 19 men from across 3 Para and Major Dennison managed to bring in a platoon-strength group of A Company, 3 Para. Yeldham set up his battalion headquarters in one of the pillboxes on the north of the bridge whilst instructing his 50 men of 3 Para to spread out and prepare to hold a defensive line that had been planned to be held by 550 men. It was shaping up to be a long hard day for the men on the northern bridgehead.

Seizing the Johnny Hills

Meanwhile, Frost's group moved south from the bridge, shadowing the main highway, where they next bumped into Mervyn Dennison who, with a small party of other members of 3 Para, was busily destroying telephone cables leading to the pillbox on the southern end of the bridge. Taking a track that split off to the west from the highway, Frost's men approached the north-eastern slopes of their first objective, Johnny II. At the bottom of the objective, as Frost was preparing his column of paratroopers to assault their first position, he met Lieutenant Tony Frank, commanding 1 Platoon A Company, who informed his commanding officer of his actions so far that night.

Landing 20 minutes earlier than scheduled onto the south edge of the drop zone Frank had managed to locate a weapons container and a handful of men. On moving off from the drop zone, they came under fire from an enemy machine gun to their east, which was also firing at the incoming paratroopers and their Dakotas. Frank and his men moved forwards to engage this machine gun before it could send any more fire into the air armada above or the landing paratroopers below. The small group closed towards the enemy position and Frank positioned the Bren gun ready to suppress the position whilst two paratroopers closed in on the position. As the flanking paras neared the enemy gun, the Bren spurted into life sending rapid fire into the enemy's position, before the two paras cleared the positions from close range with their Sten guns. Frank's number 2 on the Bren gun was shot in the leg during the exchange of fire, highlighting the accuracy of the returned enemy fire.

Frank's small force moved off towards their forming-up point to meet the rest of the battalion but as they did so they came across a farm building where two Germans were escorting four captured fellow paratroopers. Frank quickly deployed his men into firing positions and waited to engage the German guards, without hitting their own men. On his orders the Germans were engaged, with one killed and the other wounded. The four prisoners now found themselves free again and ready to join the attack, even though they had no weapons. The firefight had attracted the attention of some more Germans in a farmhouse to Frank's left flank and a further 10-minute firefight ensued. Already running low on ammunition, Frank made the decision to extricate themselves from this fight and carry on moving towards the more important Johnny objectives.

On breaking contact with the enemy, Frank now took up position in a bomb crater to check his bearings and begin moving towards the battalion forming-up point (FUP). He moved out with his small force to the FUP and there met fellow stragglers from 2 Para. Three sticks from A Company and 12 men from B Company had managed to reach the RV point. Being the senior officer of the composite group of only 22 men and three officers, he organised the group into three groups, two led by A Company officers and the third group led by a B Company officer.

The three groups firstly conducted a sweep over the slopes of Johnny II, securing it with no opposition at 02:30. On seeing no signs of enemy occupation, he decided to repeat the manoeuvre and secure the more important objective of Johnny I.

Moving to the north of Johnny I in order to sweep up and over the hill and push any enemy towards the south, Frank's group filed around the north of the hill in silence and took up their positions ready to ascend the feature. At 03:15 Frank again split his composite platoon into three groups under each officer. Moving off from a start line at the foot of the hill, the groups then conducted a sweep over Johnny I, with two groups beginning simultaneously from the north and east, and Frank taking his third group in a north-east direction upwards towards the summit. The north group moved in single file up the hill but met no opposition and managed to reach the top and collect some prisoners hiding in caves along the way.

The Italian defenders facing the 'east' group had spotted their advance from their concealed viewpoint and could see the silhouetted men of 2 Para begin their ascent up the hill. They didn't wait for the paratroopers to get within touching distance and opened fire with their machine guns from their positions hidden in the caves halfway up the hill. They fired from a distance of around 150 metres as the men had just begun to make their advance to contact up the slope. The men immediately went to ground and began to fan out so as not to present a bunched-up target to the enemy gunners. The firing was soon identified as originating from an enemy position at a small cave entrance. Fire was returned by the whole group whilst the officer and NCOs lifted their heads above the firing to get a clear view of the position and quickly formulate a plan of attack. With the enemy position being suppressed, half of the group began moving around the left of the position whilst the other half stayed where they were and continued to send suppressing fire towards the Italians to keep their heads down. The flanking group reached the hill level with the cave and then threw Mills grenades into the entrance, waiting for the explosions to go off and then firing into the position to finish off any survivors. Some 40 Italian prisoners soon emerged from the smoking cave and surrendered. Leaving only a couple of men to guard the prisoners, the 'east' group began moving off towards the summit.

As they reached the crest of the hill they came under fire from Italian machine-gun posts located in another cave just below the ridgeline. In a carbon copy of the first flanking attack, the cave was subjected to suppressing fire and then had a couple of grenades lobbed outside its entrance. The rapid attack had the desired effect and a further 80 Italian prisoners emerged. Johnny I was now secured and the men began to consolidate the position with Frank positioning an observation post to look out over the valley to the west and Highway 114.

At 04:00 the paratroopers received incoming small-arms fire from the south-east of the hill but on sending out a fighting patrol no enemy was found. At this stage, unknown to Frank, Frost had arrived at the foot of Johnny I and sent Lonsdale and his A Company up to capture the summit. They arrived unopposed to meet the men of Frank's group who were already digging in and consolidating the position. Major Lonsdale assumed command in the absence of Frost and sent a patrol back to Frost led by Frank to explain the situation and also to clear the summit of Italian prisoners who were becoming a burden. The initial group of captured Italians were put in a farmhouse courtyard on the summit of Johnny I whilst newcomers were rounded up and sent back down the hill. They were marched in two groups down to the FUP at the base of the hill so that the paras could concentrate on the defence of Johnny I. Frank was later awarded the Military Cross for leading the two assaults up Johnny II and Johnny I. This piece of airborne initiative laid the foundations for 2 Para to protect the southern flank of the entire operation and prevent their encirclement by the rapidly reorganising Fallschirmjaeger who would soon try to wrestle the Johnny positions back from 2 Para's grasp.

By 05:00, Frost's, Lonsdale's and Frank's groups were now united atop Johnny I and almost a quarter of 2 Para were now organised on the ground in Sicily and centred on Johnny I and as close to full strength as they would get for the remainder of the battle. They took over the Italians' previous headquarters in a lone farmhouse on the north summit of the feature and used this as battalion headquarters and as an observation post. The perimeter already had slit trenches dug and barbed wire deployed by the Italians. The Italian prisoners were kept in the outside courtyards surrounded by a stone wall. From this position Frost, and Lonsdale acting as CO whilst Frost received treatment for his twisted knee, had a clear view down the slope to the Primosole Bridge a little over a kilometre away. Frost was hoping the injury to his knee wasn't that severe as he was also the nominated second-in-command of the brigade if Lathbury was injured during the battle, meaning he would have to re-position himself at the bridge.

Medical treatment wasn't far away, if Frost needed attention. Under the north slope of Johnny I, some of the field ambulance had reached a farmhouse that was to serve as the MDS, where the brigade's casualties started arriving for treatment. No.4 Section of the MDS had itself become casualties after being caught up in the friendly-fire barrage over the fleet and had many of its planes shot down into the sea.

The first medic to reach the MDS farmhouse was Captain Ridler of the HQ Section at 04:45. He had been dropped 4 miles (6.5km) west of DZ3 but had managed to locate his trolley of medical supplies and wheel it over the countryside to arrive at the MDS. Accompanied by only one corporal of the RASC, on entering the farmhouse, he found 20 Italian soldiers who promptly surrendered and were then put to work in tidying up the house, ready for the expected British casualties. The Italians would then be employed as medical orderlies throughout the day and were also used to drive some Italian trucks found at the farmhouse to help transport casualties to the dressing station. Ridler was lucky to have landed on the correct drop zone, the remainder of his section was scattered on the drop and, joined by equally scattered 3 Para soldiers, were led by Captain Keesey back to Allied lines two days later.

Shortly afterwards another stick arrived at the MDS from HQ Section, led by Major Longland, and started transforming the farmhouse into an operating theatre ready for the first serious casualties, with only the supplies that they had managed to drag from the drop zone on their trolley. The farm was a single-storey building containing seven rooms. Three rooms on the east side were designated for the walking wounded, enemy wounded and those awaiting evacuation. Four rooms on the west side were designated as a pre-theatre room, operation theatre and two post-operation rooms. The kitchen was put to use immediately to start boiling water and cooking food.

Back on top of Johnny I, Lonsdale pushed the perimeter out towards the southern slope of the hill where olive groves reduced visibility to only 200 yards (180m). A platoon from A Company was established on the edge of the grove and outside of the main defensive perimeter in order to provide overwatch of the highway approaches from the south. Frost now reflected that the Germans 'remained on the low ground during the night' which 'allowed us to forestall them'.[6] This perceived slow reaction of the Germans to attack the weakened Johnny I position, however, was the intended plan of the Fallschirmjaeger. They had sited themselves on the low ground to coordinate their defence of the drop zones for the incoming Fallschirmjaeger and had chosen to post the Italians out of the way on the high ground in the vicinity. Their opinion of the Italian troops, who they termed as '*Die Spaghetti Kameraden*',[7] was that they could be used to simply provide a presence at key points to provide an early warning system until the German troops could arrive and take over the situation. However, unbeknownst to the Germans, this move would allow the British to capture the Johnny positions against light Italian opposition, forcing the Germans to counter-attack in daylight the next day.

At 05:00 the Fallschirmjaeger began sending out reconnaissance patrols to establish just what they were up against after the confusion of the previous night's airborne landings. 3 and 4 Companies of the 1st Machine Gun Battalion sent patrols out to cover the immediate area within 2 kilometres of their position south-west of the bridge. They returned with more prisoners and captured weapons. Poppel was now providing covering fire for the patrols. 'Huge numbers of weapons, along with twelve prisoners, are brought in. Another recce patrol of mine under Feldwebel Jetter brings back two prisoners and a quantity of automatic weapons. At midday, 4 Company captures a number of armoured scout cars and anti-tank guns, along with seven prisoners'.[8] Poppel's battalion would take a total of 82 prisoners from the 1st Parachute Brigade on that first night and inflicted an unknown number of casualties on the men whilst they were in their planes and as they landed straight into the German fire. Without this Fallschirmjaeger intervention in the airborne insertion, far more men would have been able to reach the bridge and formed a much stronger force to defend the objective, more in accordance with Lathbury's original plan. The small number of men that the British had to hold the bridge and Johnny features meant that they had no strategic reserve to send out as fighting patrols to gather stragglers, harass the enemy or collect the weapons and other kit dispersed on the drop. This left the Germans, who were not tied to securing any ground, free to dominate no man's land and go on the offensive.

Lathbury, despite the calamity of the air insertion, had now managed to seize all of his brigade objectives. The next problem would be to consolidate and hold these objectives against an enemy force stronger than expected, with a brigade many times smaller than expected. As the mask of night was beginning to fade away, the two sets of devils were about to clash face to face in the bright sunshine of a summer's day on Sicily.

CHAPTER TWELVE

'Green Devils versus Red Devils'

The sun was rising in the blue sky, the beginning of yet another long, hot and dusty Sicilian summer's day. The distant southern slope of the towering Mount Etna began to glow orange with the first rays of light from the rising sun. The countryside around the bridgehead began to feel the first warming rays of daylight at 05:00, followed an hour later by the first glimpses of the rising orange sun itself.

Off to the east, the shimmering Ionian Sea could be made out from atop the Johnny positions. The veil of darkness had provided good cover from accurate enemy ground-to-air fire for the parachuting phase of the operation, but it had also caused difficulties after landing for the coordination of hundreds of paratroopers in unfamiliar territory behind enemy lines. With the daylight, the paras who had made it to the bridgehead, and also the men who had been scattered in the drop, could now begin to better obtain their bearings. Landmarks appeared out of the gloom of the Sicilian night allowing the men of the 1st Parachute Brigade to orientate themselves to the ground and better understand their position and that of the enemy.

The chorus and sights of combat that had reached a cacophony throughout the night, such as tracer rounds arcing through the night sky and snaking up to towards the Allied air armada, now gave way to the pre-dawn stillness of the hills, villages and fields of the Sicilian landscape. Out of the darkness appeared the olive, lemon and carob trees which so dominate this part of the island. The wandering paratroopers passed by the burnt-out haystacks which had illuminated the countryside the previous night, allowing the anti-aircraft gunners to target their incoming planes. By this time they were just smouldering blackened ashes, spreading a thin veil of smoke over the farmers' fields. Livestock grazed around in their dusty fields as if the events of the previous night had long been forgotten. The paratroopers took the scene in as they moved stealthily across the countryside. Men used their fieldcraft skills to traverse the terrain, never walking across fields in plain sight, instead hugging the walls and hedgerows as a camouflaged backdrop, making sure that they were using all available cover. Enemy snipers and ambushes were an all-too-present threat and enforced the need to move tactically at all times, with men only moving under the watchful eye of the covering aim of their comrades. This 'pepper-potting' slowed movement down but provided a firebase with which to immediately return fire on the enemy in the event of an ambush.

Daylight brought welcome relief to the men who had been dropped miles from their intended drop zones and now littered the area in small wandering groups trying to reach the bridge and join the fight that they had trained all those months for and had flown all of this way for. Maps could now be checked in daylight – using white light to read maps at night not only lost the man his night vision but made him and his immediate comrades a potential target by revealing their position. For those miles from the bridge, or just simply lost, the onset of morning provided their best opportunity to march quickly to the bridge. The rising skyline of the Johnny features provided a main reference point for the men on the ground and could be clearly picked out as a landmark. This would allow them to start heading for known friendly locations and take their place in its defences alongside their mates, ready for the inevitable German onslaught.

Some men's rations of food, water and ammunition were already running low after the exertion of the previous night's jump, subsequent march to the bridge and then fighting already. They were all thirsty, hungry and with the effects of adrenaline fading fast, the men were becoming tired. Each man would have their own story of their journey from leaving their aircraft to arriving at the bridgehead or wherever they had managed to find their colleagues. They were suffering from injuries sustained whilst parachuting or from heavy landings. Many of the men had twists and sprains but their only option to was to just lace their boots up tighter and march with the rest of their comrades into battle. There would be a few twisted ankles, cuts and bruises suffered from the embarrassment of falling over an obstacle, much to the amusement of comrades looking on. Even in the thick of battle the paras found time to laugh at the unfortunate circumstances of their muckers. Sympathy is a quality not found in abundance in the Parachute Regiment. Individual soldiers would also be nursing blisters and rubs from carrying their packs, especially sore blisters on the lower back caused by packs rubbing with every step taken, known as 'Bergen burns'. This was where the training and general discipline installed in the paratrooper came to the forefront. Each man was a volunteer, well trained and instilled with the determination to achieve their personal and their unit's objectives. If that meant that they had been placed in a ditch and told to not let a German get past them then this is what they would do or die trying. This is where airborne training methods, now enshrined in 'P' Company – the selection process for today's Airborne Forces, was derived. The mental and physical ability to be a paratrooper, which was so rigidly tested in training, was now being tested for real on the battlefield. The *Cactus* exercises in North Africa had fine-tuned the men to land behind enemy lines at night and march to their target, overcoming any obstacles in their way, be that the enemy or being dropped miles from their drop zones. Many of the men were finding those training scenarios very real. Despite their injuries they began to cross unfamiliar terrain at night to reach their objective of the bridge, overcoming obstacles along the way such as the liberally strewn barbed wire and having to leap over countless brick walls and irrigation ditches dividing up the farmers' fields in this corner of Sicily.

Just prior to sunrise, and again at sundown, the paras, wherever they were in Sicily on that first morning, observed 'Stand-to'. This was a British military tradition, which identified the transition from day to night, and vice versa in the evening, as the most likely time of an enemy attack. All men, therefore, 'stood-to', facing outwards from their positions, watching over their weapon sights for any sign of the enemy. The men waited nervously for the first signs of the approaching enemy. They remained perfectly still and scanned the ground around them for 30 minutes, until it was fully light. This same procedure would be practised again at sunset. Once the 'stand-down' order was issued, the stragglers continued their march towards the bridge whilst those already at the bridge and the Johnny hills began to improve their defensive positions, and possibly even enjoy a brief window of opportunity for personal administration.

If time permitted any personal 'admin', the men would work in pairs, known as the 'buddy-buddy' system; one man would keep watch whilst the other man cleaned his weapon, changed his socks and powdered his feet, re-applied camouflage and mosquito repellent to his face and hands and generally checked over his kit, all whilst the hot water was being brewed in the background to make tea to go along with cold rations for breakfast. The men would take on all the calories they could, when they could. Who knows when they would have the chance to eat again? The men would take their daily Mepacrine anti-malarial tablets and roll their sleeves up during the day, rolling them back down again at night to limit the area of skin exposed for the mosquitoes to feed on. However, many of the men in Sicily didn't take their Mepacrine pills and would later suffer from malaria, including Alistair Pearson. Once the first man had as quickly as possible completed his admin he would then keep watch whilst his buddy completed his admin. Once they had both completed their admin they would keep watch together and share a mug of tea before, no doubt, a sergeant or corporal would be over with ad hoc tasks to be completed.

Whilst the men were completing their personal admin, Lathbury had established his headquarters on the southern bank of the river. He called in the officers and NCOs that were present. They now had to reform their structure and chains of command, with so many men already killed and missing this early into the operation. This provided an opportunity for an impromptu 'O' Group. The officers and NCOs swapped any information that they had picked up in order to build an intelligence picture of just what had occurred the previous evening during the chaos of the drop. Lathbury used his 'O' Group to take stock of the depleted number of men at his disposal and spread them around the bridgehead perimeter so as to best repel the most likely directions of attack from the enemy. By dawn there were some 200 men, comprising 120 men of 1 Para, two platoons from 3 Para and a handful of engineers, holding the bridge. There should have been closer to 1,200. As well as the shortage of manpower, there was also an acute shortage of firepower. The brigade could only call on the fire support of three out of the eight 6-pounders, two of the twelve 3-inch mortars, three of the 27 PIATs and a single Vickers machine gun, with much of the ammunition also being lost during the jump. Lathbury was further hampered by the lack of communications available. A single No.22 set had arrived from the drop zone but it was missing its accessories and therefore wouldn't function. The loss of the bulk of the longer-range support weapons meant that the enemy troops couldn't now be kept at bay and effectively gave them an unexpected opportunity to advance to close-quarters with the paras.

Despite the disappointingly low amounts of men and weapons at the objective, Lathbury tasked Pearson to best place them for the approaching fight. The PIATs and machine gun were sited facing the highway to the north to stop any approaching enemy vehicles or troops. During the night the anti-tank guns had already been set up at the southern end of the bridge and captured enemy artillery pieces set up to cover the north end of the bridge.

The Orders Group ('O' Group) had served to give a clear picture of just what resources the 1st Parachute Brigade had at its disposal to fend off the might of the approaching German and Italian infantry, paratroopers and armoured units. The same procedure was being carried out by Frost on the summit of Johnny I with his depleted 2 Para. A distinct lack of both manpower and firepower was immediately apparent for both commanders. The airborne ability to be as dogged in defence as

Knocked out Sherman tanks from A Squadron, 3rd City of London Yeomanry. The unit lost 6 of its 7 tanks on the same morning it was meant to be speeding northwards to relieve 1st Parachute Brigade at Primosole Bridge. (Kent and Sharpshooters Image)

they were aggressive in attack was about to be tested as they began to dig-in and let the enemy come on to them. They had no choice but to sit tight and fight it out.

Once Lathbury and Frost had finished briefing their respective 'O' Groups and they were happy that all points had been covered and that the officers and NCOs knew what was expected of them and their men, they would be dismissed back to their sections to pass on the information, known as 'gen'. Once the Officers and NCOs were back in their slit trenches and had briefed their men, they had a short admin window of their own. Officers were meant to lead by example and their admin in the field was expected to be better than that of the men. Despite being under fire on the battlefield, officers and NCOs led the way in maintaining a sense of smartness in their outward appearance, in turn promoting good battlefield admin traits in their sub-units.

Whilst the officers checked their maps, the Corporals and Sergeants would start to really earn their pay by getting the men and materiel into the best possible shape, ready for the fight to come. These ranged from monitoring the men digging in and speeding their rate of digging up through to checking their ammunition levels and redistributing ammunition as necessary, so that every man had equal amounts if ammunition and the machine guns and anti-tank weapons were positioned so that they had the best fields of fire against the approaching enemy. They would also check the general welfare of the men for injuries and made sure they had time for admin, often ensuring that the men had recharged their magazines, cleaned their weapons and had food and water.

The NCOs made sure that the men were sited correctly in positions that provided 360-degree defensive cover. Men would be given inter-locking arcs of fire, with a left and right axis depicted on the ground by the NCO by two prominent features. He would point out, for example a prominent tree as the man's left axis and a large rock as the right of axis. Any enemy that moved in this arc was the man's responsibility to engage and warn his colleagues of the danger. The men to his right and left would repeat the same process, with their own arcs of fire but ensuring that they slightly overlapped to provide additional coverage. The ground out in front of them was also 'broken-down' into near, middle and far ground, with estimates of distances to the various features in front of them calculated. Features, such as hills, woods and buildings, if not already named in the orders stage, would be given names to allow for quicker target identification and referencing points to allow one soldier to quickly bring attention to a particular area for the remainder of the unit.

Sentries were posted, as the remainder of the men started the laborious task of digging in to the sun-baked Sicilian soil. The men had learnt from their experiences in North Africa not to sight trenches at the base of trees as rain water would invariably run into the trench. However, the men intended not to be in trenches for a prolonged amount of time at Primosole and they incorporated the trees into their defensive positions for overhead concealment and also cover from artillery fire. It would soon prove to be a different sort of object raining down on them, not just rain water but airburst shrapnel from the approaching Italian and German defenders. Experience gained in North Africa against enemy tanks dictated that trenches were to be dug down to a depth of 5 feet (1.5m) to allow for a tank to pass over the position without it collapsing on its defenders. The men were expected to simply let the tank pass overhead and then reappear and continue engaging the expected accompanying enemy infantry following the tanks. Digging down to 5 feet would prove difficult in Sicily due to the lack of time before the Germans began counter-attacking, the constant need for men to be fighting and not digging and the rocky terrain of the ground itself which would prove difficult to scrape more than a few inches down into the top soil. If the men had time they would sketch out a quick 'range card', in essence a rough drawing of the ground directly in front of them with features shown, named and distances added in order to quickly orientate any reinforcements or new men to the ground out in front of them quickly. With nothing else to do, the men carried on digging to get down as deep as they could. The veterans knew how important it was going to become later in the day for a place of safety from all the flying bullets and shrapnel. The men didn't know how long it was going to be until the Germans made their first move, so they carried on digging until the sentries began calling out the target indications of the advancing enemy. Each man would then drop his shovel, pick up his weapon, put the butt in his shoulder, take up a stable firing position and begin scanning the horizon for targets.

Lastly the men were briefed on the bigger picture of the operation so far. From what scant information Lathbury had, he could deduce that the jump had been scattered due to both enemy and friendly anti-aircraft fire with only a fraction of the brigade actually in position on the ground. However, all objectives had been taken and would now have to be held from the inevitable counter-attacks from the German paratroopers and their supporting elements until the Allied relieving forces arrived.

The defensive screen around the bridge had been hastily organised immediately after its capture. After the 'O' Group, and now that it was daylight, the perimeter defences were beefed up. Hawkins mines were strung across the road approaches to prevent vehicles attacking the paratroopers. The enemy pillboxes on the north and south of the bridge were occupied and the captured guns, two Italian 50mm guns and a heavier German 75mm piece which had been unhooked from one of the destroyed vehicles in the earlier ambush on the northern end of the bridge, were set up to be re-used on the regrouping enemy. Second Lieutenant Clapham of B Troop of the 1st Airlanding Anti-Tank Battery, had been onboard Glider 129, which had struck the top of the bridge on landing. After making his way to the bridge, he had organised a party to go back out onto the drop zones and salvage three 6-pounder guns from the gliders on Landing Zone 8. Once back at the bridge he was put in charge of incorporating the 6-pounders and the captured enemy artillery pieces into the bridge's defences. Manned by his airborne gunners, complimented by glider pilots, he now waited for the first sight of the enemy.

A stock of German Teller mines was also discovered in the south-western pillboxes by 1 Para men, which were fused by the engineers and added to the bridge defences to complement the Hawkins mines. Several abandoned Italian Breda machines guns with plentiful ammunition were discovered in the nearby slit trenches and incorporated into the perimeter being set up around the two ends of the bridge by 1 and 3 Para. The Breda only fired a 20-round magazine and wasn't belt-fed but it was a welcome addition to the paras' defences.

Sergeants Anderson, Atkinson and Doig of the 1st Airlanding Brigade's Royal Artillery detachment positioned the three salvaged 6-pounder anti-tank guns and were central to keeping these weapons during the upcoming battle. Anderson's gun was placed at the southern end of the bridge slightly to the west to fire over the river to the north. Doig and Atkinson's guns were placed 20 metres apart by the highway 500 metres south-east of the bridge to cover the road. They were joined by their Horsa glider pilots who had landed them the previous night, Sergeants Protheroe and Kerr, and they showed them how to handle and load the guns. (Protheroe, along with Staff Sergeant White, was to be awarded the Distinguished Flying Medal for his actions in successfully landing his Horsa accurately on LZ1. These were the only two Horsas to land on their correct landing zones during the airborne insertion.) This fitted with the glider pilots' view of themselves as 'total soldiers' as they could land their gliders and then join the battle as infantrymen. They would remain with the battery throughout the remainder of the day, acting as ground troops now they had successfully fulfilled their glider pilot role. Under Lathbury's command the defenders at the bridgehead had spent the last couple of hours salvaging equipment and building up their defences around the bridgehead. They had nothing more to do now except wait for the Germans to make their opening move.

The first enemy activity came at 05:30 in the low-flying shape of a Feiseler Storch reconnaissance aircraft. The German plane made a low sweep over the bridge and then flew off into the distance as quickly as it had appeared. The German pilots hadn't had enough time to confirm whether the bridge was in German or British hands. They could certainly see gliders and parachutes around the bridge but the men were dug-in and held their fire to prevent giving their positions away. It had all seemed oddly quiet at the bridge from the air. To aid the Luftwaffe planes, the Fallschirmjaeger around the bridgehead had marked out their positions with red, white and black swastika flags to allow the German planes to pinpoint their positions and ascertain where the front line was. This enabled an accurate report of the front line to be passed back to headquarters and also allowed for the pilots to attack anything beyond the ground recognition flags as likely to be enemy troop formations. However, the bridge had been garrisoned by Italian troops meaning that the lack of flags on the ground couldn't therefore be taken as proof that the

North end of bridge and house. Captain Rann's group charged from behind the house, past the pill-boxes and over the bridge to secure the objective. (Kent and Sharpshooters Image)

bridge was in British hands. The Feiseler radioed back to Catania airfield with a quick intelligence picture. Messerschmitts Me109s were scrambled to fly over the bridge immediately and investigate further.

For the paras on the ground, the sight of the Feiseler had prompted the men to be on alert for further aircraft. They didn't have to wait long. Just 15 minutes later a flight of four Messerschmitts Me109s appeared and flew over the general area but without interfering. The Germans were clearly carrying out patrols to ascertain just what was happening. Due to the spread of paratroopers over south-east Sicily that night, the Germans were confused as to just what their target actually was. Reports of individual firefights had been coming into German headquarters all night. Indeed, some firefights were taking place on isolated drop zones with no real targets of value, coupled with the spread of paratroopers ranging from Mount Etna 20 miles (32km) to the north to Lentini 10 miles (16km) to the south, created a picture of a marauding force of British paratroopers landing all over south-eastern Sicily and attacking enemy forces at random. The Germans would have to move on foot against the bridge to see just who was in possession of this vital objective.

Whilst the bridgehead was being secured and the Germans planned their response to the airborne landings, Brigade-Major Hunter set out with a small party to the drop zones to salvage any further kit and direct stragglers towards the bridge. He managed to find a spare set of accessories for a No.22 radio which, coupled with the single radio set at the bridge, made up one single working radio. However, as of yet, no communications had been or could be established with any other units. They needed to keep trying to establish radio communications with other Allied units urgently. The message that the bridge was held but with very few troops, and that relief was needed immediately to prevent it falling back into German hands and being destroyed had to be sent at all possible speed to Montgomery back at his headquarters.

Whilst the paras sat and waited for their relieving force to arrive, they prepared for the inevitable battle. The medics began to set up their temporary dressing station at the north end of the bridge in preparation for the expected casualties. Staff Sergeant Stevens of the 16th Parachute Field Ambulance had arrived at the north end of the bridge at 04:50. He had immediately started to collect the walking wounded and stretcher cases that had made it to the bridge from the drop zones. Captain Rutherford and Captain Haggie, who was RMO of 1 Para, had already established another dressing station at the south of the bridge, and Stevens began to ferry casualties between the bridge and the MDS with a horse and cart.

Corporal Tynan of the RAMC was also helping to clear casualties from around the bridge. He continually moved forward under fire to help evacuate wounded men throughout the day and was awarded the Military Medal for his courage under fire. Tynan was helped by the padre, Captain the Rev Bernard Egan, who had been on the same Dakota as Frost but had landed some miles to the west of his drop zone. He had managed to lead a small group of paras back to the bridge later that day before moving to the MDS to help with the wounded. He was awarded the Military Cross not only for his actions around Primosole Bridge but for also tending the wounded at Tamera a few months previously.

The defences were ready. The attackers were finalising their attack plans. The scene was now set for the clash of the devils. The paratroopers lay in their shell-scrapes and in the pre-dug irrigation ditches of the olive groves and vineyards – a scene that would be familiar to today's paratroopers serving in Afghanistan. They could start to see the first distant shapes of German troops arriving to take over the attack from their Italian counterparts. There were still around 300 Italian prisoners who had been released by the paras wandering around the vicinity of the bridge, not quite sure what to do with themselves. They remained close to the bridge throughout the action, seemingly debating whether to approach their fellow Axis forces or wait to be recaptured by the British.

Meanwhile, 2 Para, from their position on the Johnny features overlooking the surrounding area, could see long columns of trucks, packed with German paratroopers, edge cautiously forward along the highway from Catania towards the bridge. In the distance through their binoculars they could make out the Catania airfield where rows of Messerschmitts stood, their machine guns and cannons being re-loaded in preparation for sorties against the airborne troops holding the Primosole Bridge. Without any of their heavy weapons arriving after the drop, 2 Para were tantalisingly unable to interfere with the Fallschirmjaeger forming up for their counter-attack in the valley below. The men of the 1st Parachute Brigade were undoubtedly expecting an enemy reaction to their landings and attempt to take the Primosole Bridge. They would also undoubtedly have expected some form of a counter-attack. However, they may not have expected the counter-attack to come in the form of elite German Fallschirmjaeger supported by tanks and aircraft. A sense of anticipation was now beginning to grow amongst the Red Devils as they watched the enemy forming up and advancing on their position. The fight with the enemy was now changing from small groups of lost soldiers making their way through the night to a well-planned and well-supported deliberate attack in daylight. The battle for the Primosole Bridge was about to start. The paratroopers, as per their regimental motto, were '*utrinque paratus*' – ready for anything.

CHAPTER THIRTEEN

'Incoming!'

First Contact from the South

Just after dawn had cast its warming rays over the summit of Johnny I, the men of 2 Para settled into their foxholes and grabbed a quick bite to eat and a cup of tea before the inevitable German counter-attack. They could see from their own depleted numbers present on top of the hill, that the drop had gone wrong and far fewer of their airborne comrades were on the ground, let alone at their objectives, than expected. Despite the chaos of the previous night, however, the 1st Parachute Brigade had managed to take the bridge, clear Johnny II and hold Johnny I. Optimistically they expected stragglers to steadily swell their numbers throughout the day. Unfortunately, this was about all the strength that they were going to muster for the remainder of the battle to come. They were on their own and surrounded.

In the distance was the towering mass of Mount Etna and directly below its line of sight only a kilometre away was the Primosole Bridge. Small figures of their comrades could be seen moving around and preparing the bridge for defence. From their grandstand viewing point on Johnny I, the men of 2 Para had witnessed the earlier ambush of the Italian convoy. The spectacle of the firefight and exploding vehicles would also have served as an indication for the German and Italian troops just where all these paratroopers from the night before were now gathering.

The Johnny hills provided an excellent observation point over the bridge and the surrounding area. That's why the paras had captured it as a primary objective. The Germans, too, were aware of its strategic importance in dominating the highway and bridge below. The men of 2 Para knew that this put them in the crosshairs on the planning maps of senior German officers now tasked to retake the bridge. The paras also knew the enemy were likely to move towards them from Catania to the north. Coupled with the Allied advance pushing the enemy troops away from the invasion beaches towards Catania from the south, the advance of enemy troops could only be moments away.

The 2 Para sentries on top of Johnny I could clearly see small parties of unknown troops moving around the base of the hill around a lone farm building, 200 metres to the south-east. It was not evidently apparent whether they were friend or foe in the gloomy early morning light. However, it soon became apparent as to their identity. They were German paratroopers of Laun's Fallschirmjaeger Machine Gun Battalion, the Green Devils. The British and German elite paratroopers were about to lock horns for control of Johnny I. As the men of 2 Para had been observing their enemies from afar, the Germans had also been observing their British counterparts and making notes of their hastily dug positions. The Germans carefully lined up their weapons and prepared their ammunition ready for an opening barrage. It came suddenly at 06:30. The distant thuds of mortars firing preceded dozens of mortar bombs whistling from out of the still sky, crashing into the hill and instantly bringing the sounds and sights of battle to the defenders of Johnny I. Automatic shouts of 'incoming' went up, in case anyone was unsure, that they were now under fire. The mortar bombs sent concussive shockwaves through the ground as well as red-hot shrapnel flying through the air. From behind the lone farm building opened up several machine guns, spraying the hillside with a wall of bullets. The men could see the orange snakes of tracer bullets arcing towards them before they ripped into the ground and ricocheted all around the hillside.

The barrage had been unexpected and arrived with deadly fury. C Company, supported by a platoon from A Company, had pushed forward and slightly down the slope at the south end of the hill. This had enabled them to be able to see past the olive groves and out into the open to check for any signs of the approaching enemy. Unfortunately, they had not had time to dig in before the barrage started. The flying bullets and shrapnel caused instant casualties, particularly as razor-sharp splinters from the rocky Sicilian ground added to the shrapnel as each mortar round landed. Cries for medics went up and the men had to brave the incoming fire to drag or carry the casualties to the better protection of the farmhouse where the medics were stationed. The veterans felt that same feeling of being back in battle again. The replacements who had joined the brigade in Africa, were now experiencing combat for the first time. They were experiencing emotions ranging from pure fear to the exhilaration of battle, almost willing the Germans to come on and join them in battle.

Despite the Johnny hills being in a commanding position overlooking the local area, they were not rugged hills provided with natural rocky cover or thick vegetation for defence. This reduced their ability to be held as a bomb-proof fortress but they did provide basic cover solely due to their height. The men needed to quickly scrape out some trenches into the hill, as casualties were mounting whilst they had no cover. They continued to dig in as best they could, despite the incoming enemy fire all around them.

The men had brought their famed maroon berets with them as per orders. The distinctive maroon berets of the airborne troops could also double up as ground-to-air recognition markers and were included in the planning for *Husky*. The 1st Airborne

Division's Headquarters had written to all British ground forces in the build-up to *Husky* to ensure that the message was passed on to non-airborne troops in the invasion force that:

> Red berets will be carried by all airborne troops on Operation *Husky* and will be worn when opportunity offers.
>
>   Consider valuable alternative means of recognition and request that all troops be warned accordingly.[1]

Some men had made a personal choice in whether to keep their helmets on or swap them for their more comfortable maroon Parachute Regiment berets. Wearing helmets for a prolonged period of time was disliked by the men as they soon became heavy and uncomfortable. They were provided with a cloth cap comforter to wear as an insert into the helmet but in the heat of the Sicilian summer these only added to the wearer's discomfort. As soon as the barrage had started, the men who had opted for berets were soon reaching for the better protection of their helmets amidst the rain of shrapnel being sent onto their position by the Fallschirmjaeger heavy weapons teams just out of sight and range.

Despite the dust and smoke kicked up with each explosion, which was slowly creating a smokescreen, some 30 metres long and 8 metres high, in front of the 2 Para positions, the Fallschirmjaeger were able to improve their accuracy as they adjusted their fire onto the 2 Para positions with each round.

The bulk of the initial barrage had landed on the A Company positions. The paras didn't have any heavy weapons of their own with which to fire back and try and suppress the incoming fire. The furthest ranged weapon they possessed was the medium Bren machine gun. The NCOs were running and crawling between the different trenches, encouraging their men and making sure that they were calling out the enemy positions as they saw them. This would allow for a coordinated response of fire to be sent in that direction to neutralise the threat. Sergeant Bardwell had noticed that two of his men had been wounded by an incoming artillery round and were lying wounded in their shell-scrape. He braved the bullets flying all around to run out into the open and drag the men back into cover before they were engulfed by the approaching fire. He was awarded a Military Medal for his courage.

Corporal Ashley Neville of A Company had spotted one of the German machine-gun crews as they moved to a closer position. He now shouted out the position of the target to his paras in the next shell-scrape and then moved his Bren gun forward of his hastily dug shallow cover to better engage the German machine gun. He lined up the Germans in his sights, took a breath, and then slowly squeezed the trigger, The Bren gun burst into life, sending a stream of .303 rounds ripping into the enemy gun crew, killing the enemy paratroopers and silencing the gun. The paras were now finally getting the chance to fight back as the Germans closed in.

Shortly after knocking out the enemy machine gun, Ashley and his fellow paratroopers were faced with yet another probing attack through the smoke on the hillside. Whilst the men around him fixed bayonets due to the growing proximity of the advancing Fallschirmjaeger, Ashley fired off a burst from his Bren, taking down two attacking Fallschirmjaeger who were setting up their MG34 machine gun. The Germans lay out on the field wounded whilst their comrades were forced to retreat under withering fire from the men of 2 Para above them. As Ashley took his position again behind the Bren and started scanning the ground for further targets, he noticed that the burning vegetation was spreading towards the two stricken Germans. He decided to sprint out into the firing line and rescue the two Germans. Handing his weapon over to his buddy, he asked for covering fire before running out into no man's land to drag both wounded Fallschirmjaeger away from the fire and back into cover in the 2 Para lines, before handing them onto the MDS for treatment. He was later awarded the Military Medal for his actions. This switch from fighting each other to the death, and then saving the enemy's life in the next moment, highlights the healthy respect that the Green and Red Devils held for each other on the battlefield. Ashley's actions inadvertently also provided vital intelligence for 2 Para. From the insignia on the uniforms worn by the two wounded Germans that Ashley had saved, they now understood for the first time that they were up against fellow paratroopers from the German Parachute Regiment.

By 07:00, the vegetation was well alight and giving off clouds of white-grey smoke to add to the black puffs of smoke generated by the incoming mortar rounds. The whole hill smelled like a giant bonfire and stung the eyes. The men of 2 Para were sitting atop Johnny I in their shell-scrapes and could do nothing as the smoke on the ground began to roll up the southern aspect of the hillside towards them. This gave the Germans a rolling smokescreen that they could use to remain hidden from view as they advanced to contact and reduced the distance that 2 Para could see down the hill and pick out the advancing Germans. The paras' visibility was reducing at a steady rate and thus allowing the Fallschirmjaeger to manoeuvre closer to the 2 Para positions. The closer the enemy approached, the more accurate and heavier their fire became. The Fallschirmjaeger were using all available cover to tactically move up the hill. As each man moved, his comrade covered him before repeating the process. This 'pepper-potting' technique was allowing the Germans to close in on the front 2 Para positions.

The smokescreen did, however, provide a visual reference for the stragglers still trying to locate their units after the jump. One of these stragglers was FOO Captain Vere Hodge. Hodge arrived on Johnny I out of breath and tired but immediately set up his No. 66 radio to establish communications with the waiting cruisers only a few kilometres out at sea to the east. He spent the next two hours trying to establish communications using one of the few working No 22 sets with the naval fleet whilst selecting targets on the ground for future fire missions. The men of 2 Para had been spotting enemy positions for the last hour and noting their grid references, which they now passed to Hodge.

Captain Vere Hodge (second from right) brought effective naval fire down onto the Fallschirmjaeger attacks against 2 Para. (Courtesy of Air Assault Museum)

Having earlier abandoned Johnny II in order to concentrate their forces on Johnny I, Frost's men now came under fire from the Germans who had occupied Johnny II. They brought down additional machine-gun and mortar fire onto Johnny I. The Germans were delivering wave after wave of high explosives and bullets onto the men of 2 Para with impunity, appearing to have plenty of stocks of ammunition to keep up a prolonged bombardment. They were also out of range of the paratroopers' small arms, leading to a one-sided pummelling. The weight of fire that they were bringing down on the British positions was allowing them to take their time and line up their targets, producing more accurate fire as the fighting raged on.

In contrast, the besieged paras could hardly lift their heads from their shallow shell-scrapes without risking death or injury. Shrapnel was piercing the air with bursts of machine-gun fire cracking overhead or ricocheting in all angles from hitting the hard ground. They had to quickly take their chances and raise their heads above their shell-scrapes, try and pick a target and fire, before lowering themselves back down to the earth for protection. When they weren't quick enough, or were just plain unlucky, the cry for medics went up, casualties were now trickling into a steady stream. Only fleeting glimpses of the occasional Fallschirmjaeger presented themselves before diving for hard cover behind the rocky slopes of Johnny I. Despite the worsening situation, the paras knew they had to hold on to Johnny I and prevent the Germans from securing the high ground, central to the brigade's plan to ultimately hold on to the Primosole Bridge.

A fighting patrol was sent out at 07:30 to try and neutralise enemy machine guns now sited on Johnny II and alleviate the pressure on Johnny I. The patrol consisted of five men from 9 Platoon, C Company led by Lieutenant Peter Barry. He was accompanied by Privates Irvine and Henderson, who were armed with a Bren gun, and Sergeant Norris and Private Dunkeld. Their objective was to silence a machine gun that had been firing with impunity at the 2 Para positions for the last hour. It was out of range of the paras' small arms, meaning the men would have to push forward into no man's land and attack it. On moving out to the east, the Bren gun team set up their gun and began to engage the enemy machine gun as the remainder of the patrol attempted to flank the enemy. As they stood up and moved forward they came face to face with an extended line of advancing Fallschirmjaeger. Henderson immediately switched fire to the new threat. He opened up with the Bren gun at the same time as a previously unseen German armoured car simultaneously opened up on the patrol with its own machine gun. Sergeant Norris and Private Dunkeld were killed in the opening burst of fire. Barry shouted back to Henderson and Irvine to get back to the perimeter. As they sprinted back to their own lines they were both shot and wounded in the process. Barry, meanwhile, opened fire on the advancing group of 50 Germans. They hit the ground, some for cover, and some from bullets. Other C Company men saw the drama unfolding and tried to reinforce the patrol by providing covering fire. This allowed Barry to crawl into cover after being grazed by six bullets. Sergeant Cowie ran out to Barry's position and dragged him back to his own lines.

By 08:00 the intense heat from the burning vegetation was now forcing Frost's men to withdraw from their forward positions on the southern perimeter and back into the main perimeter. This allowed the Fallschirmjaeger of Laun's Machine Gun Battalion to creep closer to 2 Para and redirect machine gun and mortar fire more accurately. The precarious hilltop position was shrouded in smoke, catching fire, under heavy fire and on the verge of being stormed by German paratroopers. Something was needed to help turn the tide of battle.

That something was provided in the shape of Captain Hodge. He had now established communications with HMS *Newfoundland*. The cruiser had spent the last few days as part of the 15th Cruiser Squadron, under command of Naval Force K, providing fire support to the amphibious landings and also picking up survivors from the ill-fated glider operations who had ditched into the sea. Whilst trying to make radio contact with the cruiser, Hodge had moved his observation post close to the forward perimeter of the 2 Para positions. From here he got to work with his map, compass and binoculars, plotting fire missions back to the warships at sea. He began by recording the grid references of friendly troops and then of likely or known enemy positions. Major features, such as the road, would be calculated and their directions and distances from the observation post calculated, so as to be ready to bring fire down any position quickly on any given piece of ground if needed. Once in contact with the *Newfoundland*, Hodge sent his first fire mission to halt the advancing Fallschirmjaeger. He gave the range and distance from his own position to that of the enemy soldiers then ordered an adjusting round to be fired first to gauge the accuracy of the fire before bringing down further artillery, mainly to prevent friendly forces from being hit but also to conserve ammunition.

Newfoundland's radio operator let Hodge know when the guns were firing and a time of flight, in seconds, to impact. Instructions were hastily shouted by Hodge to the 2 Para men that naval fire was incoming. This gave the men the chance to get their heads down and prepare for the concussion of the blasts. The first high-explosive 6-inch round from the ship landed conservatively behind the German positions. Hodge observed the fall of shot of this first incoming round. He radioed the *Newfoundland* to add extra distance and then he then ordered a further fire mission to start bringing the rounds down on the Germans in anger. The rounds were adjusted and steadily brought closer to the Johnny I positions until, at a range of 400 yards (360m) to their front, the rounds started dropping onto the Germans.

The Germans' only warning came with the last few seconds of a piercing scream of the incoming rounds as they travelled through the warm blue sky of the Sicilian morning towards them. With a loud 'crump' the rounds began to land in the midst of the advancing Fallschirmjaeger. The initial orange cloud of the fiery explosion soon gave way to a black and grey cloud of dust. The unseen shrapnel from the round, and the stone fragments that were created in the explosion, now hurtled through the air faster than the speed of sound and caused fragmentation injuries to the Germans. The screams of wounded Fallschirmjaeger and desperately barked German instructions could now be heard from the British lines. Three rounds landed very close to the paras' front line near battalion HQ, with one round landing as close as 30 yards (27m) to the Italian prisoners in the yard, injuring several of them and causing them to try and flee the hillside.

The horror of the naval shelling would, in the fog of war, be music to the ears of the paras, hunkered down in their shallow trenches and glad to be receiving the support of the Allied fleet out to sea. They hoped this would be the start of continued naval and air support for the rest of the day. After only a matter of minutes Hodge ordered a cease-fire. The paras shouted over their thanks to Hodge as the Germans could be seen running back down the hill and out of the immediate ambush zone that they had found themselves in. The naval fire had silenced some of the German heavy weapons and forced the Fallschirmjaeger to abandon the farm buildings that they had recently occupied and were using as a forming-up position to move against 2 Para's defences.

Now that Hodge had control of the *Newfoundland*'s guns, he could start to deliver their high-velocity shells against other enemy targets. He swiftly followed up the success of his first fire mission with a barrage directed at the troublesome machine guns and mortars on Johnny II that had been previously out of range of the Bren guns and therefore firing at the paras with impunity. 'Shells came crashing down onto the Germans at Johnny II'.[2] This accurate shelling was decisive in causing the Germans to climb off the top of Johnny II and seek shelter. John Frost remembered later that at 'about 09:00 Vere Hodge was tuned in and almost immediately the high-velocity medicine began to arrive with a suddenness and efficiency that completely turned the scales'.[3] The effect of the naval shells landing not only inflicted casualties on the Germans but also provided the recognition that the Allied fleet was supporting the defence of the position and improved the morale of the battered defenders of Johnny I. The Germans paratroopers, who were on the cusp of victory only moments ago, were now hurriedly retreating off the slopes of both Johnny I and II. The men of 2 Para at last had a reprieve and chance to take stock of their morning's work. They were able to push their perimeter outwards again and start the all-important task of digging in – they had seen the necessity of being able to take cover on the barren slopes of their hilltop fort.

The lull in the fighting also meant that casualties, both friendly and enemy, could be evacuated down the hill to the MDS.

An Italian medical officer, wandering around the base of Johnny I near the MDS, was taken prisoner at 10:00 and put in charge of the enemy wounded but he disappeared a short while later, not to be seen again. Red Cross flags were now flying from the roof of the MDS and red paint, especially parachuted-in with the men, was used to paint red crosses on the exterior walls and on the roads nearby so as to be visible from the air.

The commanding officer of the field ambulance unit, Colonel Wheatley, had cycled over from the bridge on a newly liberated bicycle to begin his day's work at 06:40. By now, the MDS was fully operational and already treating casualties as the 2 Para casualties were brought in. Operations in the theatre were being conducted alternately by Wheatley and his second-in-command, Major Longland. After establishing the MDS, Captain Ridler helped to provide anaesthetic for the operations and treat patients over the next two days. He was later awarded the Military Cross.

The MDS was attempting to make the men there as comfortable as possible. A pig and several chickens in the farmhouse courtyard, along with potatoes and pasta, were requisitioned by the hungry paratroopers and used to feed the patients. Several horses at the farm were coupled to carts and used to ferry supplies and casualties to and from the bridgehead. Only nine stretchers had been recovered from the drop zones, which made moving casualties from the front line to the MDS problematic throughout the day.

Casualties would be triaged into three groups depending on the severity of the injuries and their need of an operation. Priority 1 (code-named RED) would be for serious gunshot wounds, abdominal injuries or multiple injuries requiring urgent operations or resuscitation. Priority 2 (BLUE) casualties would be fractures and minor injuries that would need operations but not within the next six hours. Priority 3 (BLACK) were all other casualties, namely the 'walking wounded' who would be patched up if time allowed by the aid post but more likely would provide self-help to themselves or receive aid from a combat-trained medic on the front line. Many of the men were taught that their first action on becoming a casualty was 'self-help'. They were expected to get themselves into cover and begin treating themselves if possible. They each carried two shell dressings in their smock pockets and could use these to begin to stem the flow of blood from any wounds that they had. Their comrades were also expected to carry on with the fight in hand as a priority and then help their wounded comrades when there was a lull in the battle. The men each had a small first aid kit with which they could treat themselves. Normally the wounded would pour some sulphadimidine powder on the wound to prevent infection and then hopefully look forward to getting themselves back into the fray.

Away from the main dressing station, Captain Gordon, RMO of 2 Para, and his team had set up an assistant dressing station (ADS) at a farm building near the drop zone. This ADS was mainly dealing with wounded men being brought in from the DZs by their comrades: 29 were bought in from 2 Para as a result of the jump, and there were a further 15 wounded on DZ1 from 1 Para. The medics took the men in for treatment, allowing their comrades to hurry on to their objectives and join the fight.

Back on the top of the hill, as the men regained their perimeter after the first German counter-attack, Captain 'Bombs' Panter of S Company discovered a battery of Italian 4-inch light howitzers in a valley between 'Johnny I' and 'Johnny II'. He got some men from the Mortar Platoon, who had arrived without any of their mortar kit, onto the guns to get them into action. The men had been cross-trained in the use of captured enemy small arms but weren't expecting to fire Italian artillery pieces but with a bit of practice the mortarmen were able to translate their weapon handling skills from their own weapon systems to those of the enemy. After loading the guns with the shells that were lying around, they started putting them to good use against their former masters. They could clearly see enemy troops building up their forces around the bridge, ready to attack their comrades of 1 and 3 Para. With a quick crash course in how to load and fire the guns, they began to find their range against German targets appearing to the north of the bridge, taking care to fire away from the bridge itself whilst they found the measure of the fall of shot on the unfamiliar guns. The mortar men managed to loose off 15 rounds towards enemy positions over the bridge before switching fire to the closer target of Italians on Johnny II. Their fire began attracting a counter-battery response from enemy artillery, which was getting too close for comfort. With a lack of targets, the newly formed battery was ordered to cease fire as they were attracting more incoming fire than they could match. Private White, however, remained at his post firing the gun into the advancing enemy troops. Eventually he was ordered to abandon the gun and seek shelter. He was awarded the Military Medal for helping to break up the enemy counter-attack. The sudden intervention of artillery from Johnny I had the unexpected result of slowing down the German advance on the bridge, as they took time to ascertain if this fire was coming from the Allied ground forces, who were expected to be only a matter of hours away. For this action, as well as leading charges against the creeping assaults of the Fallschirmjaeger on the perimeter earlier that morning, Captain Panter was later awarded the Military Cross.

It had been a tough morning's fighting for 2 Para. They now had time to rebuild their defences and await the next German assault. The Germans had well and truly received a bloody nose in trying to prise Johnny I away from 2 Para. They decided to keep 2 Para bottled up on the hill and switch their focus to retaking the bridge. The weight of the Fallschirmjaeger's next blow was about to fall on 1 Para and 3 Para. The men at the bridge had heard the fighting for Johnny I and its sudden cessation of noise. They wrongly believed that 2 Para had all been killed or captured. They knew they were next in the firing line and steadied their weapons, looking over their weapon sights, waiting for the approach of the Germans.

CHAPTER FOURTEEN

'Dog Fight'

Second Contact from North

The sounds of battle from Johnny I were carried on the cool morning air down to the men at the bridge. After the ambush of the convoy on the bridge, followed by enemy air attacks some hours before, it had been relatively quiet. No sign of enemy troops had yet been seen and the paras had taken the chance to dig in as the stragglers from the drop zones continued to arrive.

News of their earlier ambush seemed not to have provoked any enemy response so far. The enemy had certainly not warned their men that the bridge was in British hands, as at 10:30 a lone German motorcycle despatch rider was seen approaching from the north again. He was riding from Stangenberg's headquarters in Catania carrying a message for Heilmann at his headquarters near Carlentini. As he tried to cross the bridge he was met by a burst of British Bren gunfire. He managed to perform a hasty U-turn and accelerate back to headquarters, promptly telling Captain Franz Stangenberg his tale.

Stangenberg listened intently. He now had confirmation of the 1st Parachute Brigade's whereabouts and their objective. Reports he had received throughout the night of their scattered drop had confused his intelligence picture. He now began to prepare an assault force to march on the bridge and perform a reconnaissance in force. His men loaded themselves into two trucks and drove down the highway towards the bridge. The trucks slowed down to a near-halt 1.5 miles (2.5km) from the bridge.

Although they knew the bridge was almost certainly still to be in British hands, the paras could not be seen. The paras, however, had seen the approaching German trucks and followed their progress on foot as they moved closer. Due to the limited range of their small arms and low quantities of ammunition, they let the Germans come on into an ambush. Mortar fire controllers (MFCs) on the edge of the bridgehead's defensive perimeter had already given mortar teams the location and distance of the enemy. The mortars now laid their barrels onto the path of the advancing Germans and waited for the order to fire.

The convoy of Germans had also been spotted by Second Lieutenant Clapham through his binoculars and he relayed the direction and distance back to his gunners manning the 6-pounders, so that they too could start laying their sights onto the enemy vehicles. As each gun reported back to Clapham that they were loaded, on target and ready to fire, he waited until he knew all guns were poised for a single explosive barrage into the German trucks. When the trucks presented the best possible targets, Clapham ordered the 6-pounders and captured artillery pieces to engage Stangenberg's trucks. Lance Corporal Osborne was manning one of these guns and he remembers 'our officer saw German lorries loaded up with infantry. We loaded up the gun and let them have four shells and it shook them up, and forced them to get off the lorries, so of course they had to come to us on foot'.[1] The shock of artillery from the bridge caused panic in the German ranks as they clambered to dismount from the big targets of their trucks and get into cover in the scrub either side of the road.

The Germans began to de-bus from their vehicles and unwittingly started taking cover right where the mortars had predicted. The MFCs ordered them to fire a barrage of high-explosive rounds. Seconds later, six mortar rounds fell from the Sicilian sky without warning and landed amongst the Germans. Stangenberg's patrol disappeared in a cloud of dust as the rounds exploded all around them. The men of 3 Para added to the ambush by opening fire with machine guns. The unexpected strength, weight and accuracy of the British fire caused them to sprint back to the vehicles at the rear of the convoy, which were panicking in their rush to turn around. Stangenberg and his troops caught their breath as they returned to the vehicles, quickly jumping into the back of them before speeding off back towards Catania. Stangenberg was furious that the bridge had been captured and that his own patrol had just been shot up. He intended to press-gang every able-bodied man he could find at his headquarters and return straight back for another fight.

Clapham's well-disciplined artillery broadside had broken up Stangenberg's assault and, coupled later in the day with using his jeep to ferry casualties under fire to the main dressing station, earned him the award of one of the first Military Crosses that day.

The defenders of the bridge had now performed two successful ambushes. If this was to be the only form of attack from the enemy, then they might be in for a much easier time than they imagined. They settled back down to their defensive positions once Stangenberg's patrol hurriedly retreated from sight. They took the opportunity to refresh themselves, someone even discovered some wine left in one of the pillboxes by the bridge's former defenders. The wine of Sicily was well-renowned and provided a nice addition to the men's rations and parched mouths. They also had access to fresh drinking water from one of the farmhouses on the northern side of the river. Water was increasingly needed by the men after their exploits under the scorching Sicilian sun. Water was also needed to help cool the remaining Vickers machine guns. For every 1,000 rounds they fired, the Vickers required 1.5 pints of water to prevent over-heating.

The successful ambushes of the morning had had the side-effect of identifying the British positions and allowing for an estimation of their strength. Stangenberg returned to Catania to organise more men for a counter-attack. He telephoned Heidrich's headquarters in Rome, asking for permission to bolster his unit with men from Captain Erich Fassl's 1st Company, 1st Fallschirmjaeger Signal Battalion. Fassl's Company had been airlifted into Catania airfield the previous evening and its task was to establish communications before the rest of the division arrived later that evening. In the event, Stangenberg had had to send Fassl's men to guard Catania harbour as its Italian garrison had fled, leaving the port undefended. He now called them back to Catania airfield to form up and march towards 1st Parachute Brigade. He also sent his NCOs around the area to press-gang all German troops, including cooks, clerks and other headquarters staff, into fighting service. This was a common feature of German battlefield ingenuity throughout the war, with ad hoc all-arms battle groups being formed and taking the name of the commander. (Major Dickie Lonsdale of 2 Para would later lead an 'all-arms' composite battle group, Lonsdale Force, in the defence of Oosterbeek towards the end of the battle of Arnhem.) Stangenberg had formed an impromptu battle group, numbering some 350 men, in barely a matter of minutes. He was ready to return to the fray.

Stangenberg was taking no chances this time though and ordered Fassl's men to lay telephone cables to a nearby Flak battery to provide fire support. This artillery would now provide some heavier firepower when Battle Group Stangenberg returned to test the paras' defences. As his battle group climbed aboard their convoy of trucks for the journey south to the scene of battle, the artillery opened up on the British defences. The first few rounds were aimed directly at the bridge for the German gunners to start acquiring their range. Red and blue coloured airburst rounds began to explode closer and closer to the bridge as the German fire controllers homed in on their targets. They then laid down a two-minute barrage of high-explosive shrapnel rounds to pepper the bridgehead. It ended as suddenly as it started. The German gunners had found their mark and would wait for Stangenberg to close on the bridge, before sending over the full 'softening-up' barrage. Any ideas of an easy day for the bridge's defenders were about to suddenly change.

At 12:10 the screech of incoming artillery sent the men around the bridge scurrying for cover. Shouts of 'incoming' were barked out to give everyone a chance to find some form of cover. Airburst rounds were exploding overhead at a height of 25 metres, showering the bridgehead area with red-hot shrapnel. The concussive effect of the rounds bursting overhead sent an outward ripple in the air pressure, bursting the ear drums of some of the men who were directly underneath it. This was not to be another two-minute ranging exercise by the German gunners. The shelling droned on for a full hour of non-stop explosions.

A Bren gun team seen in action. (Courtesy of Air Assault Museum)

Despite the incoming fire, the paras remained on constant vigil. Despite the pre-operation briefings leading them to believe that they would likely be up against second-rate Italian units, they could see for themselves that they were up against German troops now. And Fallschirmjaeger at that. The Italians had melted away. They knew they were definitely in for a fight. All they could do was settle back and wait for the end of this preliminary bombardment, which they thought likely would signal the expected follow-up ground assault.

Under this bombardment, Lathbury began to contemplate just what was happening outside of his bridgehead. He had heard the fighting on Johnny I raging all morning and then die down. He had had no communications with them and started to fear the worst. He was standing in the south-eastern pillbox, which was acting as brigade headquarters, without any working radios and was blinded as to 2 Para's whereabouts or that of the relieving 4th Armoured Brigade, which should have been arriving at any moment. He had to begin thinking just how long he would and could hold on to the bridge. He was also expecting some patrols from the Royal Marines to push north from Malati and link up with his brigade, in turn bringing news of the location of the 4th Armoured Brigade, who should have in turn relieved the Marines earlier that same morning. With no sign of either the Marines or armoured brigade, Lathbury had to assume that they were still clearing the Malati Bridge area and therefore wouldn't reach the Primosole Bridge for several more hours. He had to get his brigade to hold on to the bridge with ever-dwindling men and ammunition against a constantly reinforcing determined German enemy slowly squeezing his brigade with a vice-like grip.

Meanwhile back at the brigade's North African headquarters, news was just starting to filter back about the fate of the men on the ground. The remnants of the air fleet had landed and could retell their experiences of the seemingly disastrous drop of the men. However, HQ knew that the paras would be making every effort to organise themselves from the ashes of their drop and start heading to their objectives. Despite 1st Parachute Brigade's setbacks, Lathbury had earlier managed to get the message through at 11:15 that the bridge was secure but to prepare reinforcements and additional equipment to be air-dropped that night. Later in the afternoon, Lathbury would have to cancel this warning order for more men and kit, due to the loss of the drop zones.[2]

Lathbury was shaken from his thoughts at 13:00 by the shelling suddenly switching on to the bridge itself and the southern end of the bridge. This was the signal for the paras to once again lift themselves from the protection of their trenches and start scanning for signs of the inevitable infantry assault. Through the smoke and dust they could start to see the Germans appearing out of the haze. Once again, the 6-pounders, mortars and machine guns trained their sights on the advancing enemy before the Germans realised the danger.

Stangenberg's ad hoc battle group was advancing from the north using both sides of Highway 114 as an axis of advance towards the bridge with Fassl on the eastern side and Stangenberg on the western side. The plan was for Stangenberg's group to advance to contact with the northern bridgehead whilst Fassl's group tried outflanking the defences of the British right, held by S Company 1 Para, then move along the riverbank to capture the northern end of the bridge. They were supported by artillery in the form of an 88mm and a 5cm artillery piece firing smoke rounds to provide a smokescreen to cover their initial moving off and then high explosive to suppress the men of 1 and 3 Para manning the northern defences of the bridgehead. As they neared the bridge Messerschmitt 109s roared overhead and strafed the bridge. This was ominously developing into a well-planned and well-delivered set-piece battle by Stangenberg.

Yeldham's 3 Para, which by then numbered only five officers and 35 other ranks, was about to bear the brunt of this attack, along with S Company 1 Para. They had spotted the Fallschirmjaeger approaching under the cover of supporting artillery but without the ability to call in artillery or air support they had to let them get close to their own positions before opening fire. The loss of so much equipment during the jump was beginning to tell at this critical stage of the battle. The original plan had called for six 3cm mortars to be at the bridge but there were only two and they were already low on ammunition. The 6-pounders were too close and on too flat a trajectory to be of much use. There should have been nine Vickers machine guns present and with plentiful ammunition. These guns massed together could have created a killing field for 800 metres to the north of the bridge and prevented infantry from approaching.

If the mortars and 6-pounders had been dragged up on to the Johnny hills as planned to provide a mutually supporting firebase overlooking the bridge, these would now have proved their worth. Fire controllers at the bridgehead could have accurately directed the fire of the mortars and the 6-pounders to where it was needed. The lack of radios also prevented sentries on Johnny I relaying information on enemy movements to the defenders at the bridgehead to help them anticipate and prepare for the next probe of its defences. With a clear line of sight, they could have helped break up any attack before they had started by shelling the approaching Germans as they formed up by Catania airfield. Earlier in the day, Hodge had already displayed the power of the naval shells that could be deployed if only the paras had working radios. Naval fire could have been directed at Stangenberg's approach and broken up the attack and dissuaded any further attacks.

The failure of the previous night's drop to get the men and equipment on the ground accurately would now start to take its toll on the 1st Parachute Brigade. The role of 3 Para was planned to provide a defensive screen 1 mile to the north of the bridge and prevent the bridge itself from coming under pressure, allowing them to fend off any enemy counter-attacks from a safe distance away. Instead, Yeldham had had to fall back much closer to the bridge with his platoon-size battalion. He and his men now faced the imminent onslaught of a Fallschirmjaeger infantry attack with their backs against the river.

Despite the unforeseen circumstances in which Yeldham and his men now found themselves, they focussed on the job in hand. He silently watched the approach of the Fallschirmjaeger and managed to hold his men's fire and conceal his positions until the Fallschirmjaeger were within 200 metres. The Germans had spent nearly an hour slowly manoeuvring towards the British positions. Stangenberg shouted the order for his men to make a charge for the front line. Yeldham barked the order for his men to fire and as one single unit the platoon-size group of 3 Para and 1 Para's S Company laid down a wall of lead towards the Germans. The inexperienced rear-echelon troops that Stangenberg had cobbled together now felt their first taste of being on the wrong end of incoming fire. The short but accurate weight of fire directed at the advancing Germans halted them in their tracks. Some brave souls tried to rally their comrades and continue to press the attack but with each dash forward they were being cut down by the paras' accurate and deadly fire. In only ten minutes the British fire slackened as the targets in front of them had either been hit or were crawling back to the safety of their own lines. Yeldham reported back that the attack had been beaten off and that the line was held. Whilst 3 Para and

S Company took a chance to catch their breath, they presumed the next German thrust would be on another sector of the perimeter due to the weight of fire that they had just dished out to the Germans.

Stangenberg had other ideas though. He now directed his more experienced Fallschirmjaeger officers and NCOs to rally the men to repeat the attack again only a few minutes later. He believed the paras wouldn't be expecting an immediate counter-attack and he was right.

His battle group had seen for the first time the horrors of war and saw their comrades killed and wounded before their eyes. They had tasted battle now and their blood was up for revenge. The British positions had been located from the barrage of fire that they had just delivered at the Germans. At 14:00 the German machine guns, with belts of ammunition ready at their sides, lined up the British firing points and burst into life, pouring rapid fire into the paras' positions. While the machine-gun fire was keeping the British below their parapets, Stangenberg tried to get his troops up and moving in order to regain momentum and advance forward with a second attack. Despite being low on ammunition and outnumbered, Yeldham managed to again control the amount of return fire which resulted in the Germans soon taking cover wherever they could, simply stopping to returning fire, rather than risking trying to move forward. The attack lasted only 30 minutes. The Germans were pinned down and unable to move forward. They had lost momentum and were taking casualties. Stangenberg gave the order for them to fall back to their start line. Although they had repulsed two strong attacks, the paras had had to use large amounts of their precious ammunition. If Stangenberg kept up the tempo, the paras would run out of ammunition.

Soon after Stangenberg's attack halted against the 3 Para positions, Fassl directed his flanking attack against 1 Para. The men of S Company 1 Para had spotted the Germans moving forward under the artillery barrage and again waited for them to come onto their guns. The Fallschirmjaeger knew that they were getting closer and closer to the British front line but couldn't see their opponents. Their opponents could see them though. Each man selected a target, trained their sights on their centre of mass and then stalked them, carefully covering their target at all times, waiting for the order to squeeze the trigger and drop their targets. As the advancing Fallschirmjaeger edged closer, the paras couldn't wait any longer. As one, they opened fire and saw their bullets tear into the front ranks of the enemy. All the Fallschirmjaeger could do in response was to drop flat to the ground and try and return some fire to relieve the pressure. As Fassl's attack bogged down, another sortie by Me 109s flew over in support of the ground troops and strafed the southern end of the bridge. As soon as the planes left Fassl's men took the opportunity to again try to move forward but found themselves immediately pinned down under 1 Para's fire again. The discipline of the paras in conserving their fire and only pulling the trigger when they had a target in their sights was taking a deadly toll on the enemy as well as preserving the precious stores of ammunition.

Stangenberg's and Fassl's advances had both failed to break through the perimeter defences but had edged the Fallschirmjaeger to within touching distance of the bridge. And while they had held back the Fallschirmjaeger attacks, the British had had to expend much of their depleted stocks of ammunition just to hold their ground. They couldn't stop many more attacks of this kind before they would be out of ammunition and have nothing with which to dam the flood of Germans trying to reach the river.

At 15:00, after an hour's fighting, the German artillery barrage resumed, battering the beleaguered paras again. The paras soon noted that when a red stream of tracer was sent vertically into the air by the Germans, it was soon followed by a barrage of artillery rounds. Once spotted, this signal to call in fire became an instant signal for the paras to take cover and expect incoming artillery.

The paras were steeling themselves for the biggest attack yet on the northern bridgehead. It had become apparent that the Germans didn't have any other plan to capture the bridge other than trying to repeatedly bulldoze their way across from north to south. The men prepared their weapons and then themselves for the next round of fighting. Alastair Pearson was checking the positions of his men to keep

A section attack seen form the rear. Smoke grenades are bwing thrown to provide cover. (Courtesy of Air Assault Museum)

himself up to date with the unfolding situation on the ground. He arrived at one position scraped into the ground at the edge of a vineyard just in time to observe another four German truckloads of Fallschirmjaeger arrive, towing artillery pieces, and begin their advance on 3 Para's positions. 'He, along with other British paras, could audibly hear the advancing Fallschirmjaeger firing themselves for battle by singing their battle song, *Lili Marlene*'.[3]

Under cover of the artillery bombardment, Stangenberg was bringing up more German troops. These were the troops in the four trucks Pearson had seen arriving through his binoculars. 'As Pearson continued to observe the enemy through his binoculars, one of his veteran sergeants from North Africa, Jock Rainnie, scrambled along a roadside ditch and lobbed a couple of grenades into the first two trucks, which exploded a couple of seconds later into great balls of flame'.[4] The Germans spread out into the fields and soon cleared the area of any more lurking paras. They unhooked their artillery pieces and started to unload the shells from the two undamaged trucks. These guns were quickly dug in and positioned to take aim at the pillboxes that were housing the captured Italian Breda machine guns which were inflicting losses on the attacking Fallschirmjaeger. The paras could see the reinforcements arriving and watched helplessly as they dug in their artillery, tantalisingly out of range. They would have to wait for the Germans to again close in on their own positions until they could fight back.

They knew the next attack wouldn't be too long in coming. As soon as Stangenberg's fresh troops were in place, his intention was to launch yet another offensive on the 3 Para positions to try to punch through the paras' defences and onto the bridge. 'Suddenly there was a strange interruption to the drama. As both sides tensed themselves, for the fight an elderly Sicilian came riding down the road on an ancient bicycle, watched by hundreds of pairs of eyes. He zigzagged round the German bodies that littered the road. As he passed Pearson standing in the bushes, he shouted a cheerful '*Buon Giorno*'. Pearson politely tipped his helmet as the old man pedalled on across the bridge and out of sight'.[5] This brief interlude was one of the few appearances of civilians on the battlefield that day, it marked a short lull in the battle before, on Stangenberg's orders, the shelling increased to a new crescendo. The bridge and its defenders were engulfed in smoke and dust of the exploding shells once more. Shrapnel whizzed through the air, pinging off the steel framework of the bridge and echoing. Debris rained down on the men and sent plumes of water up from the river. Any movement above ground was becoming impossible, the paras were pinned down into their trenches.

At 15:30 the dug-in artillery now added to the defenders' problems. They had lined up the northern pillboxes and now they opened fire, scoring direct hits immediately. Once more the Fallschirmjaeger advanced to contact with the paras. This time the Germans kept close behind their own artillery barrage and used the noise and concussion of the shells to mask their advance until they were in touching distance of the British positions. Battle was joined again as the Germans came into contact with the forward British trenches. The lack of ammunition and firepower was allowing the enemy troops to advance on the British positions until they were engaged in hand-to-hand fighting. After 30 minutes, the enemy was in amongst the British positions in superior numbers. They started to evict the British from one trench after another as their weight of numbers started to tell. Sensing that they were gaining the upper hand, the German artillery now redirected its fire onto the south end of the bridge to prevent reinforcements coming to the aid of the northern bridgehead and also to stop the British withdrawing back over the bridge.

The Germans were slowly gaining ground but they were having to fight for every inch of it. Hermann Kuster was part of the Fallschirmjaeger assault on the bridge. After the battle he wrote a letter home highlighting the close-quarters savagery of the fighting:

> British Fallschirmjaeger landed and we fought a battle to hold an important bridge across the Simeto River. They fought like tigers and eventually took it with terrible losses. The fighting was horrific with men milling around and shooting and bayoneting each other they were so close together. I have never seen men fight one another the way both sides did in the battle.[6]

Despite putting up a courageous fight, the British were now on the back foot, losing momentum to the German onslaught and being squeezed ever closer to the bridge. Spent brass bullet casings lay all around them, the air was thick with cordite and the air was hazy from burning grass and buildings. The non-stop whistle of bullets of different calibres flying overhead, sometimes distant but sometimes all too close for comfort, seemed to be competing with each other for airspace. Dashing enemy silhouettes would appear and then just as quickly disappear once again, moving to get a better firing position from which they could get a clearer shot at the paras. Constant shouting between the defenders alerted them to the ever-moving positions of the enemy. Target indications were called out, bringing attention to enemy threats and allow a coordination of fire. Puffs of dust were continually being kicked up from sniper rounds landing close by. Some men were pinned down in their trenches and couldn't move an inch without a sniper reminding them that they were in his crosshairs, somewhere out there, unseen. Longer bursts of machine-gun fire tore through the air and the reeds where some men were taking cover. Mortar rounds were exploding and adding orange dust to the grey smoke of the burning vegetation. The flames were licking up into the hot air of the Sicilian summer to add to the discomfort of the beleaguered defenders of the bridgehead. The sun was beating down on the men most of whom had no shade to shelter in. The metal parts of their weapons were becoming hot to touch adding to the uncomfortable conditions. White and red phosphorous rounds added to the multi-coloured smokescreen now cloaking the battleground around the bridgehead. The weight of German fire was intended to keep the paras' heads down to allow the Fallschirmjaeger to sneak around the flanks of the bridge perimeter. All the time the paras were pinned down, the Fallschirmjaeger units were creeping forward, using any dead ground or hard cover to crawl to within feet of the British positions. Operating in small disciplined teams, sometimes only in small groups or acting alone, they were constantly probing forward in a myriad of separate infantry assaults.

One of the defenders was George Pratt of 1 Para:

> My Bren gun hardly stopped firing the whole time. Then, one of the lads next to me was shot in the face; his head literally exploded and sent bits of tissue and bone all over me. Like an automaton, he staggered backwards before colliding with the back wall, and slid down it, leaving a big blood smear where the back of his head had contacted the wall. Not five minutes later, the young lad who'd landed with me got killed; he was flung onto his back having been shot in the chest, blood pouring out of the wound. How I didn't get killed I don't know as enough bullets were coming through the slit to kill a dozen of us. Jerry was only 80 yards (72m) away by then. At that range it was difficult not to hit someone, and I can honestly say I shot quite a few, but the ammo was my main worry and I had to be very frugal when I fired to make it last.[7]

Despite the enormous pressure being exerted on the paras, they kept their nerve. They fought until the last possible moment in each trench, before shouting to their mates in neighbouring positions to provide covering fire as they moved to new firing positions, ready to resume the fight once more.

With every brief respite, or even when still under fire, the men were continually recharging their magazines with fresh rounds from their webbing pouches. Each man would reload his own magazines, or a section or fire team would give their empty magazines to one or two men to recharge all the magazines, whilst their comrades kept watch or kept fighting. Corporals and sergeants were now really earning their pay, constantly checking on the levels of ammunition held by each man. Shouts of 'ammo state' were permeating the sound of the battlefield. The ammo state would be calculated by the NCO and then ammunition redistributed as necessary to leave each man with a similar amount of ammunition. This also ensured the NCOs and officers knew just how much firepower they had left. They were using the bare minimum of ammunition required to hold back the enemy but, at any moment, they might need to provide rapid fire to fend off yet another counter-attack so they had to keep some ammunition in reserve. As ammo states lowered throughout the day, the men were repeatedly told to mark their targets clearly before firing. There was not enough ammunition to fire at possible or likely enemy positions simply to provide a sense of comfort. Only definite targets could be engaged.

Each man had become embroiled in his own personal war. Often fighting against an enemy only a few feet away and with both unaware of the bigger picture of the battle unfolding. Each man knew that his only immediate priority was to defend the ground he stood on and not allow the enemy to take it from him. Individual drills, such as clearing stoppages on weapon systems, now came to the fore. All those hours of training meant that stoppages by touch could be cleared in seconds, often while they continued to scan their arcs of fire. For any lengthier stoppages, the men would inform their comrades by shouting 'stoppage'. Another man would then provide rapid or covering fire to suppress the enemy and provide time for the stoppage to be cleared and get all weapons back into the battle. Any respite in the fighting now was a short sharp window for each man to complete some personal admin. Just a few seconds' lull in the battle would allow the men time to cover each other so that they could go to the toilet where they were, recharge magazines, have a sip of water or check over their equipment. Pearson made good use in any lull in the battle to start evacuating the wounded across the bridge. 1 Para had already lost 20 men killed and 50 wounded of the 250 men at the bridge. He knew the time was approaching to withdraw from the northern bridgehead before he and his men were wiped out.

There was glimmer of hope for the besieged paras at 16:00 when a squadron of Spitfires flew high overhead at 10,000 feet (3,000m). Yellow smoke was immediately popped to get their attention. However, the Spitfires either didn't see it or were preoccupied with their existing mission and carried on flying northwards towards Catania. This was the first and last time that any Allied air support was seen that day.

With a lack of air or armoured support, the Germans were now using over-whelming firepower to reduce one British positions after another. George Pratt remembers: 'The final blow was the shoulder-fired panzerfaust anti-tank rocket. The Fallschirmjaeger began using them once they were within range, about 60 yards (54m). First, they took out the bunker on my left, and then it was my turn'.[8] Trenches and the two pillboxes were lost in short time. There was no cover left for the beleaguered defenders to fight from.

With the loss of the northern pillboxes, the end was approaching for the northern bridgehead. The Germans were now fully encircling the northern bridgehead and were sending out constant probing attacks. The paras were hemmed into a small patch of land at the entrance of the bridge. They were almost out of ammunition, taking casualties and up against an enemy growing in numbers and firepower all the time. Despite their gallant resistance, the defenders had their backs against the river. At 17:05 a German armoured fighting vehicle arrived close to the northern bridgehead and took cover in the farmhouse closest to the bridge. Whilst the Fallschirmjaeger provided it with target information, it began engaging the pillboxes on the south end of the bridge. The Germans were planning to charge through the defenders on the northern bridgehead and straight over the bridge to start attacking the southern bridgehead. The arrival of German armour made up Pearson's mind for his next course of action. He made the decision that even if he couldn't fully hold the bridge, then he could at least recover his men to the south of the bridge and provide a blocking force there, preventing the Germans from getting across and securing the bridge for themselves. The men who had fought all day for control of the bridge, would now have to make a life-or-death surge towards the southern bank in order to continue the fight.

CHAPTER FIFTEEN

'Tactical Retreat'

With fresh German reinforcements of men, and now armour, approaching the bridge from the north, Pearson had made the command decision to pull his forces back to the south end of the bridge. Although this relinquished full control of the bridge, it still allowed the paras to deny the bridge to the enemy, and would allow the bridge to act as a springboard for the tanks of the 4th Armoured Brigade to turn the tables on the Fallschirmjaeger and launch an armoured assault against them. The hope was that as the paras fought a rearguard action, they would effectively be buying time for the 4th Armoured Brigade to arrive. This small action at the bridge, and the necessary concession to the Germans of the para's foothold on the north bank, also signalled the temporary strategic loss of the Eighth Army's foothold over the Simeto.

Pearson gave his men a rallying cry to 'fight the Barbarians off for as long as possible'.[1] This gave him time to clear the bridgehead of casualties and coordinate covering fire from the south bank of the river for when he ordered his men to make the dash across the bridge and into the river for the relative safety of the southern bridgehead.

The determination of the paras' defence of the northern bridgehead, coupled with the vast number of aircraft they had seen in the sky the previous evening, led the Germans to believe that they were up against a much larger force than was actually present. In addition the paras had put up a barrage of fire to meet every enemy attack, which hadn't given the impression that they were low on ammunition. The paras were changing their firing positions after every couple of rounds that they fired, in order to prevent an enemy sniper zeroing in on their position, but also serving to give the overall impression to the Germans that they were dealing with more firing positions, and hence paras, than there actually were. The Germans were probably expecting a full-strength brigade to be on the Primosole Bridge, as that would be the numbers required to take and hold an objective of this size according to military doctrine. As a result, the Germans now began to consolidate their recent gains and bombard the bridge again, so that they could recover their own strength ready for a final push against the bridge. However, they were only fighting against

A Vickers machine gun. Despite a lack of ammunition, they were key to holding back the German attacks against the bridgehead. (Courtesy of Air Assault Museum)

two companies' worth of under-gunned and low-on-ammunition men who were about to perfect a tactical withdrawal under the noses of the Fallschirmjaeger.

The pace of the battle was reaching a crescendo as the Fallschirmjaeger inched ever closer to the bridge with the paras unable to lay down enough fire to hold them off due to lack of ammunition for all the weapon systems. In contrast most of the Germans and Italians had been transported to the battlefield by truck with extra loads of ammunition, enabling them to outgun the weight and length of the British fire being aimed at them in return. The sole Vickers machine gun was down to its last belt of ammunition after having provided invaluable fire support throughout the day's fighting, and was only able to provide shorter and shorter bursts of fire as the afternoon wore on. Ammunition had to be conserved, only definite targets were receiving a one-second burst from the Vickers.

In contrast, as more and more Germans arrived they brought more ammunition and more machine guns with them. The scales were constantly tilting further and further in the Germans' favour as the fight wore on.

The paras were well trained, like their Fallschirmjaeger opponents, and were difficult targets to spot. The paras were leopard-crawling between what little cover there was in order to keep the enemy guessing their whereabouts and also to attempt to find a clear shot to return at the enemy. The men were crawling with their heads down and their bodies as close as possible to the ground to avoid becoming a target. They rested their weapons across their forearms, ensuring the barrel stayed out of the dirt, so as to prevent a blockage to the muzzle.

Pearson began to issue orders for the men to draw close back to the bridge. Some men now had to sprint under fire to disengage from the enemy. As they crossed open ground they were covered by their comrades' fire. After a couple of rounds of covering fire to get the enemies' heads down, the man breaking cover would, if possible, take a few steps back in order to provide a run up and so break cover with a rolling start then launch himself at full pace with his weapon in one hand or still on the shoulder ready to fire, towards the next piece of cover. The first few yards were run in a zigzag fashion, known as 'hard-targeting', to make it more difficult for any enemy snipers to get a fix on their prey before they could take cover again. Often the cover near the riverbank was only tall grass, reeds and bushes. Whilst this provided cover from view, it did not provide cover from fire. So, the men had to rely more on firing accurately back at the enemy to keep their heads down. Once the first man had taken a bound and found some cover, he began sending suppressing fire back towards the enemy, allowing his buddy to make a bound backwards. This process continued until Pearson's men were in touching distance of the bridge.

As well as avoiding the snipers' bullets, the 88s now resumed their campaign of sending high-explosive shrapnel rounds against the paras. With each incoming artillery round a cloud of earth was kicked up leaving its signature of a smoking shell crater, whilst the men in the area of the explosion were covered with another layer of Sicilian soil. The ground became littered with broken branches from the vineyards and lumps of earth and rock thrown up by explosions. Having learnt their lessons from North Africa the men had dug in and prepared defensive positions during the night, and these precautions saved many casualties from the effects of the airburst shrapnel rounds but still the noise and concussion of artillery rounds landing close by was enough to test any of the paratroopers' nerves. The combination of rounds could be distinguished by some of the more experienced men on the ground. The distant plop of mortars launching and then the whistle of their near-vertical descent could be told apart from the high-velocity screech of the 88 rounds coming in on a much flatter trajectory. The roar of the friendly naval rounds – although far too few were being delivered from the paras' point of view – could be heard roaring towards the battlefield around Johnny I from miles out to sea and then exploding in a ground-shaking concussive blast sending shock-waves through the ground for hundreds of metres.

Pearson constantly positioned himself at the front line. It aided his decision-making, as he could see first-hand the enemy's advance, but it also allowed his men to see him, moving around under fire and encouraging them to fight back. He came across one private who was taking cover at the bottom of his trench, apparently deciding that he had had enough.

"What's wrong?' asked Pearson, kneeling beside him.

'I've got a sore head,' said the man. 'The noise is driving me mad. I cannae go on.'

Pearson straightened up and as he did so his boot flashed out.

'And now you've got a sore backside as well. Get on with your job.' The man, grinning, picked up his rifle again as a great roar of laughter came from his mates. A hundred yards away, the Germans listened to the mad *Britischers* enjoying a joke in the midst of battle, facing almost certain annihilation, and they shook their heads in amazement".[2]

Whereas the last few casualties were returned across the bridge to the MDS, those who had been killed were hastily buried in shell-scrapes with a rudimentary cross or weapon dug into the ground bayonet-first with their helmet on top to signify the burial place. Some unfortunately had to be left where they had fallen until they could be properly recovered after the fighting.

Pearson made his final tour of the perimeter and decided that the Germans were drawing breath – this was his best chance of getting his troops intact across the river. His plan for a tactical withdrawal, which married up the remnants of 1 and 3 Para into a single force concentrated on the southern bank, was now put into action.

As the order was given for the men to wade across the river and back to the southern bridgehead, they began to organise themselves so that a platoon at a time crossed the river whilst being covered from a rearguard on the northern bank. Yeldham would lead the remnants of 3 Para straight across the bridge first. With covering fire, they ran across the bridge and were almost in cover before the enemy could react. It wouldn't be possible for 1 Para to follow the same route now that the Germans had lined their sights up on the bridge. 1 Para elected to wade across the river underneath the bridge as the safest means of crossing back over the Simeto. They moved through the smoke and thunder of war to the river's edge whilst a few men stayed by the bridge to provide covering fire.

Sergeant Padureano, a Spaniard whose parents had moved to Norfolk before the war and who coveted gaining his British citizenship, was helping to cover the withdrawal of his comrades. He had already earned the Military Medal in North Africa for carrying out similar actions and was now repeating his heroic feat at the northern end of the Primosole Bridge. However, before the withdrawal was complete Padureano was hit and killed under the weight of incoming German fire. His determination was an inspiration for the paras to keep up the fight.

Pearson's withdrawal of his battalion needed to be quick whilst he still had the element of surprise on his side.

The remaining Vickers and Bren guns were concentrated around the southern end of the bridge to give covering fire for the north-bridgehead men to move under the cover of the bridge itself back to the south bank. Ammunition for essential weapon systems, like the Bren guns, was now being expended. Luckily, due to the men's training, captured enemy weapons were being employed into the defences.

Sergeant Douglas-Kerr ran out of ammunition for his Bren gun but then switched to using a captured MG42 to provide covering fire for men to move back across the bridge. He continued firing until the MG42 too ran out of ammunition. He then withdrew to the southern side of the bridge when ordered to do so. He was awarded a Military Medal for his actions.

Likewise, Private Lewis of 1 Para manned his Bren gun all day and covered the retreat of the brigade away from the bridge, inflicting heavy casualties on the advancing Germans. He too was awarded the Military Medal.

George Pratt of 1 Para was manning his Bren gun when the order came to evacuate the north side of the bridge:

> I got the order that I had to hold on and give the wounded men cover as they withdrew over the bridge. I was praying that they would get a move on so that I could get the hell out of there before the bunker got flattened. When I heard the whistle, I knew it was time to move, and none too soon, as the moment I skedaddled out that door there was a huge explosion and I was thrown to the ground. I got up and sprinted across the bridge.[3]

The wall of covering fire put up by the rearguard allowed the bulk of the defenders to cross the Simeto and begin digging in once more on the southern bank.

Whilst being covered by a few of their brave comrades at the bridgehead, the remainder of 1 Para were entering the cool water of the Simeto. Clutching their rifles, machine guns and any remaining precious ammunition, the paratroopers moved through the reeds and down the banks of the river to the water's edge. Here they waded through the Simeto and up the southern bank. NCOs from 1 Para were there to direct the men into covered positions as quickly as possible, to get them out of harm's way and also to maintain the element of surprise for the remainder of the rearguard to begin their withdrawal without too much Fallschirmjaeger attention.

The men who had been on the south bank, watched their fellow paratroopers approaching across the river, with wounded men being helped across, bringing home the intensity of the fighting that they had endured on the other side of the bridgehead against the most determined attacks of the Germans. The Germans were taken by surprise at the swift extraction of the northern defenders to the southern bank. They continued to probe the northern perimeter defences for 30 minutes after the paras had evacuated their positions. As soon as the Germans realised their mistake they immediately moved up to the bridge in order to resume the fight. An earlier minefield which had been laid by the engineers with captured German Teller mines now exploded and threw a cloud of dust into the sky above the bridge.

It is testament to the discipline of the men that they withdrew in an orderly fashion from the north side of the bridge to the south side. Many units who were under-gunned against a superior force of Fallschirmjaeger supported by tanks, artillery and airpower may well have surrendered or been routed and retreated in a mass of confusion. The fact that the paras were able to maintain a steady tactical withdrawal whilst holding their front line against Fallschirmjaeger attacks was due to the discipline of the men who unquestionably followed orders and of the officers who withdrew the men in a timely fashion. The low numbers of British prisoners taken attests to the fact that they were not routed or overrun but withdrew tactically as a cohesive unit. This allowed the paras to conduct a phased withdrawal before they were overrun but also slowed the German advance whilst inflicting maximum damage on the enemy. The pillboxes on the south side of the bridge also managed to use some of the last of their ammunition to put down a wall of covering fire to hold the Fallschirmjaeger back and allow the paras to withdraw in an orderly fashion.

Once the paras had safely withdrawn to the south of the bridge to strengthen the bridgehead there, they were not actively pursued by the Fallschirmjaeger. When they finally appeared at the north end of the bridge and looked like preparing a dash across the bridge, they were met with volleys of rapid suppressing fire from the regrouped paras which put paid to thoughts of charging across the bridge.

As quickly as they had left their positions and crossed the river, the paras were straight back into new defensive positions and ready to continue the fight. The Germans would have noted the professionalism of paras as they continued the fight despite being outnumbered and pushed back, a skill that the Fallschirmjaeger themselves had to learn in Russia. The British decision to reorganise their defences on the south of the bridge allowed them to still deny the bridge to the Germans, thus protecting the Allied push towards Catania from a German counter-attack but by clinging on to the southern bridgehead, as well as the Johnny features, they were also providing a springboard to recapture the bridge and breakout towards the Catania Plain once the supporting infantry and tanks arrived from main invasion force.

The cover on the south side of the river did not provide protection from enemy bullets and artillery. The men were trying to dig in to fresh positions or increase the size and depth of existing trenches but they also had to have one eye looking out for a sudden German rush across the bridge or across the river at any moment.

The main defensive points on the southern bridgehead were the two pillboxes, as at the northern bridgehead. The pillboxes stood at a junction of the main road heading towards the bridge and a side track joining from the west. The two pillboxes were covered in the debris from the shelling. Telegraph poles, jumbled telegraph wire and splintered trees lay all around as well as an Italian mule-train of seven dead mules which added to the stench of the battlefield. This junction was known to the men as Dead Horse Corner. The ad-hoc units were placed in an all-round defensive position with 360-degree inter-locking arcs of fire, to prevent the Fallschirmjaeger from attempting to move round to the flank and pour fire onto the paras from the side. The paras' positions were slightly spread to avoid artillery shells destroying their positions but also to provide fall-back positions and allow for mutually supporting fire positions to support each other in the face of rushing German assaults.

The fighting quickly became a cross-river duel between the Bredas, Brens and Vickers on the British side of the Simeto and the MG42s on the German side. The

Germans, realising that they had been out-smarted and that the bridge's defence was now centred around the southern end, waited for their 88s and a Sturmgeschutz self-propelled gun to be brought up closer to the north end of the bridge in order to pound the defences of the southern bridgehead prior to a Fallschirmjaeger assault.

In the meantime, the German artillery focussed once again on the pillboxes on the south side of the river. Lieutenant Bob Gammon, was inside the pillbox on the eastern side of the road on the north bank:

> I remember the bead curtain as in a continental barber's shop hanging over the open doorway, and I thought at the time of the good old training tag: 'Cover from view but not from fire.' I picked up an Italian carbine and started to sharp-shoot across the river until Sergeant Baber suggested that I desist before the enemy observed the flash of the puerile weapon. He was right. The others with their good British rifles could do the job better and without revealing our position. Time wore on. At any moment the 8th Army must come. At any moment their armoured cars would come sweeping down the road and up to the bridge, but time wore on and no 8th Army came… I suddenly noticed that the pillbox on my extreme left, fortunately empty, was taking a bashing. To this day I swear as each round of solid shot struck it heeled over and bounced up again. Perhaps it was the heat haze or the dust, or my fevered imagination, or perhaps – it was made of reinforced concrete – it did. I realised that each pillbox in turn was to take its punishment, and that mine was next… I watched the dusty white bridge, keeping my head well to the side of the embrasure… Suddenly there was a crash, fumes, dust, and something hit me in the chest. I could hardly see… Where's the door? Had it collapsed? A shaft of light and I groped my way out into the blinding sunshine'.[4]

Dazed, he picked himself up out of the debris and staggered back over the bridge in a hail of rifle fire. A medical orderly stepped out from the surgical post at the side of the bridge and dragged him in for treatment.

The Germans occupied the north end of the bridge after realising that the Red Devils had withdrawn to carry on the fight from a better position. Some stragglers were still trying to cross the bridge though. Corporal Stanion had fought all day at the northern end of the bridge:

> We went back, and I got hit in the back of the neck. I was knocked out for some length of time. When I came to I saw a couple of German machine gunners in the ditch where our troops should have been. A shell burst in front of me and under cover of this I ran back to the bridge. The battalions had gone. Some Italians I met with tried to explain that they had gone over to the other side. I could not cross the bridge because it was under fire, so I went into the reeds and there ran into some Jerries and was captured. I sat there for an hour or two while they argued amongst themselves as to who was to take me back. Then apparently our chaps started firing into the reeds. Two Jerries got hit in the head straight away. The others ran back and I crawled along through the reeds, which were smouldering in parts. I got down to a point where they went into the water, into which I slipped and dog-paddled over to the other side, where I lay. I was in full view of both sides and feared that, if I tried to identify myself, I would be shot. It was then about four-thirty in the afternoon. I lay there waiting for darkness to come.[5]

The Germans occupied the northern pillboxes and used these defensive positions to begin engaging the southern pillboxes in preparation for a charge across the bridge. Sergeant Anderson's 6-pounder had been in action throughout the day and now used some of its last rounds engaging the northern pillboxes. After two direct hits the fire coming from the pillboxes fell silent and allowed the paras to reorganise themselves without the burden of heavy machine-gun fire sweeping over their heads. Shortly, a Sturmgeschutz self-propelled gun appeared on the battlefield from the barns on the north side of the river. It began to engage the southern pillboxes and within a few shots had destroyed both. Lance Corporal Osborne recalled 'they brought up a short range direct hit, pillbox buster, and he just lined them up on our pillboxes one after the other, and he blew them flat to the ground. Some men escaped from the blast'.[6] With the enforced evacuation of the pillboxes, the German firing switched to the trenches of the dug-in paras amongst the reeds of the riverbank.

The intensity of the bullets flying now increased as the Germans focussed on suppressing the southern bridgehead. The incoming zip of rounds slashed their way through the reeds towards the defenders' positions. The crack of bullets whistled as they passed overhead. Thuds could be heard and felt as rounds dug into the ground. Pings echoed through the air as rounds and shrapnel ricocheted off the metal structure of the bridge. Warnings were shouted in both English and German as both sides tried to identify enemy troops firing at them from new positions, to avoid friendly troops from being hit from unexpected angles or out-flanked. The concussive force could be felt of both incoming and outgoing grenades exploding. The blasts were kicking up fragments of stone and shrapnel, which then rained down on the surrounding area. The smoke and dust from explosions added to the fog of war covering the battlefield. Wounded men's shouts for medics rang out and were audible to both sets of troops as both sides tried to recover their wounded colleagues and get them out of the line of fire so that they could be treated. Heads of men popped up from cover and then disappeared just as quickly, to reappear moments later in a different position as the fighting men tried to ascertain what exactly was happening and where the enemy were.

This all added to the confusion of pin-pointing each other's positions and estimating numbers of attackers and defenders. The fluidity of the front line didn't allow for a second's rest. The men had to be alert not only to prevent their own position from being attacked but also to take advantage of any mistake made by the enemy. A single wrong move could be lethal as both sides were crack shots and were actively scanning the ground for the briefest glimpse of their opponents. Some men became pinned down and found themselves in the hopeless position of having to play dead or simply lie very still behind the thin cover of the reeds in order not to attract any further fire. They could see their mates in safe positions only a matter of metres away but knew that they couldn't move until the Germans switched their attention and fire to another area of the battlefield. Some would take the chance of a quick sprint to get into cover or crawl, whilst remaining as flat as they could to the ground, to make themselves as small a target as possible.

After an hour of suppressing fire, at 18:00, Stangenberg now planned a charge across the bridge with the intention of securing the southern end of the bridge and dispersing the defenders. Stangenberg also knew, unlike his British opponents, that 2 Para were bottled up on Johnny I, which meant that the defenders had nowhere to go other than surrender or head for the delayed Allied ground forces. He planned a direct infantry assault on the bridge, supported by artillery and machine-gun fire.

As the Fallschirmjaeger tried to surge across the bridge they were repulsed by heavy rapid fire from the paras on the south bank. The bridge was swept with fire, ricocheting off the steel girders, and causing mass casualties for the Germans. As quickly as the attack started, it ended, with the dead littering the bridge and the living and wounded crawling back to their lines for safety. If they didn't know already that the 1st Parachute Brigade would continue to stand and fight from the south bank, they did now.

Following the attempted dash across the bridge, Stangenberg ordered Fassl to attempt a flanking manoeuvre to the east by crossing the river 400 yards (360m) downstream to attempt to turn the British flank. Stangenberg had realised that that a very slow battle of attrition was taking place and he was keen to take the bridge as soon as possible. His own attack on the northern bridgehead was proving costly and at this stage he decided to stretch the tight perimeter of the paras. He called on supporting heavy machine-gun fire from Laun's unit to the south, still occupying Johnny II, to be directed against the bridgehead.

1st Parachute Brigade was now being attacked from north, east and south in an ever-shrinking perimeter. Fassl's Signals Battalion moved closer to the edge of the north bank of the Simeto, 400 metres to the east of the bridge. Using the reeds and raised riverbank, they managed to stay out of view of the paras. Here they began observing the southern bank to check for any British presence and whether they had been spotted themselves before they began attempting to ford the river. Whilst the officers and senior NCOs scanned the far bank for signs of enemy movement, the junior NCOs were busy getting the men organised to begin crossing the river when the signal was given. After waiting for five minutes to ensure that the bank was clear, the decision was made to proceed with the crossing and carry out the flanking manoeuvre against the paras' eastern flank. No British movement was detected as they were still busy fighting off the Fallschirmjaeger around the more immediate area of the bridgehead.

A platoon-size advance party slowly slid down the six-foot-high (2m) north bank and began wading through the cool waters of the Simeto, covered by their comrades in over-watch positions on the north bank. The hunched figures of the Fallschirmjaeger moved cautiously but as quickly as possible across the open water of the river fearing a possible ambush whilst in this compromised position. Once the platoon gained the far bank they immediately fanned out and began the process of scanning the ground ahead of them again for any further signs of the paras. After satisfying themselves that they had caught the paras by surprise they signalled back to the remainder of the battalion to begin crossing whilst they kept watch on the south bank. Section by section the Germans crossed the river and collected on the south bank. Fassl left a small rear party to guard the fording point then moved his battalion out into the cover of the reeds and begin their advance to contact with the paras' flank positions.

The Fallschirmjaeger had the opportunity to gain surprise on the paras and they attempted to maintain the secrecy of their upcoming manoeuvre by crawling through the cover of the reeds, sacrificing speed for maintaining the element of concealment. Their movement had been spotted by the British though, and once again highlighted their fire discipline by waiting for the best time to strike at the Germans. At the single word of command, a barrage of well-aimed mortar and machine-gun fire halted the advancing Germans. The ground around was erupting under the impact pf mortar rounds, whilst the flimsy cover of the reeds was being raked with machine-gun bullets. Some Fallschirmjaeger stood up and sprinted back to the riverbank to get themselves out of the killing zone. Others chose to crawl back and stay in the cover of the reeds. Their direction of travel was all one way though, backwards. Fassl's failed flanking manoeuvre had stopped short of reaching the bridge but it had succeeded in gaining a foothold on the southern bank and building the pressure on the defenders of the bridgehead even further. This action had also used up precious ammunition – machine guns and mortars now had their firing pins removed and were abandoned.

By 18:45, only 24 hours after leaving North Africa, the defenders of the bridge had survived a horrific parachute drop and then fought all day. Their ammunition, and energy, was now exhausted. The reeds all around them were on fire and the smoke and flames were slowly closing in on them like a noose. Behind this smokescreen was the ever-lurking presence of the advancing Fallschirmjaeger.

Lathbury now had to make an all-important decision. His and Pearson's earlier plan to withdraw his forces into a concentration on the southern bridgehead had only lasted a mere two hours before ammunition was dangerously low again and the threat of being out-flanked and captured was increasing with every passing minute.

The lull from the firing on the Johnny positions earlier in the day had led Lathbury to believe that the Germans had overrun the Johnny positions and that 2 Para were now out of the fight. The ridgeline could be clearly seen from the bridge and Lathbury had watched in the morning as small-arms fire and mortar rounds crashed into the 2 Para positions. With the reduction in firing in the afternoon, as the Fallschirmjaeger instead began to focus on the bridge and leave 2 Para bottled up, Lathbury had taken this as a sign that the ridgeline had been taken. With no sign of the approaching 4th Armoured Brigade, Lathbury had to choose between a fight to the death at the bridge or attempt a second tactical withdrawal to the Johnny hills. From there, he could provide a fire base to continue to harass the Primosole Bridge, ready for when ground forces approached, and then they could launch a counter-attack for control of the bridge once again.

With a dwindling number of defenders at the bridge and an even more dwindling supply of ammunition, at 19:35 Lathbury made the decision to pull back towards the Johnny hills and continue to provide suppressing fire onto the bridge from there. He called in all available officers and senior NCOs in the vicinity of the brigade headquarters and ordered them to pass the withdrawal warning order onto the men still hunkered down in their various foxholes. The men were to wait until after last light and then start covering the distance of just over one kilometre back to Johnny I. As the sun began to set at 20:15, he would wait a further hour until 21:15 to start moving the men to safety under the cover of darkness.

The men maintained their positions, covering their arcs and waiting for yet another German attack. As they settled into their positions for the evening and waited for the onset of the Sicilian night they were resigned to a hard fight throughout the next ten hours from an enemy creeping forward under the cover of darkness. Many of the men expected to be dead or prisoners by the time the sun next came up in the sky. However, the transition from day to night gave the men an opportunity to have an impromptu stand-to at dusk and provided a window to take a breath from the fighting and check their kit and themselves over. Ammunition states were taken by the NCOs and ammunition redistributed to where it was needed the most. Much of the rifle ammunition was moved to the Bren guns, leaving the riflemen desperately short. The Vickers gun guarding the southern end of the bridge was also down to its last belt of ammunition and could only reply with short bursts of fire at enemy movement over on the opposite bank.

The men took it in turns to slide down into the bottom of their foxholes and have a brief moment away from the battle raging all around them. Just those few inches of cover below ground seemed like a safe place to be right now after the day's heavy fighting. They just had time to take a few swigs of water, have a quick snack and check their kit before slowly rising once more to their ground-level look-out points of their positions so that their mates could then take their turn to carry out their own admin.

Stainforth remembers Brigade-Major Hunter appearing at his position and relaying Lathbury's order. 'The Brigadier has given the order to abandon the bridge. Collect as many men as you can and make your way back to our own forces over the hills to the south. Our tanks can't be far away now. Clear out of here and go like hell before the enemy comes through'.[7] The bulk of the brigade moving as a single unit would soon be spotted by the Germans. It was better for the men to spread out in small groups and thus present smaller targets for any watching snipers. Hunter stayed with a small rearguard to cover the men's withdrawal before heading south himself. His actions around the fighting for the bridgehead throughout the entire day earned him an immediate Military Cross.

At each position the order was relayed and the men were told to pass the message onto neighbouring positions. New shell-scrapes and trenches had been dug throughout the day by a mixture of different sub-units within the perimeter. The paratroopers now had to make sure that the order was passed to everyone that they could find, so as to not leave any man behind. Each man now became a link-man and crawled to all the positions in their immediate area to pass the message and confirm that their neighbours had received, or had already received, the message to withdraw to the Johnny I.

As soon as they received the message they began to organise themselves into small groups and formulated a quick plan on what to do next. The firing from Johnny I had died down during the afternoon and many of the men at the bridge were aware of this and assumed that the hill had been overrun by the Fallschirmjaeger. Some still decided to head for the 2 Para positions in the hope that the Fallschirmjaeger had instead been fought to a standstill and retreated. As no enemy incoming fire was received from the hills behind the bridgehead during the afternoon, it was felt that 2 Para must be low on ammunition but still holding firm on the hilltop otherwise, surely, the Fallschirmjaeger machine guns and mortars would have been sweeping the bridgehead by now. Other believed that the Fallschirmjaeger were atop the hill and instead opted to skirt around the hills to the east and west in order to regain Allied lines in the form of the advancing 50th Division. The division was already eight hours late arriving at the bridge and so must surely be not too far away by now.

Once each group had made their decision on what to do next, they began to cautiously emerge from their positions and began to tactically move towards the numerous irrigation ditches criss-crossing the southern open ground leading towards the Johnny hills. Each group split itself into two halves, with one half covering whilst the other half moved to the next piece of cover. They repeated this pattern until they were far enough away from the bridgehead to then start moving in patrol order over the countryside.

Pathfinders Joe Smith and Stan Brown had remained for most of the day in a slit trench near the southern end of the bridge. Once the Sicilian sun was high in the mid-morning sky, they had moved to the shade under a Horsa wing and there they dug a fresh slit trench. They remained there until 19:00 when they realised that there was noise and movement from the other slit trenches. On moving to the neighbouring slit-trench they found it empty. They crawled along a ditch to find out was happening and were told by Captain Gammon, sitting by the pillbox where he had been recently wounded, to join the rest of the brigade in moving in small groups up to the high ground of the 2nd Battalion's position. Using an orange grove as cover they made their way up the slopes of Johnny I. Upon arrival they were greeted with a cup of tea and given a position to defend on the hilltop's perimeter.[8]

The discipline and professionalism of the brigade still held firm during this dangerous manoeuvre as they could expect to bump into German formations at any time. The officers and NCOs had to control the men and ensure that they resisted the temptation to send a final volley of fire at the Germans. They needed to maintain the element of surprise in order to melt away and also needed to conserve their precious ammunition as they did not know whether they would be walking into another battle once they reached the Johnny hills.

The Germans remained blissfully unaware of the paratroopers withdrawing from right under their noses. The remaining Bren and Vickers machine guns kept up a suppressing fire on the far bank in order to keep the Germans' heads down and unable to observe the paras' movements. The machine-gun fire also gave the impression to the Fallschirmjaeger that the bridge would be contested until the Germans attacked and overran the paratroopers once and for all.

The 6-pounder of Sergeant Anderson was left in situ and engaged the pillboxes around the bridgehead to provide not only covering fire but also noise to conceal the movement of the paras southwards. The remaining two 6-pounders were wheeled by their crews back in the direction of Allied lines where they met up with the advancing Eighth Army the next morning. Once the bulk of the men had slipped away into the dark of the night, then Anderson was to hook his gun up to the jeep and head straight down Highway 114 to safety. He eventually managed to leave just as the Germans began to react and send incoming small-arms in the direction of his gun. The three 6-pounders rendezvoused near Johnny I and made their way through the night to a farmhouse to the south and waited for the advancing Allied ground forces. Shortly after reaching the farm, they were joined by a group from 2 Para led by Lieutenant Tansley, commander of the Airborne Artillery's B Troop, along with a haul of Italian prisoners that they had captured on their way to the bridge after being dropped miles to the south during the jump.

One unit that couldn't be moved, however, was the 16th (Parachute) Field Ambulance main dressing station, due to the amount of equipment that had been set up and the number of seriously injured. The dressing station remained in situ, which was now in no man's land between the bridge and the 'Johnny' hills. The operating theatre had dealt with all its serious casualties and was closed down for the night at 21:00 so that the staff could rest. At 05:45 the next morning an Italian officer appeared and 'captured' the MDS. On seeing that enemy and friendly troops were being treated, he left the medics to continue their work unopposed. Negotiations were completed in French as a common language and it was agreed that the Italian and German casualties would be collected later and moved to Catania. Only 30 minutes later though a patrol from 2 Para arrived to liberate the MDS once more. The medical teams would go on working through the night. In total they had 71 British casualties admitted, 31 Italian, five Germans and two civilians. Thirty-five operations were completed on the most serious casualties. Despite the large number of casualties only four British and three Italian casualties died once admitted to the dressing station and only two casualties died after being operated on.[9] Wheatley's devotion to duty in treating the serious casualties and patching up the men to return to the fight would earn him the DSO.

Whilst the Germans considered their next move towards finally dislodging the paratroopers from the southern bridgehead, most of the defenders were clear of the bridge and dispersed across the open ground to the south. Only when the Vickers and Brens delivered a final prolonged burst of fire until they ran out of ammunition and fell silent, did the Germans realise that it had been a ruse to merely give covering fire whilst the remnants of 1st Parachute Brigade melted away. The firing mechanism for the remaining Vickers was removed and thrown into the Simeto, whilst the gun itself was tossed into the nearest bush before the gun's crew, their rearguard job complete, began their own withdrawal.

Whilst the British completed their tactical withdrawal, the Fallschirmjaeger to the south of the river themselves were worrying about being cut off between the paratroopers at the bridge and the advancing land forces approaching from the south. At 18:00, the battalion HQ of the 1st Machine Gun Battalion was reconnoitred by two British scout cars arriving unexpectedly from the south. After a brief engagement, the vehicles withdrew but it was enough to convince the Fallschirmjaeger that they needed to start moving to the north bank of the river and live to fight another day.

At 19:30, Hauptmann Laun gave the order to make a tactical withdrawal to the north bank of the river. The Fallschirmjaeger had to leave their heavy kit behind and burn it. They marched with their prisoners northwards as the British paratroopers were moving southwards towards 2 Para's positions. 'To avoid being recognised by advancing enemy units, Hauptmann Laun resorts to a trick. He makes us take off our helmets and gets the Tommies marching between us to keep theirs on. It seems to work'.[10] After the hard fighting of the day, both sides now needed to link their units up and reorganise for the next phase of the battle. After the small-scale actions of the day, with small groups of Red and Green Devils fighting small, almost private, wars with each other, both sides knew that heavier support and numbers were approaching the battlefield and the battle would resort to a more set-piece strategic combat in its next phase. The Germans tidied up their newly captured north bank and evacuating their own wounded, as well as the captured paras, back to the hospital in Catania.

Back on top of Johnny I, the closeness of the fighting at the bridge had been readily apparent to Frost and 2 Para from their grandstand position. They were unable to make radio contact with 1 and 3 Para and also unable to directly offer the help of Captain Vere Hodge's naval firepower. However, Hodge did manage to bring down naval fire, scoring a direct hit on an enemy coastal artillery battery to the north-west of the bridge towards Catania which had been firing airburst rounds over the 1 and 3 Para positions. One further naval round scored a direct hit on the battery's ammunition dump, which exploded, silencing the battery. The black cloud signalling its destruction could clearly be seen from Johnny I and the bridge. Between 15:00 and 16:00 naval fire was also called down on a farm building to the south of Johnny II where enemy troops and transport were observed gathering. This was close to Martin Poppel's position with the 1st Company 1st Machine Gun Battalion. Poppel's unit took three casualties under bombardment. Oberjager Fischbeck and Jager Bader were both killed, whilst Feldwebel Jetter suffered a head wound. The Fallschirmjaeger removed themselves quickly from the area once they knew they had been spotted and their position made known to the British naval guns. Poppel and his men weren't impressed by the Allied navies' involvement in the land battle, seemingly out of harm's way at sea. 'Those dogs out there in their tubs can fire just like they are on manoeuvres and we're just sitting targets'.[11] The fleet, however, was suffering from Italian and German air attacks and HMS *Newfoundland*, which had provided such important fire support that morning, was torpedoed by Italian submarine *Ascianghi* only a few days later, in turn having to limp back to Britain for repairs using only her propellers to steer. Captain Hodge later received a Military Cross for his skill in bringing vital naval fire into the battle to support the paratroopers fighting that day.

The men of 2 Para had heard the bridge defenders approaching their hilltop positions. They began peering into the darkness for their comrades, trying to attract their attention to bring them into the new perimeter. The number of 1 and 3 Para survivors now entering the Johnny I perimeter meant there was much room to accommodate all the men in the limited slit trenches. Therefore, the Italian prisoners being kept in the battalion HQ yard were released but told to report back at first light.

The battlefield was now a fluid scene of moving parts as at around 19:45, as 1 and 3 Para were moving towards the 2 Para positions, the lead elements of the 6th DLI and their Sherman tanks began to appear to the south of Johnny I from the direction of Lentini.

Whilst the paratroopers were fighting for their survival at the Primosole Bridge, the DLI were leading their relieving force in the shape of the 50th (Northumbrian) Division and were expected at the Primosole Bridge by noon. They had begun their advance at dawn, just after the 1st Parachute Brigade had secured the Primosole Bridge. Slowed down by a series of delaying actions by the Germans, their timetable was behind schedule almost as soon as they started.

First they had to relieve the No. 3 Commando at the Malati Bridge 8 miles (13km) to the north of their start line.

Whilst the 1st Parachute Brigade had been approaching the Sicilian coastline, below them on the dark waves the landing craft of No. 3 Commando were also heading for the Sicilian coastline. They, similar to the paras, were tasked with capturing and holding the Malati Bridge, before being relieved by the 50th Division who were heading inland from their landing beaches at Avola and approaching Lentini. Some men of the 1st Parachute Brigade were actually dropped so far off course that they landed on top of the commandos.

The 50th Division didn't manage to reach the commandos until the afternoon, by which time they too had had to relinquish the bridge that they had captured but couldn't hold. The 50th Division, now hours behind schedule, then set off northwards for the Primosole Bridge, a further 6 miles (10km) to the north-east. Pearson's men were by this time fighting for their lives and withdrawing across to the southern bank. With another bridge destroyed in the Carlentini area, the infantry's support vehicles and armour were delayed whilst the infantry began to march to their objective. The vehicles of the 4th Armoured Brigade did not start moving again until 19:00 that evening, shortly before Brigadier Lathbury ordered the Primosole Bridge defenders to withdraw to 2 Para's positions on Johnny I. The 50th (Northumbrian) Division managed to reach Lentini later in the afternoon and were continually held up by enemy sniper fire, blocked roads and rearguard actions. The lead elements of the division, the 6th Durham Light Infantry with Sherman tank support, eventually reached a position only 1 mile (1.6km) from Johnny I but rather than link up with the paras or attempt to secure the bridge, they instead harboured up for the night.

Just after another German artillery round of shells exploded at midnight, a Sicilian farmer approached the 2 Para positions on Johnny I to inform them of approaching tanks from the south. Presuming this to be another German attempt to dislodge the remaining paras from the Primosole area, the men stood-to. The tank soon came into view and it was immediately identified as a Sherman of 4th Armoured Brigade. Men from 2 Para were sent down to link up with the advancing tanks and supporting infantry of the Durham Light Infantry (DLI). They told the paratroopers that they were to hold-up for the night 2 miles (3.2km) short of the bridge and then attack at first light with artillery support. However, their orders, which had been explicitly delivered directly from Montgomery, were to proceed at all speed to not only relieve 1st Parachute Brigade but also secure the bridges over the coastal road to allow for Montgomery's Army to race to Messina. The decision not to attempt to take the bridge by an armoured brigade at this critical time when the bridge was lightly defended by infantry, may well have allowed for an armoured thrust straight over the bridge that very night. Instead, the relieving force waited for daylight, giving the Fallschirmjaeger plenty of time to sight their 88s and MG42s, so that they were ready and waiting for the expected dawn attack on the bridge. There were chilling echoes of this incident in the failed ground force link-up with 1st Parachute Brigade at Arnhem only 15 months later.

Lieutenant Hoyer-Millar, 2 Para's intelligence officer, insisted to the newly arrived Durhams that the Johnny I position was weakly held by the under-strength paratroopers and required some of the tanks and Durhams to move up and help hold the position in case of a German counter-attack. He also stressed that the Durhams could use the high ground for an opportunity to see where they would be advancing in a few hours' time. As they sized up the task ahead of them, they were soon seen and welcomed to the fight. German tanks sent some speculative pot shots towards them from the northern bridgehead. Although the incoming rounds were off target, they succeeded, however, in keeping the British infantry and armour sight-seers off the ridgeline for the rest of the night.

Meanwhile, in his foxhole, Major Lonsdale finally had time to reflect on the actions of the day. He had taken over temporary command of 2 Para whilst Johnny Frost was receiving treatment and had led them in their desperate fight for survival on the top of Johnny I, for which he was later to be awarded the DSO for his leadership. Barely had he had time to reflect though, when he heard the rumble of approaching tanks in the darkness to the south. 'I thought I'd better say my prayers. Fortunately, they were the 44th RTR and the fellow who stuck his head out of the turret of the leading tank was in the First XV at Sandhurst with me'.[12] The sight of British armour arriving on the battlefield convinced the Germans to cancel any plans they had to attack the paratroopers on Johnny I again.

From their sentry positions on Johnny I, the British could see the Germans walking over their newly acquired bridge. Out of range of their small arms, the paras could only watch as they strung together a string of Teller mines in the middle of the bridge and detonated these. The resulting explosion sent an orange fireball into the still night sky. The paras expected the bridge that they had fought so hard for to simply collapse into the Simeto river below. The sound of the explosion took only a few seconds to reach travel the distance from the bridge to the ridgeline. Despite its impressive-looking explosion, when the smoke had cleared, it had in fact only blown a small hole in the centre of the road over the bridge but didn't damage the structure of the bridge itself. It was still possible for tanks and vehicles to pass over the damaged road to the other side.

After failing to destroy the bridge, the Fallschirmjaeger used the cover of darkness and lull in the battle to reorganise themselves, ready for a resumption of hostilities in the morning. Reinforcements in the form of the 1st Fallschirmjaeger Pioneer Battalion, led by Hauptmann Heinz Paul Adolff, had parachuted near Catania that evening and now arrived at the northern bridgehead to be briefed by Stangenberg. Adolff took up responsibility for the southern bridgehead. He placed his 2nd Company in reserve on the northern bank and moved his 1st and 3rd Companies forward over the bridge to take up positions on the southern end of the bridge. Fassl's Signal Battalion was now redeployed after their day's fighting to guard the harbour defences of Catania, as the Italian garrison had deserted. One of his companies remained in the sunken road to the north-west of the bridge, to help shore up the northern bridgehead, as a mobile reserve. The fresh Fallschirmjaeger troops were now ready and waiting for the next British attack.

Whilst the paras reorganised themselves, the two halves of the 1st Parachute Brigade which had been fighting separately at the bridge and at the Johnny hills, linked-up for the first time since leaving North Africa. They had a brief window to look for their mates and swap tales of how they had come to be on Johnny I. Only a small proportion of the men had managed to take part in the fighting. For those that had taken part in the battle, their losses had been high. Of the 295 men who had defended the bridge, more than one in three had become a casualty – 27 had been killed and 75 wounded[13] with a further 13 captured.[14]

It was now the turn of the DLI to attempt to force their way across the bridge.

CHAPTER SIXTEEN

'Relief at Last'

The forward elements of the DLI had caught their first glimpse of Primosole Bridge from their overnight sentry positions on top of Johnny I. It appeared to them to be a quick armoured drive for the bridge and then spread out into the fields on the other side of the river. There was an obvious chance that they would attract heavy fire as they crossed the bridge but the lack of demolition charges applied to the bridge implied that it wouldn't be blown as they crossed its steel framework.

After the previous night's evacuation of the bridgehead, the bulk of the 1st Parachute Brigade from around the bridge was still arriving on the Johnny hills in the early hours of 15 July. Lathbury, being one of the last to leave the bridgehead, only arrived at 2 Para's headquarters at 06:00 after marching through the night to evade capture. He wasn't too pleased to see the tanks of the 4th Armoured Brigade sitting behind the ridgeline when he eventually reached the 2 Para positions. He was further angered when he learned that they had been there since almost the same moment that he had given the order for his men to abandon the bridge just over 1km away. Support from the Sherman's guns would have been a welcome reply to the constant unanswered bombardment of the German guns for the last 24 hours and could well have helped to at least hold the bridge until further reinforcements arrived. Whilst the Durhams started to relieve the paras' positions the officers and senior NCOs of 1st Parachute Brigade now went to work to obtain some food and water for their men from the supplies on 50th Division's vehicles. Most men had parachuted into Sicily 24 hours before and had had little time to eat but had drunk most of their water ration under the unblinking heat of the sun. Medical supplies had been used up for the most severely wounded men and now there was a chance for the walking wounded to get attention from medical staff, to have their wounds cleaned and fresh bandages applied to prevent infection.

Just after Lathbury arrived, further tank fire was heard from the south of their position around Johnny I. Brigadier Lathbury sent out a reconnaissance patrol to investigate, which located the tanks and infantry of XIII Corps, which had halted short of the bridge the previous night. The tanks now positioned themselves for an assault on the bridge.

Whilst the relieving 4th Armoured Brigade was arriving, the paras could at last catch up on some much-needed rest and admin. After passing over temporary command of the brigade to Frost, at 09:15 Lathbury finally reported to the MDS for an operation on his wounds, 30 hours after being wounded by shrapnel from a grenade blast.

Pearson had sent his men back to rest under the command of 3 Para's second-in-command Major Cleasby-Thompson whilst he remained at the front with his provost sergeant, 'Panzer' Manser, and his batman Jock Clements, hoping to see the 9th Durham Light Infantry finish the job now that they had arrived with their complement of fresh troops, supported by Sherman tanks belonging to the 44th Royal Tank Regiment.

The Germans had likewise seen the arrival of the DLI and their supporting Sherman tanks, and feared that the tables had turned on them; their Fallschirmjaeger would now have to face enemy tanks and superior numbers of accompanying infantry.

Despite the heavy fighting for the bridge, the German strategic plan had called for the bridge to be abandoned and the pre-defined defences south of Catania, the Hauptkampflinie, to be manned as part of the overall plan for the defence of Sicily. However, Captain Stangenberg managed to convince his superiors that the bridge had been won back from the paratroopers and could be held, or at least used to delay, the Allied advance. That night three companies of Fallschirmjaeger,

Primosole Bridge seen from the west just after the fighting. (Kent and Sharpshooters Image)

The defences at the southern end of the bridge. The Johnny hills are in the distance. (Kent and Sharpshooters Image)

a battalion each from the 1st Fallschirmjaeger Pioneer Battalion, the 1st Battalion of the 4th Fallschirmjaeger Regiment and a battalion of the 1st Fallschirmjaeger Artillery Regiment, in total numbering some 450 men, were parachuted onto Catania airbases as reinforcements. These Fallschirmjaeger were hurried down to the Primosole Bridge. Two companies were moved to the south of the bridge to bolster the perimeter there, whilst the third company remained on the northern side of the river as a reserve. The 1st Fallschirmjaeger Machine Gun Battalion, after having borne the brunt of the fighting of the previous day, was moved to the west and remained in a defensive position on the northern bank. Fassl's remaining company from the Signal Battalion was placed on the sunken road as a mobile reserve.

The DLI's First Attack

Following a quick briefing from the para officers on what to expect at the bridge, at 07:30 the 9th Battalion DLI's advance moved off from its start-line. The 9th Battalion, Durham Light Infantry, supported by A and B Squadrons of the 44th Royal Tank Regiment, took the lead in the attack. They moved down the slopes of the Johnny I towards the bridge with the main road as their axis of advance. A Squadron was on the right and B Squadron on the left, supported by infantry from

9th DLI with bayonets fixed. The guns of the 24th and 98th Field Regiments RA were to provide fire support to the advance. The amount of military hardware at disposal for this counter-attack was in stark contrast of the firepower that the paras had been able to call on in the previous day's fighting. A smokescreen was also fired to cover the final approach to the bridge.

Their first objective was to secure Dead Horse Corner. Once this road junction was cleared they then moved towards the bridge and attempted to drive straight over it to the northern bank. The infantry were well spread and advancing at walking pace. The Fallschirmjaeger of Adolff's Pioneer Battalion on the north bank of the river marked their targets through their weapon sights but waited to open fire until the enemy approached the bridge. Suddenly, a wall of machine-gun fire began to scythe down the ranks of the DLI. MG42s opened fire on the exposed infantry from only 50 yards (45m) away whilst the 88s and 7.5cm Italian guns engaged the Sherman tanks. The Fallschirmjaeger also kept up constant machine-gun fire directed at the Sherman tanks, thus ensuring that they kept their hatches battened down and were therefore unable to spot targets to neutralise for the supporting infantry.

The Shermans and DLI infantry managed to rush the bridge and make it across to the north bank. Hand-to-hand fighting ensued but heavy casualties forced the DLI to retreat to the south of the bridge. Casualties numbered over 100, with 34 killed.[1] Three Sherman tanks accompanying them were knocked out by the German 88s, with one knocked out by an impromptu minefield laid on the east of the road

Men of the DLI dug-in just to the north end of the bridge. (Kent and Sharpshooters Image)

during the night. The DLI were forced to move back towards Johnny I to reorganise themselves for a second attempt that night.

The paras had had no access to tank support or concentrated artillery fire support over the past two days of battle. Yet even with this support, the Durhams were unable to take the bridge. This highlights the tenacity of the paras as they fought against the odds to hold the bridge for as long as they had.

The Germans, having inflicted a bloody nose on the DLI, now suffered an error in communication which caused 1 Company of the Fallschirmjaeger Engineer Battalion to withdraw to the north bank of the river. This allowed the Durhams to establish a position on the southern end of the bridge. This fortunate withdrawal by the Germans allowed the DLI to cover the bridge and prevent any enemy attempt to blow it up. Both sides took to sniping and mortaring each other from opposing ends of the bridge. The sniping became so intense that most of the men were pinned down in the slit trenches that they had recaptured from the 1st Parachute Brigade's original positions. Even basic actions were hampered by the sniping. An 'O' Group between an RTR troop commander and a DLI battalion commander in the cover given by a Sherman tank was abruptly interrupted when an artillery shell containing urine was poured onto the two officers' heads by one of the tank crew above. The tank crew, not wishing to take the chance of leaving the tank and exposing themselves to enemy fire, had taken to using their empty shells as a toilet, highlighting the lethal atmosphere around the bridge.

Planning for Second Attack

As stragglers returning to the ridgeline from the DLI's attack, Major Fitch, officer commanding B Company 2 Para, arrived with eight other men at the brigade HQ on Johnny I at 11:00 after having made their way back to the feature through enemy lines after being dropped on the slopes of Mount Etna nearly two days ago.

It wasn't just men still arriving on the battlefield. After the failed attack of the morning, the artillery of XXX Corps had caught up with the front line. Their firepower was now brought to bear and fire missions were immediately called down onto the enemy positions north of the bridge at 12:00. The captured Italian guns that Captain Panter had brought into action the previous day were again used. Captain Panter directed a team of men from the Mortar Platoon who proceeded to engage German targets to the north of the bridge towards Catania. Once the gun had expended its stockpile of 20 rounds, it was then abandoned for good.

Under cover of this barrage, 1st Parachute Brigade and 50th (Northumbrian) Division were able to move forward together and liberated the MDS at 14:00. The remaining casualties being treated there were carried back up to the safety of Johnny I, where at 17:00, ambulances arrived from behind the front line and managed to finally evacuate the wounded back to hospitals and dressing stations behind the lines. Some men had now lay wounded for three days and required urgent treatment and operations.

German reinforcements were beginning to appear to bolster the bridge defences as well. Fassl returned with the rest of his company from Catania port during the afternoon. He had decided that his small force could not hold Catania on its own anyway but could still make a difference back at Primosole Bridge. Fassl's men now returned to the scene of their tough fighting the day before and took up positions north-west of the bridge to support Adolff's flank. There they waited for the DLI to move up against the bridge again.

Plans for the DLI's attack were now underway. Pearson and Frost were invited to the DLI's 'O' Group, led by the Durhams' CO Lt Col Lidwell, to formulate the plan of attack against the bridge for that night. Lidwell's plan called for A and D Companies of the 8th DLI to repeat the full-frontal assault that had been tried that morning, at 16:00. Pearson couldn't help but raise his opinion, 'Well if you want to lose another bloody battalion that's the right way to do it.' The 'O' Group turned around to see who had interrupted the proceedings. Lidwell replied, 'All right Alastair, how would you do it?'. To which Pearson responded, 'I think I would take that battalion across the river tonight'.[2] Lidwell agreed to the proposal on the spot

Armoured units are seen here reinforcing the bridge soon after its eventual capture. A Horsa glider can be seen to the left of the picture. (Kent and Sharpshooters Image)

and informed Pearson that he would act as the guide to lead the DLI across the ford that he had reconnoitred the previous morning soon after reaching the bridge. It was to become an invaluable recce in the battle for Primosole Bridge.

Pearson called in the company commanders of the DLI. He explained his plan to use the ford 800 yards (720m) to the west of the bridge as a crossing point. He assumed that the German forces would concentrate around the northern bridgehead to prevent another attack directly over the bridge. Pearson's final words of encouragement to the DLI commanders were, 'I will take you across the river and put you on the bridge, but after that you are on your own. I will cross that bridge and I'll be up that road as hard as I can bloody well go!'[3] Pearson knew the ability of the Germans to counter-attack. If the DLI attack achieved surprise and captured the northern end pf the bridge, then it needed troops to pour across from the south and spread as far as they could past the northern approaches to the bridge to hold back the inevitable German counter-attack.

As night began to fall, the route to the fording point was marked out with three miles (nearly 5km) of white mine tape. As the DLI moved forward, their supporting battalions now finally relieved the paras from Johnny I for the final time. The DLI headed off into the darkness to start their attack on the bridge, and the paras could finally get some much-needed sleep before the transport arrived in the morning to take them to Syracuse and from there to sail back to Africa.

The DLI's Second Attack

The DLI moved off in a file formation into the darkness at midnight. The column was led by Pearson's batman, Jock Clements, who guided them on their way towards the riverbank. Clements had been in battalion HQ with Pearson through the North African campaign and Pearson knew that he could be trusted. He had witnessed Clements lead an ad hoc platoon of men in a bayonet charge counter-attack against the Germans during the battle of Tamera, where the enemy had got as close as 50 yards (45m) of the battalion's headquarter positions.

Behind Clements was 'Panzer' Manser, rolling out the white mine tape as he went forward. Manser had undertaken a similar task a few months previously, unrolling white mine tape under the direction of Captain Coxen prior to 1 Para's assault on Djebel Mansour in Tunisia.[4] Lidwell and his three company commanders then followed behind Pearson. Pearson recalled that 'they were very distressed, as they had never been so near the front in their lives!'[5] The noise of their approach was covered by a two-hour artillery bombardment of the German positions, which was being witnessed by the paras from atop Johnny I.

The DLI managed to reach the cover of the reeds at the riverbank at 02:30 and were making good time. Suddenly, a rifle shot rang out into the silence of the night. A DLI soldier near the front of the snaking column had just accidently shot one of his colleagues in the head, known as a negligent discharge (an 'ND' or a 'Neil Diamond' in regimental parlance). The entire column froze, went to ground and waited for the Germans to react. After a few minutes went by without any further sound or movement, Pearson decided that the Germans hadn't heard the sound or weren't coming to investigate. Either way he needed to get the men over the river to maintain the element of surprise before anything else happened to compromise their silent approach.

Pearson ordered Clements to wade across the river and scout the far riverbank for signs of the enemy. On reaching the far bank Clements shone his torch back across the river. Pearson whispered as loud as he dared, 'Don't just wiggle that torch about. Away on and have a look around'.[6] Clements crept forward into the darkness. After straining his eyes and ears into the darkness, he reappeared minutes later to confirm to Pearson that there was no sign of the enemy.

Pearson had some final words of warning for Lidwell, 'Now, for Heaven's sake get your men out to the edge of the scrub because they'll (the Germans) be here in the morning. You can guarantee that. Remember what happened to the other battalion'.[7] Lidwell and his DLI disappeared across the river, Pearson, his job done, led Clements and Manser back towards Johnny I.

The DLI now crossed the river, with each company 50 yards (45m) apart, and made their way down to the bridge on the north bank. They stayed by the riverbank using the vineyards as cover, although they proved difficult to navigate in the dark and they had to call out their platoon and section numbers on the dark in order to maintain contact with each other. This attracted some enemy machine-gun fire from the Fallschirmjaeger who had pulled back 400 yards (360m) from the riverbank. The two wireless sets belonging to A and D Companies failed to work after they were submerged during the river crossing, providing communication problems for Lidwell. He would have to take the bridgehead on himself and rely on his sister battalion to push forward over the bridge to support him.

The Durhams waited by the riverbank and listened to the final artillery bombardment which preceded their attack. For 80 minutes the artillery pounded known and suspected German and Italian positions, mainly concentrating on the north end of the bridge and the adjoining olive groves spreading 500 yards west from the bridge. The final 10 minutes of the bombardment was supported from Johnny I by the tanks and heavy machine guns of the Cheshire Regiment, which had moved up during the night.

After the bombardment the Durhams moved forward to find that the northern end of the bridge had been abandoned and the enemy forces had withdrawn to the north. D Company secured the bridge whilst A Company pushed a further 400 yards (360m) to the east of the bridge and started digging in 100 yards (90m) north of the river. They didn't push out from the bridge as Pearson had warned them to do. The early morning brought probing attacks from the Fallschirmjaeger as they again used the dense scrub to crawl forward and attack the Durhams. The remainder of the 8th DLI needed to move over the bridge and reinforce the northern end. However, neither A and D Companies on the north side had a working radio. Lidwell had ordered two officers to stay with a Bren gun carrier on the south side and wait for a 2-inch mortar flare round as a signal to then drive across. But the mortar flares had been lost in the river crossing in the dark and the Bren gun carrier had been knocked out by a German shell, killing the driver, wireless operator and one officer, and leaving the other officer seriously wounded. Eventually a War Office observer pedalled across the bridge on a bicycle, blissfully unaware of the attempts to signal across the bridge. On arriving at the northern end, he was immediately sent back to pass a message for the remainder of the 8th DLI to advance across the bridge and exploit northwards.

The delays in moving B and C Companies across the bridge meant that they were now advancing on the German positions north of the bridge in daylight and not under the cover of darkness as planned. The Fallschirmjaeger let the Durhams come on until they were within 100 yards (90m) of their positions. All of a sudden, the MG42s roared into life against the advancing infantry and cut down the leading sections and platoons. B Company took heavy casualties and could only dive for cover and attempt to return some suppressing fire. C Company managed to move on the right flank of the Germans, supported by their Bren gun carriers. The Fallschirmjaeger were now centred around the sunken road and B Company

Various battle-damaged vehicles are being recovered from the south end of the bridge in the days after the fighting. (Kent and Sharpshooters Image)

fixed bayonets and moved forward to clear the position. The Fallschirmjaeger and Durhams clashed in the close vegetation of the sunken road. The ensuing hand-to-hand fighting only lasted for 20 minutes but incurred almost 100 per cent casualties on both sides, leaving the dead and wounded from both sides intermingled on the ground. However, the Fallschirmjaeger just managed to stand their ground and hold the sunken road.

C Company now moved forward again in the light of the day, unaware of the Fallschirmjaeger strongpoint in the sunken road. They were hit with enfilading machine-gun fire and forced to go firm out in the open before crawling back to a farmhouse near the riverbank.

Meanwhile, A Company was overrun by Fallschirmjaeger at first light. Two platoons were captured or became casualties. The third platoon and Company HQ had to swim back across the river to safety.

The Fallschirmjaeger were undoing the DLI's hard work. The perimeter on the north side was now 330 yards by 330 yards (300m). The only movement across the bridge was by armoured vehicle. The 88s were still engaging moving targets from 800 yards (720m) away. A charge by two Shermans was ended by 88-fire forcing them back. The Mortar Platoon was ferried across in Bren gun carriers and set up their barrels to bring some suppressing fire down on the Fallschirmjaeger. Self-propelled 'Priests' now arrived on the south bank to provide additional fire support. One 88 was knocked out by a Priest. Another three Shermans charged the bridge, this time two were knocked out by 88s.

Lidwell set up an impromptu headquarters in one of the captured farmhouses and urged his men forward. The Fallschirmjaeger even employed a captured British Sherman tank to drive up to the DLI's lines whilst everyone held their fire to see if it was friend or foe. As it got to within 200m of the DLI, it fired a high-explosive round from its main gun and sprayed the forward trenches with its machine gun before driving up the road and disappearing.[8]

Montgomery and Dempsey arrived at 13:30 to view the battle from the Johnny hills. A larger set-piece battle was now called for. The same fording point would be used that night to push across the 6th and 9th DLI supported by tanks of the 3rd City of London Yeomanry. The attack was supported by 19 guns and scheduled for 01:00 on 17 July. As the DLI crossed the river they were engaged by the Fallschirmjaeger's machine guns and heavy fighting ensued. However, like the 1st Parachute Brigade in previous days, the Fallschirmjaeger were now low on ammunition and were finding themselves becoming overrun purely on overwhelming numbers. By 07:00 the Shermans of the Yeomanry rolled over the bridge and their weight of fire forced the Fallschirmjaeger to surrender or withdraw to fight another day.

In one final show of defiance as the Shermans approached the bridge, Hauptmann Adolff personally drove a truck laden with explosives onto the bridge in an attempt to destroy the structure. He was stopped and killed by a merciless weight of fire.

The bullet-riddled truck came to rest on the north end of the bridge and failed to detonate. Adolff was mortally wounded and died soon after. He was posthumously promoted and awarded the Knight's Cross for his actions.

The bridge was now secure. The Fallschirmjaeger, despite not destroying the bridge, had delayed the entire advance on the eastern side of the island by clinging on to the Primosole Bridge. Their actions even made headlines in wartime British media coverage of the event.

The London Times of 27 August 1943 stated that the Fallschirmjaeger had '... fought superbly. They were troops of the highest quality, experienced veterans of Crete and Russia: cool and skilful, Nazi zealots to a man and fanatically courageous. To fight against them was an education for any soldier'.[9]

A Bren gun carrier crossing the bridge soon after its capture. Note the damage to the bridge on both the left and right sides of the railings. (Kent and Sharpshooters Image)

As the few Fallschirmjaeger prisoners were marched back over the bridge to captivity, the 9th DLI Commander, Colonel Clarke, shook hands with the Fallschirmjaeger commander as a mark of respect. The cost of final battle to capture the bridge was 300 dead Germans found around the bridge, whilst the 151st Brigade suffered 500 casualties for their gain of 1,000 yards (900m).

The DLI history states that 'men who had experienced the fiercest fighting of the North African campaign at Alamien and Mareth said they had never seen so much slaughter in such a small area'.[10] This slaughter was inflicted against an armoured brigade by an exhausted enemy with limited ammunition. It is testimony to the strength of the lightly armed 1st Parachute Brigade, who had been up against this ferocious level of fighting for the previous two days with no air or armoured support. The 50th Division after the battle of Primosole Bridge were a unit in need of a rest. The 5th Division now passed through their lines in order to continue the offensive towards Catania and ultimately Messina.

The Paras Head for Home

Whilst the DLI undertook their second attack led by Pearson, the remainder of 1st Parachute Brigade now began their journey back to North Africa. They were being pulled out of line now that they had done their job.

At 06:30 on 16 July, as the fighting was still raging at the bridge, the paratroopers finally left Johnny I after handing over their positions to the DLI and Cheshire Regiment. They marched 3 miles (5km) down Highway 114 towards Syracuse where they were met by trucks at 10:00 to drive them to the port of Syracuse. Long-lost colleagues now began to swap their war stories and try to piece together just what had happened to their brigade over the last day and a half.

Even though they were no longer on the front line, they weren't altogether safe; their convoy was strafed on the way to the port. As Gordon Mitchell recalls, 'we came under attack several times and had to bail out and run for cover to return fire. I always felt sorry for the wounded, who had to be left on the wagons while gunfire landed all around them.'[11]

Pearson managed to catch up with his battalion as they were boarding the trucks bound for Syracuse and home. The convoy wound its way to the outskirts of Syracuse where the men waited in the cover of an olive grove for the order to move down to the harbour for their ship back to Africa. Seventy-five men from 1 Para had to be diverted to Lentini to escort 800 POWs to the main holding cage at Syracuse before they too met up with the remaining survivors of 1st Parachute Brigade. On the way to Syracuse they passed Montgomery's staff vehicle coming the other way. Montgomery's greeting was full of enthusiasm for the paratroopers. 'Ah, Pearson,' said Montgomery, 'I'm delighted to see you. You've made a big difference to my campaign'.[12] Montgomery's sense of victory wasn't shared by all the men, with some seeing their heroic failure to hold the bridge as just that, a failure, not a victory.

The approach to bridge from the south. A Horsa glider can again be seen in the background. (Kent and Sharpshooters Image)

Montgomery walked between the trucks and his staff officers handed out cigarettes to the paras, before the convoy rumbled on once more for Syracuse. Pearson addressed his men before they boarded their ship and he headed for the hospital in Syracuse, suffering from the first signs of malaria. In the hospital the DLI casualties from the Primosole Bridge began to fill the wards. The adjutant of 9th Battalion DLI spoke with Pearson and told him how the DLI's attack had nearly failed. The adjutant told Pearson, 'I was there when you told my commanding officer not to stay where he was but push out to the edge of the scrub. But as soon as you disappeared he changed everything. And by Christ we suffered'.[13] It was disappointing for Pearson to discover that his advice hadn't been followed and that the men of the DLI had suffered as a result. This was war. He had to move his thoughts on to the safe return of his battalion to their camp at Sousse.

From Syracuse, the Paras were embarked the troop ship HMTL V 424 at 16:00, ready to sail for Sousse in the morning. However, that night the port of Syracuse suffered an air attack by the Luftwaffe. The troop ship put up a smokescreen, Gordon Mitchell remembers: 'that night we were heavily bombed – terrifying when you are below deck – and they let off smoke as a screen. Half of it came down on us. There we were, huddled together, lights out, choking on the smoke'.[14] The ship wasn't damaged, however, and weighed anchor the next afternoon at 15:30 for the voyage back to Africa. The ship harboured in Malta overnight before leaving again on the morning of the 18th at 07:00. There was a scare that night as the ship had to avoid drifting mines but arrived safely in Sousse harbour at 06:30 on the 19th. The men were offloaded from the ships at 07:15 onto waiting trucks which took them back to the camp that they had left only a few days before. The sea journey had given the men that had landed in Sicily a chance to talk to each other. However, only a fraction of the brigade had even made it on to the ground after the drop. On arrival at Sousse, the survivors were pleased to see so many of their comrades already there. The men of 1 Para were now told that 189 men of the battalion hadn't even managed to jump over Sicily. The men were once again in high spirits as their feared number of casualties was reduced on seeing whole platoons intact waiting for them as they neared the camp. Roll calls were carried out for each battalion at 10:00 before the men were given lunch, their first hot meal in days. In contrast to how they had spent their last few days in combat in Sicily, they were all driven to Sousse to spend the afternoon swimming in the Mediterranean.

The next morning Browning visited the men at 08:30. Such an early visit so soon after the men's return from battle highlighted his concern at the airborne insertion

The Sunken road. Scene of bitter hand-to-hand fighting between the DLI and the Fallschirmjaeger. (Kent and Sharpshooters Image)

phase of the operation. As news of the operation was still being analysed, it was clear at this stage the operation had been severely compromised by the failure of the aircrews to drop their paratroopers correctly. Browning stressed the point that 'it was most necessary to keep on friendly terms with the American crew'.[15] The rumours spread by the men that had landed back at camp without jumping had been damning of the American pilots' response to the flak. These rumours were now being supported by the men who had been dropped inaccurately over the target and who were telling the same stories of excessively evasive action by pilots, rather than dropping the men at the drop zones and braving the flak in the process.

The official debrief started in earnest to dissect the operation from start to finish, beginning with corroborating the men's stories, to piece together just what had happened in the few days between an elite parachute brigade leaving North Africa and returning as a battered fragment.

CHAPTER SEVENTEEN

'The Race for Messina'

On 16 July, General Hube arrived on Sicily with orders from Hitler to effectively take over operations on the island, including both the German and Italian forces there. He officially was working alongside Guzzoni but was allowed control of all German forces on Sicily. The stalling of Allied operations around Primosole gave the Germans time to bring over from the mainland the remainder of the 1st Fallschirmjaeger Division and the 29th Panzergrenadier Division. Hube now concentrated these forces on a defensive line running from Catania and across to the base of Mount Etna, effectively forming a 'hard crust' to fend off the Allies. Behind this defensive screen, he instructed the rest of his formations to retreat to Messina in an orderly fashion to be shipped back to Italy. The first defensive line the Allies had to breach was the Hauptkampflinie which ran from Catania over the north of the Catania Plain and on to Santo Stefano. The line was defended by the 29th Panzergrenadier Division, the 1st Fallschirmjaeger Division and Hermann Goering Panzer Division. The line was also overlooked by German forces based in observation posts on the slopes of Mount Etna which provided a massive strategic advantage to the defenders as they could observe Allied troop movements and predict Montgomery's next moves.

Two further defensive lines were added behind the Hauptkampflinie in a pattern of ripples decreasing in size towards Messina: 15 miles (24km) behind the Hauptkampflinie was the Etna Line, running from San Fratello to Troina, then from Adrano then Acireale. The third and final defensive line ran from Mount Pelato to Cesaro to Bronte to Riposto. All three lines were defended mainly by German troops in prepared positions. The delaying tactics that the German Army would employ so well in the battles on the Italian mainland were about to be perfected in the closing stages of the battle of Sicily.

The Hauptkampflinie was being attacked by the British in the east, the Canadians in the centre and by the Americans in the west. The lynchpin of the defences was Catania and the bulk of the German elite troops were positioned here. It blocked the advance up the east coast of Sicily by dominating the coastal plain running between Mount Etna and the coast. It couldn't be outflanked but had to be taken in head-on assaults over open ground. Consequently, heavy and slow fighting developed in the towns and villages that had been fortified as part of the main defensive line. The Canadians struggled through hilltop town after hilltop town against an enemy who inflicted heavy casualties on the attackers as they worked their way up each hill but then skilfully vanished by the time the Canadians reached the top. Despite this war of attrition, they managed to methodically squeeze the line up against the slopes of Mount Etna.

In the west, the American forces were up against Italian units and were making the most progress. Unlike the confines of the line around Catania, the Americans were able to capture large tracts of land and thus spread their forces out in order to attack on a wider front and with a network of supporting roads available to them. Patton was now sensing that he might just be able to achieve the impossible. After being sidelined to Montgomery's Eighth Army, there was a chance that, up against the Italian defenders and not the Germans, he could perform a left hook around Etna from the direction of Palermo and capture Messina before Montgomery.

As a further sign of the Axis' attempt to merely use Sicily as one large delaying tactic, they now began to evacuate their aircraft. On 16 July, all Italian aircraft stationed on Sicily were ordered to fly for Italian mainland bases. About 160 Italian planes had been lost in the first week of the invasion, 57 lost to Allied fighters and anti-aircraft fire in the first three days of the invasion alone. Despite these losses, the Italian air force were still very much in the fight and were able to inflict losses on the Allied fleet. That day, HMS *Indomitable* was damaged by an Italian torpedo bomber and put out of action for almost the rest of the war.

The Italian navy was also still taking the fight to the Allies despite evacuating all of its Sicilian bases. On the night of 17 July, the Italian light cruiser *Scipione Africano* was patrolling the Straits of Messina and managed to use its radar to detect four British motor torpedo boats. Opening fire on the small British craft, the *Scipione Africano* manged to score hits on two of the boats, sinking one and damaging a second. Twelve British sailors were killed as a result.

Back on land the fighting continued to grind on. On the night of 17 July, Montgomery renewed his attack towards Catania with a two-pronged offensive by two brigades of the 50th Division. Montgomery held his position firm around Primosole and instead sent a left hook slightly inland towards Misterbianco, in order to cross the Simeto river and Gornalunga canal further downstream. As the lead troops left their cover and heading out towards the open space of the plain, they were heavily engaged by the waiting German troops. With casualties mounting and no ground being taken, Montgomery had no choice but to call a halt to the offensive on 19 July.

Montgomery believed that the Hauptkampflinie was weaker the further inland that he probed away from Catania. He, therefore, planned a second left hook further inland again, this time using the Canadians. The Canadians managed to fight their way uphill and take the well-defended town of Enna on the 19th. They only narrowly beat American troops to take the town, whose arrival so close to the Canadians caused some surprise, particularly to Montgomery. He could clearly now see that the Americans were moving across the island at speed and that the enemy in front of them was on the run. Montgomery's forces on the other hand were bogged down in front of an entrenched German enemy and had little momentum forward. Montgomery doubled his efforts in urging the Canadians on and on the 21st they managed to advance on and take Leonforte.

Just as it seemed that progress was being made by the Canadians, on 20 July the 51st Division, 11 miles (18km) further west, launched an offensive to capture the Gerbini airfields. Despite making initial gains, they were driven back to their original start-lines by German armoured counter-attacks the next day. It became clear to Montgomery that he needed to revise his strategy. Rather than pushing forwards along the east coast towards Catania and Messina, whilst simultaneously driving a left hook around Etna to attack Messina from the north-west, he only had enough troops to pursue the coastal advance on Catania and Messina. He now gambled on calling up his reserve division from North Africa, Major-General Evelegh's 78th Infantry Division, and going all out for a direct assault up the coast, whilst ceding the northern advance to Patton, hoping to beat him into Messina. The race between the commanders to reach Messina was now well and truly on.

The Americans were initially used as diversion on the north coast road to draw enemy forces from around Etna but the taking of Palermo and drive on Messina now needed clear discussion between the commanders to agree a cohesive strategy.

Whilst the British and Canadians were slogging it out with the Germans around Catania, the Americans had organised themselves into two corps. The Provisional Corps, under Major-General Geoffrey Keyes, was to push to the west and soon captured Porto Empedocle and Agrigento. Agrigento's Italian garrison put up strong resistance to the first probing attacks of the American advance, until Colonel William Darby's 1st and 3rd Ranger Battalions of the 3rd Infantry Division managed to fight their way into the town and secure it. The Second Corps, under Major General Omar Bradley, was tasked with advancing north towards Caltanissetta to cut Route 121, the main highway crossing the centre of Sicily.

With the British advance on the east of the island attracting the attention of Hube, he shifted the 15th Panzergrenadier Division to the east to maintain the delaying tactics on Montgomery's push. This cleared the path ahead of Patton's troops and allowed them to advance northwards to cut Route 120. With such momentum, Alexander encouraged Patton to push northwards again, tasked with capturing the port of Palermo and cutting the northern coastal road linking Palermo and Messina, effectively cutting the island in two. Catania and Messina were the two main ports considered necessary to capture first on Sicily. Palermo was believed to be too far west, meaning that it would be captured after that if Catania and Messina. An

Montgomery and Patton in Sicily. (Battlefield Historian Ltd @ battlefieldhistorian.com BHC 003034)

opportunity had now arisen though, where the quicker than expected seizure of Palermo would provide a much-needed port to ferry supplies into Sicily. The Allied planners now had one eye already on the invasion of Italy itself.

Patton ordered Keyes' corps forward to attack the outskirts of Palermo on 21 July. Despite heavy resistance by the Schreiber Battle Group and several battalions from the Aosta and Assietta Divisions, Keyes' men were soon overlooking the city. They pushed forward the next day and managed to drive into the heart of the city meeting only light resistance. Patton now ordered Keyes to mop up the west of the island whilst he urged on Bradley's corps to turn east for Messina and race along the coastal road to beat Montgomery to the prize of declaring victory on Sicily.

With the differing fortunes of the two advances on the island, the commanders agreed to a conference, and on 24 July Montgomery, Patton and Alexander met for the first time since arriving in Sicily at Montgomery's headquarters in Syracuse. Here it was decided that Montgomery would continue to push around Etna only, whilst Patton moved towards Messina along the northern coast. The air forces would also focus on the north-east corner of Sicily, attacking the concentration of German forces that were undertaking their evacuation of the island. They concluded the meeting with plans for a second meeting, three days later at Patton's headquarters in Palermo.

On 25 July King Victor Emmanuel of Italy took the steps to officially remove Benito Mussolini as *Il Duce*. He was immediately replaced by the Head of the Army, Marshal Pietro Badoglio. He announced to the Italian public that Italy was not surrendering and that the fighting would go on. Behind closed doors, however, he reached out to the Allies to enter into secret negotiations for a cessation of hostilities.

Hitler could now see the end approaching in Sicily and that Italy was the obvious next Allied target. If the Allies could move through Italy, they would potentially be at the borders of the Reich within months. Hitler, therefore, wanted to save his forces for the impending Italian campaign. The Sicilian campaign was delaying the Allies and inflicting casualties but it was now time to order the evacuation of the German troops back to the Italian mainland and to live to fight another day. Under Operation *Lehrgang*, 70,000 German troops moved towards Messina and embarked for Italy. General Baade had been appointed to prepare for the evacuation days previously and had carefully built up the anti-aircraft defences and prepared 'receiving areas' for the troops so that that they could be swiftly embarked and sail across to Italy. General Heidrich, commander of the 1st Fallschirmjaeger Division, had been appointed as the receiving commander of the evacuation on the Italian side of the evacuation.

Allied fighter aircraft, previously based at Malta, began to arrive at Sicilian airfields, allowing them to concentrate on attacking the evacuation areas whilst heavy bombers in turn deployed to Malta to attack southern Italy. The increase in Allied air power resulted in Rome's main train marshalling yards being bombed on 19 July. An air-drop of leaflets over the city warned civilians of the impending air raid, countering Mussolini's denials. The air raid undermined Mussolini's authority and helped seal his fate. In coordination with raids by aircraft based in England which targeted northern Italy, the Allies now used their bomber force on Malta and in North Africa to pummel Italy, instead of attacking the evacuation from Sicily, a less favourable target due to the density of the air defences around Messina – nearly 250 anti-aircraft guns provided an overlapping arrangement of anti-aircraft defences across the Straits.

With the Allied naval forces also refusing to attack due to the strong coastal batteries, the Germans had an unexpected window to evacuate their forces under minimal Allied interference. The Allied fighter planes further eased the evacuation by switching from day to night attacks owing to the heavy flak. This allowed the Germans to use daylight hours to ferry troops across the Straits of Messina, increasing their rate of evacuation.

On the 27th Montgomery flew to Patton's headquarters at Palermo and narrowly escaped disaster when the B-17 bomber that was carrying him nearly landed off the short runway at the airfield. Recovering himself after his shaky landing, he discussed

Tanks of US 2nd Armoured Division are greeted as conquering heroes by the civilian population of Palermo. Before the invasion it was thought that Allied troops might receive a cold reception from the Sicilians, but once they arrived it soon became clear that the locals were tired of the conflict and wished for peace to return to their island. (Battlefield Historian Ltd @ battlefieldhistorian.com BHC 003021)

with Patton the two-pronged attack on Messina. Both commanders were happy for their two armies to continue their advances as previously agreed. Alexander arrived late to the meeting. On entering the planning room to discuss his strategy with his subordinate commanders, he was promptly informed by both Patton and Montgomery that they had already decided matters and reiterated that the British would continue the push for Etna and Messina whilst the Americans continued their north coast road advance towards Messina also.

With the Patton now bearing down on Messina from the west, Montgomery knew that time was of the essence if he was to break through the Hauptkampflinie and beat Patton to Messina. Adrano had been seen as the anchor of the defences around the base of Mount Etna. The small town sat on a rocky outcrop and provided cover over the approaches around Etna. Its capture would effectively split the German forces in half around Etna and leave the coastal defenders isolated, allowing Montgomery to increase the pressure against them and push for Catania. Roy Urquhart's 231st Brigade Group, along with the 1st Canadian Division, began an eastward advance from Leonforte towards Adrano, taking the town of Agira along the way. At the same time, Montgomery launched Operation *Hardgate*, which involved a second advance from the south by the newly arrived British 78th Division, with the 3rd Canadian Brigade as support, to break the Hauptkampflinie and head for Adrano. The advance managed to secure a bridgehead over the Dittaino at Catenanuova and allowed the push to continue towards Centuripe, which formed the southern perimeter of the Agira defences. Here at Centuripe, they encountered the dug-in Fallschirmjaeger of 1st Battalion of the 3rd Parachute Regiment, along with elements of the Hermann Goering Panzer Division. After two days of hard close-quarters fighting, the town eventually fell and undermined the position of Agira. Allied forces were now on the brink of breaking the Hauptkampflinie at last.

Seeing that Montgomery was making progress after calling up his reserve division from North Africa, Patton also called forward his reserve division, Major-General Eddy's 9th Infantry Division. With the capture of the main highways leading from Palermo to Messina, Patton replaced two of his original divisions with fresh divisions, the 45th Division with the 3rd Division and the 1st Division with 9th Division, and pushed them on towards Messina. The Hauptkampflinie had not been fully established in the north of the island and therefore Patton's forces first test against dug-in German troops came at the second defensive line, the Etna Line. Whilst the British and Canadians were fighting for Adrano, the Americans had a tough fight of their own to capture the hilltop town of Troina from the 15th Panzergrenadier Division, supported by four battalions of the Italian Aosta Division.

For six days, the Germans and Italians conducted a costly rearguard defence of the town. In a battle which constantly swung like a pendulum, the Americans reached the outskirts of the town on 24 occasions, only to be beaten back. Eventually the Americans conducted a large-scale dawn assault on the town, only to find that the Germans had withdrawn during the night. Immediately after the battle, 1st Division's commander, General Allen, and his deputy, Brigadier Roosevelt, were relieved of their commands, creating controversy on whether they were being relieved for a rest or for poor performance in their costly capture of Troina.

With the capture of Troina, the Americans now held a commanding position from where to site their artillery and begin to bombard enemy positions to smooth their advance. Coupled with the Hermann Goering Panzer Division being forced to retreat back to their final defensive line, the Tortorici Line, by the British advances around Etna, the ground was opening up in front of Patton's army. Patton became bolder in his bid to reach Messina. When his troops came up against the 29th Panzergrenadier Division at the coastal towns of Santa Agata and San Fratello, he ordered a flanking amphibious assault to get behind the enemy positions. This move by Patton, known as an 'end-run' in American football terminology, involved Patton catching the Germans by surprise by landing 7 miles (11km) behind the front line and cutting the main road.

Patton repeated the manoeuvre on 11 August at Brolo, a further 15 miles (24km) behind the front line. They managed to entrench themselves atop Mount Creole

Scottish troops of the 51st Highland Division move up to the front line during their advance inland through Sicily. (Battlefield Historian Ltd @ battlefieldhistorian.com BHC 003019)

which dominated the area but were pinned down there by German forces supported by tanks. Naval firepower was called in from the sea and air power was used to break up German attacks in a show of inter-service firepower that was sadly lacking on Operation *Fustian* for 1st Parachute Brigade.

The speed of advance of Patton's ground forces now overshadowed his third 'end-run' on 15 August. His amphibious assault force duly landed behind enemy lines again, 25 miles (40km) west of Messina, only to find on arrival that their fellow infantrymen had already overrun the landing site. Patton was now poised to strike at Messina.

Meanwhile, Montgomery had begun to gain some momentum on the eastern side of the island. The assault on Adrano finally prevented the enemy from freely moving on the battlefield and reinforcing their front line as the Allies struck. The slow grind towards Catania was met with success when the British troops entered the city on 5 August, followed the next day by the capture of Adrano. The enemy had held up the Allied advance, allowing their forces to be evacuated from Messina. They weren't issued with orders from Hitler to fight in the ruins of the cities, instead they could fall back to their next defensive line.

With town after town now being captured on the southern approaches to Etna, Montgomery's front line was shortening all the time. He even now began to rotate his divisions, including allowing the 5th Division to begin preparing for the invasion of Italy. The real end-game came in Sicily, not due to the Allies, but because the Axis forces had completed their evacuation.

On 18 August, the German High Command declared Operation *Lehrgang* at an end. They had successfully shipped from Sicily to Italy around 60,000 German troops and a further 75,000 Italian troops, together with over 14,000 vehicles, 50 tanks, 100 artillery pieces and thousands of tons of stores. All of this huge amount of men and materiel would now be employed in the defence of Italy. It would prove to be a costly missed opportunity for the Allied forces. They could have broken the back of the upcoming Axis defence of Italy on the battlefields of Sicily already. In contrast, the last German troops to leave Messina, sensing a victory snatched from the jaws of defeat, towed a bottle of wine behind their boat to cool in the sea, so that they could toast their arrival back in Italy.

With only the remnants of an Axis defence left around Messina, Montgomery's forces were now at last able to race for their prize. However, the Americans were already there. On 16 August, the US 3rd Division entered the city and accepted its surrender. A victory ceremony was then hastily arranged for the arrival of Patton himself the next morning. Patton completed his victory ceremony in Messina at 10:00 on the 17th. Shortly afterwards the senior British commander arrived and declared to Patton 'It was a jolly good race. I congratulate you'.[1] The closeness of the race for Messina and the bragging rights to claim victory on Sicily had gone to Patton. The repercussions of this were felt throughout the ranks of the Allied forces. No longer could the British claim to be the senior partner in the coalition. Although the British had been fighting for longer in the war, the Americans had now been blooded and, coupled with the vast amounts of men and equipment that they were pouring into Europe, they were increasingly seen as the main players in the European theatre of operations.

The invasion of Sicily had succeeded in achieving its key objectives. It had captured Axis land and established a foothold on continental Europe, providing a springboard for the assault on Italy. It also saw the first combined operations of the Allies, putting ashore an amphibious assault supported by airborne operations. Lessons learnt from Sicily, and again from Italy, were to be put to good use in future operations, notably the Normandy landings. Importantly, in the grand strategy of

The winning team at Montgomery's HQ in Taormina at the end of the campaign, Eisenhower and the Americans were there to invest Eighth Army's Commander with the highest order which America can bestow upon a soldier of a foreign nation, that of Commander of the Legion of Merit. Seated from left to right: Patton, Eisenhower and Montgomery: Standing Bradley, Truscott, Gay (Patton's Chief of Staff), Keyes and Dempsey. (Battlefield Historian Ltd @ battlefieldhistorian.com BHC 003045)

the war, the Allied invasion of Sicily showed the Russians that the Allies were pulling their weight and had well and truly opened a second front in order to relieve the pressure on the Eastern Front.

The invasion of Sicily had also served to effectively knock Italy out of the war. Bardaglio's continued secret negotiations with the Allies resulted in a truce and unconditional surrender for Italy on 3 September. It was signed at Cassibile on Sicily, scene of one of the original invasions weeks earlier. The main failing of the Sicilian campaign for the Allies, however, was the missed opportunity to firmly put a cork in the bottle of the escaping German army. The Germans were allowed to make a run for it and live to fight another day. The invasion of Italy began six days later with amphibious landings at Salerno, met with strong resistance from German troops recently evacuated from Sicily. A long hard fight up the spine of Italy would now hold the Allies away from Germany's borders until the end of the war.

The cost of men in Sicily had not been cheap either. Montgomery's army suffered 11,843 casualties, 2,062 killed or missing, 7,137 wounded, and 2,644 captured. Patton's army had lost 2,237 killed or missing, 5,946 wounded, and 598 captured. The Canadian forces had suffered 562 killed, 1,664 wounded, and 84 captured. German losses were estimated at 9,000 killed or missing, 13,500 wounded and 5,500 captured. The Italians incurred 4,300 killed and with a large proportion of their conscript army – 116,500 men – captured.

Conclusion

In the Parachute Regiment's short history, the battle of Primosole Bridge had once again illustrated the regimental traditions that were being forged on the battlefield, with an addition of yet another battle honour for the fledgling regiment. The Parachute Regiment had once again shown its coolness in the heat of battle.

The battle of the Primosole Bridge had been a hard-fought encounter between two of the most elite formations of World War II. It was the first time in the history of warfare that two forces had parachuted onto the battlefield and engaged in close-quarters combat. Both sides can claim a victory but also a defeat. The 1st Parachute Brigade managed to seize the bridge but then couldn't hold it in the face of overwhelming numbers and firepower of the Fallschirmjaeger. The Fallschirmjaeger in turn couldn't hold the Primosole Bridge once they were out-gunned and outnumbered by the Allied ground forces.

The battle of Primosole Bridge was ultimately a heroic failure. Lathbury stated that 'this operation against the Primosole Bridge was a disappointing one. Of the brigade group less than one third arrived at the right place. More than one-third were taken back to North Africa without being dropped, and the remainder were dropped in other parts of Sicily'.[1]

The men of the 1st Parachute Brigade fought in the true spirit of the Parachute Regiment against overwhelming odds, a better equipped enemy, including artillery and armour, and without support from their own approaching land forces. Despite the odds being stacked against them, they still managed to highlight the potential of Airborne Forces. General Browning stated that 'My conclusion is that these operations were probably the most difficult that will ever be carried out by airborne troops but they completely achieved their objectives and a corner of the veil of future possibilities has been lifted'.[2] This clearly demonstrates that, despite the failure to deliver the paratroopers on the correct drop zones coupled with the failure to reinforce their position by ground forces, the paras still managed to capture all of their objectives with only a small nucleus of the original force.

Montgomery's plan to insert the 1st Airborne Division in three operations to capture three key bridges clearly shows the desire to employ the paratroopers to achieve 'vertical envelopment' on the battlefield and to fully utilise their element of surprise in landing behind enemy lines to pave the way for the advancing ground troops. Despite the airborne troops not being relieved in time and the advance stalling as a result, Montgomery would use the Parachute Regiment to spearhead the four major campaigns in the European theatre, namely the invasions of Normandy, southern France, Arnhem and the Rhine Crossing.

The overall Allied invasion had been a huge success. It was a complex and vast undertaking and involved immense inter-service coordination for the first time, a strategy that would be improved later in the war, notably for the Normandy landings. The capture of Sicily had massive implications in the grand strategy of the Allied war plan. Firstly, the first piece of Axis land had been captured, leading to the overthrow of Mussolini, the surrender of Italy and the opening of sea lanes in the Mediterranean. Secondly, it had shown the Russians that the Allies were serious about opening a second front to relieve the pressure on the Eastern Front. Thirdly, the opening of a second front offered the opportunity to advance towards the borders of the Reich itself through Italy whilst weakening the Atlantic Wall defences of Northern France prior to an Allied invasion less than a year away.

The delay in capturing the Primosole Bridge ultimately delayed Montgomery's advance northwards and allowed Patton to win the race for Messina. In turn, the Americans took over as the superior Allied power now that they had a bloodied army in Europe and were providing the bulk of the Allied equipment and logistics.

At the time, Montgomery didn't let it outwardly show that his advance had been halted. He handed out cigarettes to the men of the 1st Parachute Brigade and exclaimed, 'Well done! You have saved me a week. That week will make all the difference later on!'[3] In reality, the delays at Primosole Bridge had allowed the Germans to use elite divisions to bolster the Hauptkampflinie and fight the British and Canadian Armies to a halt for a week. If the ground troops had successfully linked up with 1st Parachute Brigade by noon, as planned, on the day they took the bridge, the Allied tanks would have reached the outskirts of Catania and been able to spread out their forces on the Catania Plain only an hour later, instead it took a further week of heavy fighting.

Despite the overall strategy of the Operation *Fustian* not concluding as planned, it had served to sharpen the skills of the planners of airborne operations and of the Parachute Regiment soldiers themselves.

The delivery of parachute troops to the battlefield needed urgent review. General Alexander had suspended any future airborne operations until better inter-service work was completed. All three airborne operations during the Sicilian campaign had attracted friendly fire and been widely dispersed as a result. Even after the friendly fire incidents of Allied aircraft flying over the fleet, the Allied Naval Commander, Cunningham, still urged his gunners that 'an aircraft in a position to menace the fleet must be instantly engaged unless it has identified itself in the most positive manner'.[4] So even after the debacle of the shooting-up of the air armadas, the policy was to fire first and ask questions later. More coordination and air lanes were incorporated into future operations to clearly delineate friendly from enemy aircraft.

Churchill himself was keen to find out why the airborne troops, both British and American, had been so badly delivered to the battlefield during the Sicilian campaign. On receiving the figures for the campaign and noting that 1,100 paratroopers were missing of the 3,637 who had taken part in the campaign in Sicily, Churchill angrily replied to the War Office that '1,100 – This is a very serious disaster'.[5] The Allies knew that they couldn't afford these high levels of casualty rates if airborne operations were to continue. Hitler had already stopped the Fallschirmjaeger from mass drops due to the high level of casualties during the invasion of Crete.

The aircrew also clearly needed better training in night navigation and dealing with flak. Group Captain Cooper was tasked to fly over Sicily during Operation *Fustian* in his Beaufighter and observe the air armada as it approached the coast. He noted light flak but 'it did not seem that this flak was more than was to be expected under the circumstances, nor such as to cause greater losses than we had always considered inevitable on this operation. The refusal of the Americans to face flak which not only caused quite a number to turn back, but also it is thought may have been responsible for some of the inaccuracy in dropping, must be contributed to the fact that firstly that most of the crews were Transport crews, whose training and mentality were not such as to make them take readily to being shot at, and also to the fact that they had no previous experience of flak'.[6] As a result of Allied investigations into the delivery of airborne troops to their drop zones, it was recommended that Allied aircraft have white and black stripes painted on their wings to identify them to the naval gunners as friendly aircraft. A smaller number of larger drop zones was also recommended in order to make sighting them easier for the navigators to find and the pathfinders to mark them.

Post-action debriefs between the aircrew and paras highlighted that the offensive spirit of the paras had not been quite so well understood prior to the operation by the aircrews. 'It is apparent that preliminarily liaison would have been welcomed by the aircrew. It would have served to impress upon the Air Force the determination of parachute troops to do their job at all costs. The return of complete sticks without dropping would have been substantially reduced thereby'.[7] This clearly highlights that the aircrews had not been fully aware of the importance of their role of delivering the troops to their drop zones. The primary objective of aircrews was to deliver the troops to battle, and if they couldn't locate the drop zones, they needed to give an honest estimation of their position, so that the men could then jump and be roughly orientated once on the ground, even of it was not on the correct drop zone.

The Parachute Regiment now also received its own dedicated air fleet. No.38 Wing RAF was expanded, becoming No.38 Group with its Halifax squadrons, now supported by four squadrons of Albemarles and four squadrons of Stirlings. A second RAF transport group, No.46 Group, was formed, and was equipped solely with Dakotas, instead of the mixture of aircraft in No.38 Group. After these changes, the RAF Groups could supply 88 Albemarles, 88 Stirlings, 36 Halifaxes and 150 Dakotas, a total of 362 planes, for airborne operations.

The role of the gliders was also placed under scrutiny. The 1st Airborne Division's commander, General Hopkinson, was still supportive of gliders after the Sicily campaign and championed their use over the employment of paratroopers. 'The Albermarle pulls a Horsa with 32 passengers or carries but 10 parachutists'.[8] He went on to state that the glider forces for Operations *Ladbroke* and *Fustian* landed in 35mph winds, which would have been unsuitable for parachute operations. In summing up the future of airborne warfare he added that 'the conclusion to be drawn from these considerations is that the general tendency of airborne development will be towards the glider and away from the parachute'.[9] The gliders had also suffered heavy losses though, with entire gliders and their troops lost at sea. A recommendation was adopted to ban the release of gliders over water again at night.

One bonus for the glider-borne troops that Hopkinson brought out in his summary of the *Husky* operations was that there should be equal pay between the glider and parachute troops. 'The invidious distinction between the parachutist and glider-borne soldier in the matter of pay should be removed once and for all. An all-round rate of 2 shillings a day is surely the least reward that can be offered to officers and men who accept the implications of the duties of an airborne soldier'.[10]

Once on the ground, important lessons had been learned which would be incorporated into future airborne operations. Hunting horns were employed to rally the men on the drop zones after Sicily, notably by John Frost at Arnhem. Once the element of surprise was lost, the sound of the hunting horns proved effective in quickly rallying the men.

Radio communications had also been a big problem in Sicily. Improvements were requested of the available radios. Airborne troops needed lightweight kit that still had the range and efficiency of vehicle-based radio units. The paratroopers found themselves isolated and unable to call in air, sea or ground support with their short-range radios. One new policy adopted was that of automatic drop zones. In the event of no radio communications, resupply aircraft would drop their loads onto a predesignated drop zone. This system was used at Arnhem, however the drop zones had been overrun, resulting in the bulk of the resupply equipment being delivered to the enemy forces.

Communications with the relieving ground forces also needed improving. The use of a liaison officer from the Parachute Brigade could have been utilised to instil some momentum in the ground forces. Airborne forces were employed to capture key objectives, such as bridges, to enable the ground forces to continue their advance. Too often the ground forces saw the airborne link-up as the finish line itself and failed to exploit the initial success of the airborne shock troops' gains. At Primosole and then again at Arnhem, the paratroopers had completed their part of the mission, only to have to relinquish their objectives when the delays of the relieving force meant

Arnhem one year later - Men of No 3 Platoon, R Company, 1st Parachute Battalion armed with Bren gun and No. 4 rifles defend a large shell hole. (Courtesy of Air Assault Museum)

that they were overrun. In Sicily, despite the chaos of the delivery of the troops, all airborne objectives were captured intact by smaller than anticipated forces and the demolition charges removed. They were then defended against ground forces superior in numbers and weaponry. Despite having to complete a staged withdrawal, the 1st Parachute Brigade stoutly defended the Primosole Bridge until a tactical withdrawal was the only option. At the very least, the Primosole Bridge operation, as well as the Malati and Ponte Grande operations, proved that small groups of elite troops could indeed capture and hold key installations from the enemy and hold them until land forces arrived. Later at Arnhem, John Frost's 2 Para took and held Arnhem Bridge for four days against SS panzer divisions without any support. The urban environment of Arnhem had granted them at least some level of defensive cover,

Horsa gliders pictured at Pegaus Bridge during the Normandy landings. The distinctive black and white stripes were added after the friendly-fire incidents in Sicily. (Battlefield Historian Ltd @ battle-fieldhistorian.com BHC 007034)

only a year before, the same 2 Para had managed to hold onto Johnny I despite having no cover other than shallow shell-scrapes.

The missed intelligence picture of what enemy forces the men of the 1st Parachute Brigade were expected to face on the ground was also another factor that hindered their operational plans at both Arnhem and Primosole Bridge. The enemy in Sicily was thought likely to be Italian conscript troops. The fact that the Fallschirmjaeger parachuted into the Sicily theatre to support the Hermann Goering Panzer Division almost at the same time as the 1st Parachute Brigade was, even by Kesselring's standards, a 'fluke success'.[11] The men still battled against the elite Fallschirmjaeger but importantly were missing their support weapons with which to fight back against the out-of-range Germans. At Arnhem, the 1st Parachute Brigade were told to expect only 'old men and boys'. Instead they faced armoured panzer divisions.

The experience and lessons had come at a high price though. Only 295 men out of 1,856 took part in the battle for Primosole Bridge. Only 20 per cent had been delivered accurately to their designated drop zones. A further 30 per cent landed back in Africa. Casualties incurred in the fighting for the bridge and the Johnny hills were 27 killed and 78 wounded. The full cost of the operation would not be learnt until weeks later due to the dispersal of the drop. Eventually, it was assessed that 2,095 men from the brigade had been killed during Operation *Fustian*. Others suffered longer-term illness as a result of the Sicily campaign. Alastair Pearson, along with 11,500 other soldiers of the Eighth Army alone, contracted malaria. Pearson was sent back to the UK to recuperate but returned to fight in Normandy with 8 Para at Breville, where he would earn his fourth DSO, to go along with the award of his third DSO won at Primosole Bridge. Within a year, every officer who had served alongside Pearson at Primosole had been killed, wounded, taken prisoner or had gone on the run after Arnhem. Lathbury himself was shot in the back in Arnhem and temporarily paralysed.

Gallantry awards for 2 Para alone for the action at Johnny I were one Distinguished Service Order for Lonsdale, five Military Crosses and seven Military Medals for a single morning's fighting.

After Sicily the 1st Parachute Brigade was shipped to Taranto in Italy to guard the harbour before being withdrawn back to the UK – for some men it was the first they had stood on home soil for three years. They next went into battle for Operation *Market Garden*, their next bridge too far.

Their opponents, the 1st Fallschirmjaeger Division, went on to the brutal defence of Monte Cassino after fighting a delaying action on Sicily all the way back to Messina. After the heavy losses of the 'graveyard of Crete', the role of the Fallschirmjaeger changed from an airborne force to that of an elite infantry unit which continually fought delaying actions. The only and final jump of the Fallschirmjaeger after Crete was to be in the Battle of the Bulge on 16 December to capture the Malmedy crossroads. A combination of poor planning and fresh recruits caused that operation to end in a scattered drop with no objectives, and heavy losses for the inexperienced Fallschirmjaeger.

Life around the Primosole Bridge soon returned to normal after the battle. The wave of destruction soon passed over Sicily and moved onto the Italian mainland, leaving the farmers to regain their fields and continue their way of life. Despite the damage to the Primosole Bridge, it continued to be used until the 1970s, before being replaced by a modern structure. Further west of the Primosole Bridge is the modern motorway of Highway 1 and this carries today's road traffic away from Primosole on its route between Catania and Syracuse, making the Primosole Bridge area a quiet backwater compared to its busy days during the war. The Johnny hills have been encroached upon by mining companies and to the north of the bridge the urban sprawl of industrial estates is reaching down to the north bank of the Simeto all the way from the international airport in Catania to the north.

It is difficult today to picture that such a bloody battle occurred in such tranquil surroundings between two elite sets of airborne warriors. For both the Red and the Green Devils, the Primosole Bridge had proved to be the first bridge too far.

1st Parachute Brigade Order of Battle

Divisional HQ and Defence Platoon

Commander: Major-General Hopkinson
GSO-1 (Operations): Lieutenant-Colonel R. F. K. Goldsmith
GSO-1 (Air): Lieutenant-Colonel W. T. Campbell
Assistant Adjutant and Quartermaster General: Lieutenant-Colonel J. A. Goschen
Assistant Director Medical Service: Colonel A. A. Eagger
Assistant Director Ordnance Services: Lieutenant-Colonel G. M. Loring
Commander Royal Artillery: Lieutenant-Colonel Charles Crawfurd
Commander Royal Engineers: Lieutenant-Colonel M. C. A. Henniker
Commander Royal Signals: Lieutenant-Colonel R. J. Moberley
Commander Royal Army Service Corps: Lieutenant-Colonel T. H. Jefferies
Commander Royal Electrical and Mechanical Engineers: Lieutenant-Colonel R. T. L. Shorrick

1st Parachute Brigade

Brigade HQ and Defence Platoon
Commander: Brigadier Gerald Lathbury
Brigade Major: Major David Hunter
Deputy Assistant Adjutant and Quartermaster General: Major C. D. Byng-Maddicks
Signals Officer: Captain G. Rowland
Second-in-Command: Lieutenant L. Golden

1st Parachute Battalion

Battalion Headquarters
Commander: Lieutenant-Colonel Alastair Pearson
Second-in-Command: Major Peter Cleasby-Thompson
Adjutant: Captain J. A. Jessop
Intelligence Officer: Lieutenant J. J. MacFadden
Quartermaster: Lieutenant T. Brown

Regimental Medical Officer: Captain M. Haggie
5 Pl S Company Captain Bingley

2nd Parachute Battalion

Battalion Headquarters
Commander: Lieutenant-Colonel John Frost
Second-in-Command: Major J. H. S. Lane
Adjutant: Captain Victor Dover
Intelligence Officer: Lieutenant Francis Hoyer-Millar
Medical Officer: Captain R. Gordon
Chaplain: Captain/Reverend Bernard Egan

Headquarters Company

Commander: Major K. Mountford
Quartermaster: Lieutenant J. T. Parker
Regimental Signals Officer: Second Lieutenant J. G. Blunt
Assistant Regimental Signals Officer: Second Lieutenant G. F. W. Ellum

A Company

Commander: Major Richard Lonsdale
Second-in-Command: Captain J. D. Brayley
No.1 Platoon: Lieutenant Tony Frank
No.2 Platoon: Lieutenant A. Roberts
No.3 Platoon: Lieutenant R. B. Woods

B Company

Commander: Major John Fitch
Second-in-Command: Captain Doug Crawley
No.4 Platoon: Lieutenant Peter Cane
No.5 Platoon: Lieutenant W. E. Tite
No.6 Platoon: Lieutenant D. J. Pye
Spare Officer: Lieutenant D. N. Grove

C Company

Commander: Major J. G. Ross
Second-in-Command: Captain F. E. Kite
No.7 Platoon: Lieutenant M. K. Dunkeld
No.8 Platoon: Lieutenant M. P. H. Barry
No.9 Platoon: Lieutenant J. C. Horner

Support Company
Commander: Captain Stanley Charles Panter

3rd Parachute Battalion
Battalion Headquarters
Commander: Lieutenant-Colonel E. C. Yeldham
Second-in-Command: Major Smith
Adjutant: Captain R. M. D. Thesiger
Quartermaster: Lieutenant S. W. Burnard
Signals Officer: Lieutenant J. I. Pryce
Transport Officer: Lieutenant H. D. Burwash
Regimental Medical Officer: Captain John Rutherford
Regimental Sergeant Major: RSM John Lord
B Company
Commander: Major David Dobie
? Platoon: Lieutenant Richard Dorrien-Smith

1st Airlanding Anti-Tank Battery, RA
Commander: Major W. F. Arnold
Second-in-Command: Captain N. McLeod

A Troop
Commander: Lieutenant Hogan

B Troop
Commander: Lieutenant Tansley
Second in Command: Second Lieutenant Edward Eric Clapham

1st Parachute Squadron, RE
Commander: Major D. C. Murray
Captain T. J. Livesey
Captain T. C. Brockington
Lieutenant C. E. P. Sankey
Lieutenant C. G. Cox
Lieutenant A. E. Houghton
Lieutenant P. T. Stainforth
Lieutenant G. C. Buchanan
Lieutenant A. H. Scott-Fleming
Squadron Sergeant Major: CSM J. Bannerman

Strength on *Fustian*: 76

16 Parachute Field Ambulance, RAMC

Commander: Lieutenant-Colonel Percival Ross Wheatley
No.3 Section: Captain J. H. Keesey
No.4 Section: Captain A. Percival
Second-in-Command: Captain R. Wright (Attached R Company, 1 Parachute Battalion)

HQ Sticks including a Surgical Team in each

Captain Derek Hughes Ridler (Army Dental Corps)
Captain Alexander Lipman-Kessel (Surgeon)
Major C. J. Longland (Surgeon)
Padre: Captain/Reverend R. T. Watkins
Regimental Sergeant Major: RSM E. W. Brock

Every Man an Emperor

'What Manner Of Men Are These That Wear The Maroon Beret?

They are firstly all volunteers and are toughened by physical training. As a result they have infectious optimism and that offensive eagerness which comes from well-being. They have 'jumped' from the air and by doing so have conquered fear.

Their duty lies in the van of the battle. They are proud of this honour. They have the highest standards in all things whether it be skill in battle or smartness in the execution of all peace time duties. They are in fact – men apart – every man an emperor.

Of all the factors, which make for success in battle, the spirit of the warrior is the most decisive. That spirit will be found in full measure in the men who wear the maroon beret'

— Bernard Montgomery

Fallschirmjaeger Ten Commandments

The Ten Commandments of the German Fallschirmjaeger

1. You are the chosen ones of the German Army. You shall seek combat and train yourselves to endure any manner of test. To you, battle shall be the fulfilment.
2. Cultivate true comradeship, for by the aid of your comrades you will conquer or die.
3. Beware of talking. Be not corruptible. Men act while women chatter. Chatter may bring you to the grave.
4. Be calm and prudent, strong and resolute. Valour and enthusiasm of an offensive spirit will cause you to prevail in the attack.
5. The most precious thing in the presence of the foe is ammunition. He who shoots uselessly, merely to comfort himself, is a man of straw who merits not the title of Fallschirmjaeger.
6. Never surrender; to you death or victory must be a point of honour.
7. You can triumph only if your weapons are good. See to it that you submit yourself to this law - first thy weapon, then thyself.
8. You must grasp the full purpose of every enterprise, so that if your leader is killed you can fulfil it.
9. Against an open foe, fight with chivalry, but to a guerrilla, extend no quarter.
10. Keep your eyes wide open. Tune yourself to the utmost pitch. Be nimble as a greyhound, tough as leather, hard as Krupp steel. You shall be the German warrior incarnate.

The Parachute Regiment Battle Honours

Bruneval
Oudna
Tamera
Primosole Bridge
Normandy
Breville
Southern France
Arnhem
Rhine Crossing
Athens
Falkland Islands
Iraq

Endnotes

Introduction

1   Ambrose, *Pegasus Bridge, D-Day: The daring British Airborne Raid*, Pocket Books, London, p.xi.

Chapter 1

1   Whiting, Slaughter over Sicily, p.84.
2   Cherry, *Tunisian Tales*, p.44.
3   Peatling, *Without Tradition*, p.20.
4   Dover, *The Silken Canopy*, p.20.
5   Saunders, The Red Beret, p.85.
6   Parker, *The Paras: The Inside Story of Britain's Toughest Regiment*, p.67.
7   Frost, *A Drop Too Many*, p.90.
8   Cherry, *Tunisian Tales*, p.133.
9   Frost, *A Drop Too Many*, p.171.
10 The National Archives, CAB 106/687.

Chapter 2

1   The National Archives, CAB 106/687.
2   Devlin, *Silent Wings*, p.77.
3   Bailey, *Target: Italy*, p.177.
4   Molony et al, *The Mediterranean and Middle East: The Campaign in Sicily 1943 and The Campaign in Italy 3 September 1943 to 31 March 1944.*

Chapter 3

1   The National Archives, CAB 106/691.
2   The National Archives, CAB 106/687.
3   The National Archives, CAB 106/687.
4   The National Archives, CAB 106/687.
5   The National Archives, CAB 106/689.
6   Thompson, *Ready for Anything: The Parachute Regiment at War*, p.96.
7   Cherry, *Tunisian Tales*, p.122.
8   Cherry, *Tunisian Tales*, p.122.
9   Frost, *A Drop Too Many*, p.172.
10 Whiting, Slaughter over Sicily, p.85.

11 Devlin, *Silent Wings*, p.84.
12 Arthur, *Men of the Red Beret: Airborne Forces 1940–1990*, p.81.
13 Dover, *The Silken Canopy*, p.46.

Chapter 4

1   The National Archives, AIR/23/5436.
2   The National Archives, CAB 106/687.
3   Stainforth, *Wings of the Wind*, p.144.
4   The National Archives, WO 204/10397.
5   The National Archives, CAB 106/687.
6   The National Archives, WO 204/1072.
7   The National Archives, CAB 106/691.
8   Frost, *A Drop Too Many*, p.177.
9   The National Archives, AIR 23/5436.
10 Whiting, Slaughter over Sicily, p.140.
11 The National Archives, WO 169/10343.

Chapter 5

1   Pack, *Operation Husky: The Allied Invasion of Sicily*, p.71.
2   McNab, *German Paratroopers in Action: 1939–1945*, p.37.
3   Blandford, *Green Devils – Red Devils*, p.15.
4   Villahermosa, *Hitler's Paratrooper*, p.15.
5   Villahermosa, *Hitler's Paratrooper*, p.24.
6   Blandford, *Green Devils – Red Devils*, p.15.
7   Blandford, *Green Devils – Red Devils*, p.16.
8   Whiting, Slaughter over Sicily, p.136.
9   McNab, *German Paratroopers in Action: 1939–1945*, p.67.

Chapter 6

1   Thompson, *Ready for Anything: The Parachute Regiment at War*, p.98.
2   Pack, *Operation Husky: The Allied Invasion of Sicily*, p.87.
3   Pack, *Operation Husky: The Allied Invasion of Sicily*, p.87.
4   Devlin, *Silent Wings*, p.99.
5   The National Archives, AIR 23/5527.
6   Ford, *Assault on Sicily, Monty and Patton at War*, p.76.
7   Devlin, *Silent Wings*, p.101.
8   Pack, *Operation Husky: The Allied Invasion of Sicily*, p.73.
9   Ford, *Assault on Sicily, Monty and Patton at War*, p.97.
10 Whiting, Slaughter over Sicily, p.130.
11 Whiting, Slaughter over Sicily, p.132.

Chapter 7

1   D'Este, *Bitter Victory*, p.354.
2   D'Este, *Bitter Victory*, p.354.

3 Poppel, *Heaven and Hell*, p.117.
4 Poppel, *Heaven and Hell*, p.122.
5 Peters, *Glider Pilots in Sicily*, p.225.

Chapter 8

1   The National Archives, CAB 106/687.
2   The National Archives, WO 169/10343.
3   The National Archives, WO 169/9639.
4   Frost, p.178.
5   Kent, *First In! Parachute Pathfinder Company*, p.49.
6   Stainforth, p.152.
7   Parker, *The Paras: The Inside Story of Britain's Toughest Regiment*, p.73.
8   Atkinson, p.127.
9   The National Archives, CAB 106/687.
10 Kent, *First In! Parachute Pathfinder Company*, p.50.
11 Parker, *The Paras: The Inside Story of Britain's Toughest Regiment*, p.71.
12 Thompson, *Ready for Anything: The Parachute Regiment at War*, p.103.
13 Greentree, *British Paratrooper versus Fallschirmjaeger*, p.60.
14 Kent, *First In! Parachute Pathfinder Company*, p.51.
15 James, *A Fierce Quality, A biography of Brigadier Alastair Pearson*, p.73.
16 Kent, *First In! Parachute Pathfinder Company*, p.49.
17 Thompson, *Ready for Anything: The Parachute Regiment at War*, p.102.
18 Saunders, The Red Beret, p.119
19 Saunders, The Red Beret, p.119
20 Saunders, The Red Beret, p.120
21 The National Archives, CAB 106/691.
22 James, *A Fierce Quality, A biography of Brigadier Alastair Pearson*, p.78.
23 D'Este, *Bitter Victory*, p.362.
24 Peatling, *Without Tradition*, p.113.
25 The National Archives, CAB 106/691.
26 The National Archives, CAB 106/691.
27 The National Archives, CAB 106/691.

Chapter 9

1 Saunders, The Red Beret, p.119.
2 Cherry, *Tunisian Tales*, p.52.
3 Peters, *Glider Pilots in Sicily*, p.234.
4 Peters, *Glider Pilots in Sicily*, p.237.
5 Carruthers, *By Air to Battle*, p.101.

Chapter 10

1 Kuhn, *German Paratroops in World War Two*, p.78.
2 Poppel, *Heaven and Hell*, p.122.
3 Poppel, *Heaven and Hell*, p.122.

4   Poppel, *Heaven and Hell*, p.123.
5   D'Este, *Bitter Victory*, p.371.

Chapter 11

1   D'Este, *Bitter Victory*, p.364.
2   Kurowski, *Jump into Hell*, p.251.
3   The National Archives, WO 169/10345.
4   Stainforth, *Wings of the Wind*, p.161.
5   Greentree, *British Paratrooper versus Fallschirmjaeger*, p.62.
6   Frost, *A Drop Too Many*, p.180.
7   Villahermosa, *Hitler's Paratrooper*, p.134.
8   Poppel, *Heaven and Hell*, p.123.

Chapter 13

1   The National Archives, AIR 23/5436.
2   The National Archives, CAB 106/691.
3   Frost, *A Drop Too Many*, p.89.

Chapter 14

1   Greentree, *British Paratrooper versus Fallschirmjaeger*, p.63.
2   The National Archives, CAB 106/690.
3   James, *A Fierce Quality, A biography of Brigadier Alastair Pearson*, p.82.
4   James, *A Fierce Quality, A biography of Brigadier Alastair Pearson*, p.82.
5   James, *A Fierce Quality, A biography of Brigadier Alastair Pearson*, p.83.
6   Payne, *Paras: Voices of the British Airborne Forces in World War II*, p.113.
7   Payne, *Paras: Voices of the British Airborne Forces in World War II*, p.72.
8   Payne, *Paras: Voices of the British Airborne Forces in World War II*, p.72.

Chapter 15

1   James, *A Fierce Quality, A biography of Brigadier Alastair Pearson*, p.78.
2   James, *A Fierce Quality, A biography of Brigadier Alastair Pearson*, p.79.
3   Payne, *Paras: Voices of the British Airborne Forces in World War II*, p.72.
4   Saunders, The Red Beret, p.123.
5   Saunders, The Red Beret, p.122.
6   Greentree, *British Paratrooper versus Fallschirmjaeger*, p.66.
7   Stainforth, *Wings of the Wind*, p.171.
8   Kent, *First In! Parachute Pathfinder Company*, p.55.
9   The National Archives, CAB 106/691
10 Poppel, *Heaven and Hell*, p.124.
11 Poppel, *Heaven and Hell*, p.124.
12 Thompson, *Ready for Anything: The Parachute Regiment at War*, p.106.
13 Greentree, *British Paratrooper versus Fallschirmjaeger*, p.63.
14 Mitcham, *The Battle for Sicily*, p.157.

Chapter 16

1　Mitcham, The Battle for Sicily, p.161.
2　James, *A Fierce Quality, A biography of Brigadier Alastair Pearson*, p.79.
3　James, *A Fierce Quality, A biography of Brigadier Alastair Pearson*, p.79.
4　Cherry, *Tunisian Tales*, p.180.
5　James, *A Fierce Quality, A biography of Brigadier Alastair Pearson*, p.80.
6　James, *A Fierce Quality, A biography of Brigadier Alastair Pearson*, p.81.
7　James, *A Fierce Quality, A biography of Brigadier Alastair Pearson*, p.81.
8　Whiting, Slaughter over Sicily, p.160.
9　Blackwell, *The Battle for Sicily Stepping Stone to Victory*, p.147.
10　Whiting, Slaughter over Sicily, p.161.
11　Parker, *The Paras: The Inside Story of Britain's Toughest Regiment*, p.75.
12　James, *A Fierce Quality, A biography of Brigadier Alastair Pearson*, p.82.
13　James, *A Fierce Quality, A biography of Brigadier Alastair Pearson*, p.82.
14　Parker, *The Paras: The Inside Story of Britain's Toughest Regiment*, p.75.
15　The National Archives, WO 169/10343.

Chapter 17

1　Blackwell, *The Battle for Sicily Stepping Stone to Victory*, p.191.

Conclusion

1　Saunders, The Red Beret, p.126.
2　The National Archives, WO/204/1072.
3　Stainforth, *Wings of the Wind*, p.122.
4　Pack, *Operation Husky: The Allied Invasion of Sicily*, p.133.
5　The National Archives, AIR 8/1316.
6　The National Archives, AIR 23/6630.
7　The National Archives, CAB 106/691.
8　The National Archives, CAB 106/692.
9　The National Archives, CAB 106/692.
10　The National Archives, CAB 106/692.
11　Porch, *Hitler's Mediterranean Gamble*, p.43.

Bibliography

Ailsby, C. (2001) *Hitler's Sky Warriors*, Spellmount Limited, Kent.

Ambrose, S. (2003) *Pegasus Bridge, D-Day: The daring British Airborne Raid*, Pocket Books, London.

Arthur, M. (1990) *Men of the Red Beret: Airborne Forces 1940–1990*, Century Hutchinson Ltd, London.

Atkinson, R. (2007) *The Day of Battle: The War in Sicily and Italy 1943–1944*, Henry Holt and Company, LLC.

Bailey, R. (2014) *Target: Italy*, Faber and Faber Limited, London.

Blackwell, I. (2008) *The Battle for Sicily Stepping Stone to Victory*, Barnsley, Pen & Sword Books.

Blandford, E. L. (1993) *Green Devils – Red Devils*, Barnsley, Pen & Sword Books.

Carruthers, B. (2012) *By Air to Battle*, Barnsley, Pen & Sword Books.

Cherry, N (2011) *Tunisian Tales*, Helion & Company Limited, Solihull.

D'Este, C. (1988) *Bitter Victory*, Harper Collins Publishing, New York.

Devlin, G. (1985) *Silent Wings*, Mackays of Chatham Ltd, Kent.

Dover, V. (1979) *The Silken Canopy*, Cassell Limited, London.

Ferguson, G. (1987) *The Paras: British Airborne Forces 1940–1984*, Osprey Publishing Ltd, London.

Ford, K. (2007) *Assault on Sicily, Monty and Patton at War*, Stroud, Sutton Publishing Limited.

Frost, J. (1983) *A Drop Too Many*, London, Sphere Books Limited.

Greentree, D. (2013) *British Paratrooper versus Fallschirmjaeger*, Osprey Publishing Ltd, London.

Guard, J. (2007) *Airborne: World War II Paratroopers in Combat*, Oxford, Osprey Publishing.

Harclerode, P. (1992) *Para! Fifty Years of The Parachute Regiment*, London, BCA.

James, J. (1989) *A Fierce Quality, A biography of Brigadier Alastair Pearson*, London, Leo Cooper

Kent, R. (1979) *First In! Parachute Pathfinder Company*, London, B. T. Batsford Ltd.

Kuhn, V. (1978) *German Paratroops in World War Two*, Ian Allan, Shepperton.

Kurowski, F. (2010) *Jump into Hell*, Pen & Sword, Barnsley.

Lucas, J. (2001) *Storming Eagles: German Airborne Forces in World War II*, London, Cassel Military Paperbacks.

Lucas, J. (1997) *The Silken Canopy: A History of the Parachute*, Shrewsbury, Airlife Publishing Ltd.

McNab, C. (2000) *German Paratroopers in Action: 1939–1945*, London, Aurum Press.

Mitcham, S. (1991) *The Battle of Sicily*, Orion Books, New York.

Mitcham, S. (2007) *Rommel's Desert Commanders: The Men Who Served the Desert Fox, North Africa, 1941–1942*, Greenwood Publishing Group.

Molony, Brigadier C. J. C.; with Flynn, Captain F. C. (RN); Davies, Major-General H. L. & Gleave, Group Captain T. P. (2004) [1st. pub. *HHMSO*: 1973], Butler, Sir James, ed., *The Mediterranean and Middle East: The Campaign in Sicily 1943 and The Campaign in Italy 3 September 1943 to 31 March 1944, History of World War II*, United Kingdom Military Series, V, Uckfield, UK, Naval & Military Press.

Norton, G, G. (1971) *The Red Devils: From Bruneval to the Falklands*, London, Arrow Books Limited.

Pack, S. W. C. (1977) *Operation Husky: The Allied Invasion of Sicily*, David & Charles, Devon.

Parker, J. (2000) *The Paras: The Inside Story of Britain's Toughest Regiment*, Metro Books, London.

Payne, R. (2014) *Paras: Voices of the British Airborne Forces in World War II*, Amberley Press, Stroud.

Peatling, R. (2004) *Without Tradition*, Barnsley, Pen & Sword Military.

Peters, M. (2012) *Glider Pilots in Sicily*, Barnsley, Pen & Sword Military.

Poppel, M. (1988) *Heaven and Hell*, Spellmount Limited, Staplehurst.

Porch, D. (2004) *Hitler's Mediterranean Gamble,* Weidenfeld & Nicholson.

Saunders, H. St George. (1949) *The Green Beret*, London, Michael Joseph.

Saunders, H. St George. (1971) *The Red Beret*, London, Michael Joseph.

Stainforth, P. (1952) *Wings of the Wind*, Arms & Armour Press Limited, London.

Thompson, J. (1989) *Ready for Anything: The Parachute Regiment at War,* George Weidenfeld & Nicholson Ltd.

Villahermosa, G. (2010) *Hitler's Paratrooper,* Barnsley, Pen & Sword Military.

Whiting, C. (1974) *Hunters from the Sky*, Stein and Day.

Whiting, C. (2006) *Slaughter over Sicily,* Barnsley, Pen & Sword Military.

Index